FORGOTTEN BATTLEFRONTS

OF THE FIRST WORLD WAR

MARTIN MARIX EVANS

SUTTON PUBLISHING

First published in 2003 by
Sutton Publishing Limited · Phoenix Mill
Thrupp · Stroud · Gloucestershire · GL5 2BU

British Library Cataloguing in Publication Data
A catalogue record for this book is available from the British Library.

ISBN 0-7509-3004-7

Endpapers, front: Italian troops in a trench near Monfalcone, 1916; *rear*: the burial of the first American soldiers to be killed in action, 1917.

Typeset in 11/14 pt Sabon.
Typesetting and origination by
Sutton Publishing Limited.
Printed and bound in England by
J.H. Haynes & Co. Ltd, Sparkford.

CONTENTS

Introduction and Acknowledgements   v

THE BELGIAN FRONTS   1
1.   INVASION AND SIEGE   3
2.   RETREAT TO THE YSER   29
3.   THE COAST   57

THE VOSGES   75
4.   THE FIGHT FOR THE SUMMITS   77

THE ITALIAN FRONTS   109
5.   ITALIA IRREDENTA   111
6.   BATTLES OF THE TRENTINO AND ISONZO   129
7.   BATTLES OF CAPORETTO AND PIAVE   149

THE SALONIKA FRONT   183
8.   BRIDGEHEADS IN THE BALKANS   185
9.   BALKAN VICTORY   217

Bibliography   251
Index   253

A patrol setting off at dusk, Struma valley, Salonika front, 4 October 1916. (*Imperial War Museum Q32439*)

INTRODUCTION AND ACKNOWLEDGEMENTS

My interest in the European fronts of the First World War other than the Ypres to St Mihiel frontage was stimulated by family connections and the chance offered by the discovery of a collection of unpublished letters and diaries. The family connection is my great-uncle Robert, who was born in Paris in 1895 and died there in 1970 having survived various unpleasant events in two wars. In the first of those he was in the Chasseurs Alpins. The discovery was of the papers of Guy Turrall by his godson who is, luckily, a friend of mine. The curiosity thus awakened led to the tracing of the career of a distant cousin, Reginald Marix, who first distinguished himself in the early days of the war in Belgium. Coverage of the Italian campaign then came naturally into the sequence.

The nature of the terrain over which these campaigns were conducted seems to me of central importance in seeking an understanding of how the war was fought. Given the very different kinds of source I have been able to use, the coverage of the four regions is inconsistent, but I can see no reason to exclude an excellent trench map from one section only because I have no similar map for another or skimp on good photographs where they are numerous merely to preserve a notion of equality. Similarly, original, previously unpublished accounts are quoted in the Salonika section while previously published, though perhaps somewhat obscure, sources are used elsewhere. To this unevenness I trust the reader will be willing to extend indulgence. The spelling of placenames has altered a great deal since the early twentieth century. I have reproduced quotations exactly as written and tried to use the contemporary British version when in doubt.

More substantial details of the sources are given in the listing at the end of the book. I am particularly grateful to Ian Lyster and his brother for permission to make use of their father's memoir and to Ian for access to Guy Turrall's papers, maps and photographs. For permission to quote from these I am indebted to Dr Ann Turrall. Cleone Woods has kindly given permission for Geoffrey Malins to be quoted. I am also grateful for permission to quote from published sources but, at the time of going to press, the status and ownership of copyright in some of the material remains uncertain and I would be grateful for information to enable me to resolve these matters.

The modern, colour photographs are intended to convey the nature of the terrain and to tempt people to visit the battlefields. I am fortunate to have had help from a number of people who have guided my research, provided information or given permission to use their pictures. Robert Gils of Simon Stevinstichting was generous in his provision of plans and data, more than I could find room for, and with his introductions to the photographers J.-P. Lacroix, Rudy van Nunen and Bart van Bulck who have allowed me to reproduce their work. Alex Deseyne of the Raversijde Museum, Ostend, undertook a photographic tour expressly to make good my deficiencies in illustration and also provided essential information. Guy Cavallaro, whose eagerly awaited new work on the war in Italy is at press at the time of this writing, has lent both modern and contemporary photographs. The British campaign in Salonika is the subject of a substantial and important study, as yet unpublished, by Alan Wakefield, Simon Moody and Andrew Whitmarsh. They have kindly allowed me to reproduce photographs taken recently on their research trips to the region, generously putting aside what must have been an inclination to reserve them for their own, exclusive use. I am grateful to Philippa Carling for allowing me to use photographs she has taken in difficult terrain in the Dolomites and to John Chester for his pictures of the Trentino sector.

Private archive illustrations have come from the Turrall collection, Brian Kibby and the family album kept by my father, Jean-Paul. I am grateful to the administrators of the public archives at the Imperial War Museum, London, the In Flanders Fields Museum, Ypres, the Provinciale Biblioteek en Cultuurarchief, St Andries, and the United States Army Military History Institute, Carlisle, PA, for their contributions to this work. The captions to the illustrations include credits as appropriate. Unattributed pictures are either from my own collection or were taken by me. I have had the advantage of access to Leo Cooper's extensive library and enjoyed the benefit of his advice. It was he who first sparked my interest in the First World War and I am deeply indebted to him. The patience my wife, Gillian, has summoned up to read and correct the text, not to mention soothing the fevered brow and carting spare cameras across mountains, has been heroic.

Martin F. Marix Evans
Blakesley, 2003

THE
BELGIAN FRONTS

'All day long stretcher-bearers were picking up the dead and wounded, while we continued to fire from time to time. All the wounded we have picked up are young men, sixteen to twenty years old, of the last levy.'

Observations of a French Marine based at Dixmude, October 1914

Overleaf: French Marines on their way to the front.

ONE

INVASION AND SIEGE

On Sunday 4 August 1914 Germany invaded Belgium. The possibility had long been foreseen, but other options had been given equal weight. The Belgians were so eager to preserve the purity of their neutrality that they were ready to contemplate each of their neighbouring countries as prospective invaders, for while the threat of a German incursion was likely enough, might not France strike against Germany and violate Belgian sovereignty, or Britain land at Antwerp to do the same? The result was that Belgium enjoyed a supportive military relationship with no one and was obliged to fend for herself.

The defence of the country rested on the existence of three strong fortified areas, Liège and Namur on the River Meuse in the east and south respectively and Antwerp in the north-west. The cities were surrounded with rings of forts, massive, subterranean structures now some forty years old. The river-based complexes could be by-passed if not supported by armies in the field alongside them and the North Sea link to Antwerp depended on passing through the territorial waters of the Netherlands, also a country fixed on remaining neutral in which case belligerents were barred from the Scheldt. As late as 1913 steps had been taken to increase the size of the army. The conscription level of 1909 was raised with a view to creating a field army of 180,000 men and having 200,000 older troops for the garrisons of the forts while the rest of the adult males would serve in the Garde Civique. This new programme was designed to reach its full effectiveness in 1926. The effort to expand the army to meet the crisis of the summer of 1914 magnified the problems of poor training and shortage of qualified officers that dogged the Belgian forces when war came upon them. At the start of August the commander-in-chief, King Albert of the Belgians, had a Field Army of 117,000 men, 324 guns, 108 machine-guns and 12 aircraft.

The question then arose of how the troops Belgium did possess should be deployed. The twelve forts around Liège, for example, needed extensive fieldworks between them to make a defensible entity of the position. In the event Lieutenant-General Gérard M.J.G. Leman had a single field division, the 3rd, to deploy in support of the garrison troops facing Germany. The remaining five were placed with the 1st Division at Ghent facing the North Sea coast (against the British), two, the 4th and 5th, near Namur (against the French) and two, the 6th and the Cavalry, near Antwerp in reserve and ready to take position on the River Gette if the attack from the east materialized.

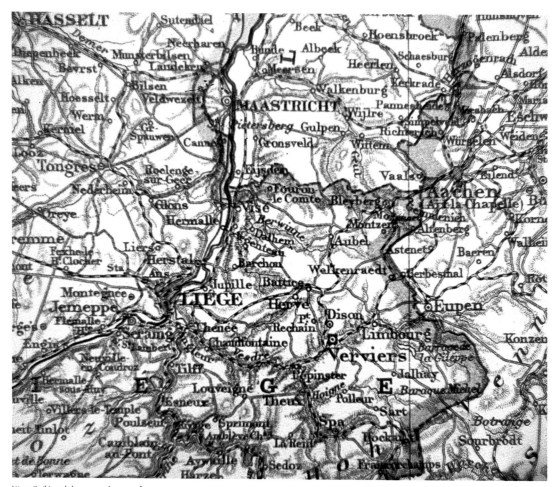

Liège (Luik) and the surrounding area from a contemporary map.

There they could be joined by the 5th if a concentration of the army to protect Brussels and the west was needed.

The Germans' modified Schlieffen Plan called for their First Army to thrust westwards on the right or northern flank before turning south, as the originator of the scheme had put it, 'with their sleeve brushing the sea'. Alongside, to their south, the Second Army would also advance to the west. The German First Army, under General Alexander von Kluck, had 320,000 men, 910 guns and 396 machine-guns organized in 14 infantry and 3 cavalry divisions. General Karl von Bülow's Second Army had 260,000 men, 796 guns and 324 machine-guns in 12 infantry divisions. They expected little difficulty in passing through Belgium. With any luck the puny Belgian Army would be ordered to offer no resistance at all.

The immediate pretext for action was the allegedly imminent march of the French from Givet northwards along the Meuse to Namur with the presumed intention to attack Germany. Germany therefore demanded passage to oppose this advance and promised to respect Belgium's rights at the conclusion of hostilities. However, any resistance would show that Belgium was an enemy. The demand was rejected with the contention that France had no such plans. Germany did not allow this to interfere with the invasion. The Belgians blew bridges over the Meuse and tunnels on the Luxembourg border.

The German cavalry led the advance and took Visé, between Liège and Maastricht. The special task force under General Otto von Emmich struck out for Liège on a frontage of 15 miles (24 km). As attempts were made to cross the river the Belgians had the effrontery to resist. The Germans were both surprised and angered. On 5 August the eastern-most of the twelve forts surrounding the city was attacked. The continuing efforts were futile, for the field artillery accompanying the army was too light to have any effect on the forts and the machine-guns cut down the gallant but imprudent frontal assaults. A Belgian officer described how they advanced, shoulder to shoulder and fell in great heaps, behind which they re-formed and came on yet again. That night six brigades formed up to attack under cover of darkness, the 14th Brigade in the centre and with them Major-General Erich von Ludendorff of the Second Army's staff. The advance was tentative and poorly directed. Ludendorff came across an orderly leading a horse and discovered that the commander of the 14th had been killed. He took over and pushed the men forward into the gap between Fort d'Evegnée, immediately to the south of the Aachen road, and the more southerly Fort de Fléron. The latter failed to fire on them and the progress in the space between the forts was

German field artillery at the gallop near Visé, August 1914.

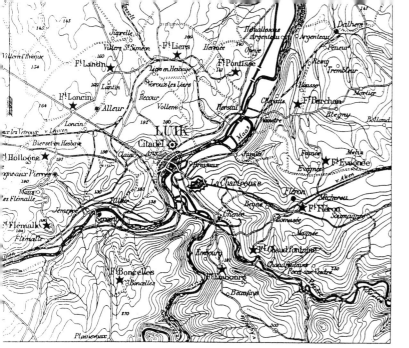

The fortifications of Liège (Luik) in August 1914. The River Meuse (Maas) flows from the direction of Namur (Namen) to the south-west to Visé in the north. Forts are marked with stars. *(Van der Hout, W., Breda, 1924)*

heartening. By the afternoon of 6 August they had penetrated far enough to see across the Meuse into the city of Liège itself.

Efforts were made to persuade the Belgians to capitulate. Lieutenant-General Leman had refused the day before and on this day he was given encouragement by a Zeppelin attack when artillery shells were dropped as bombs, killing nine civilians. A second offer of terms was still rejected, but it had become clear to Leman that, with his fortress line jeopardized, the single infantry division could not stand against the German strength and he therefore sent it west to join the main body of the Belgian Field Army. Leman himself remained in command, based in Fort de Loncin. The Germans pushed forward into the town and, more by luck than judgement, von Ludendorff himself took the surrender of the citadel. The forts, however, remained in Belgian hands, more vulnerable as, while they were designed for frontal defence, they now had the enemy to their rear, but still resisting. Von Emmich had no artillery that could hurt them.

Aware of the strength of the Belgian installations, the Germans had made provision by ordering from Krupp a mortar of unprecedented calibre, 420 mm. By 1914 five were available and to supplement these four batteries of Skoda 305-mm howitzers had been acquired from the Austrians. Moving these monsters was an immense task and the Krupps required specially built concrete emplacements from which to fire. It was not until 12 August that these guns could be brought into action, but one fort, Barchon, fell to light artillery and infantry attack on 8 August.

The defiance of Liège did not mean that the German progress was halted. The advance up the Meuse on the southern flank of the city progressed and on 12 August the town of Huy, with its hill-top fortress, was taken. On the northern flank the Belgian positions on the River Gette were challenged. The line had been formed between Hasselt and Diest on 10 August and in the centre of it was the village of Haelen (Halen). Two days later the Belgian Cavalry Division, screening the approach of the 1st Division from Ghent, deployed to oppose the advancing German cavalry which was seeking their enemy's left flank. The Belgian strength was some 2,700 men, 2 brigades, each of lancers and guides regiments. There were also a cyclist battalion of carabineers, three horse artillery batteries, a pioneer company and transport and telegraph sections. German cavalry divisions comprised about 3,600 men. They had

An Austrian 305-mm Skoda howitzer on the move.

Belgian infantry with their dog-cart transport for the machine-gun.

three brigades of two regiments of horse, cuirassiers, dragoons, hussars or *uhlans*, and a *jäger* battalion, that is, a rifle unit. In addition they had a machine-gun unit, three horse artillery batteries and pioneer and signals units.

The terrain at Haelen is flat and open, affording little protection, but the Belgians wisely elected to fight dismounted, using what cover they could find. General de Witte deployed his 2nd Brigade, 4th and 5th Lancers, his artillery and his Carabineers across the line of the German advance. The Lancers left their horses in the village with the Carabineers, while the 1st and 2nd Guides of 1st Brigade kept their mounts when they took position to the right of 2nd Brigade, ready to fall on the German left. The German 17th Lancers began the action by charging the Belgian 5th Lancers and some of the Carabineers. The defenders' 1899 Mauser carbines were of limited range and the need to hold fire until the last minute must have been very trying. The Belgian

nerve held and the assault failed bloodily. Renewed efforts met a similar fate. The
German 18th Dragoons and 2nd Cuirassiers were repulsed in their turn and the
9th Uhlans were also thrown back. As the jäger regiments came into action the
Belgian 1st Division's infantry came up to reinforce the cavalry. The 4th Infantry
had scarcely arrived before they faced a charge by the 9th Uhlans and 2nd Cuirassiers
and they took serious casualties. After a 10-hour action the Germans withdrew,
leaving 1,700 horses killed and
having suffered more than 3,000
casualties. The Belgian dead
numbered 263. The vulnerability
of cavalry to modern weapons,
known to others since the Boer
War, was now clear to the Germans
as well. This success was no more
than a short pause in the general
retreat of the Belgian Army, for the
village fell to the Germans six days
later.

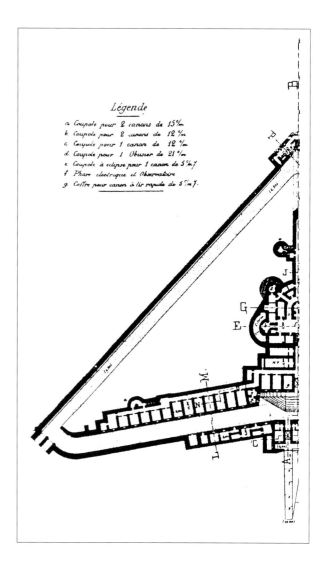

Liège's forts came under heavy
fire for the first time that day. The
arrival of the guns had been
delayed by the damage done to the
railway tunnels and the final part
of the journey to the front was a
laborious and tedious progress by
road, but from this day on the
reduction of the forts was steady
and inevitable. Fort d'Evegnée was
the first to fall to the big guns.
On 13 August the magazine of Fort
de Chaudfontaine was hit and fire
swept the casements. The combined

Detail from a diagram of Fort de Loncin showing the installation in
profile and in plan. *(Robert Gils/Simon Stevinstichting)*

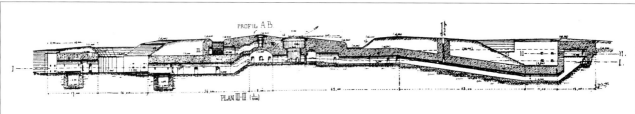

The crater at Fort de Loncin; the result of the explosion of the magazine remains evident today. *(J.-P. Lacroix)*

power of Krupp 420-mm mortars and Skoda 305-mm howitzers ground Fort d'Embourg into submission by 1730 hours that same day. Fort de Pontisse was assaulted by two Krupps and surrendered at 1230 hours. North of the city on 14 August Fort de Lierres fell and the next day Fort de Lantin surrendered soon after midday. The magazine of Leman's headquarters, Fort de Loncin, was hit and the unconscious general

The 120-mm gun inside the turret at Fort de Loncin. *(J.-P. Lacroix)*

was discovered among the ruins. Boncelles, south of Liège, had been taken earlier in the day. The two remaining strongholds, shocked by the violence of Loncin's demise, gave up on 16 August. Liège, a vital railway link for future German supplies, was lost and now, later by a few days than intended, the full force of the German advance across Belgium was released.

As the defences of Liège were crumbling under German shells, an American newspaper correspondent, E. Alexander Powell of the *New York World*, was arriving in Antwerp. He was soon joined by a press photographer from Kansas, Donald Thompson. While Powell was in possession of a *laissez-passer* issued by the governor of Antwerp, Thompson's documentation consisted of his American passport, a certificate of membership in the Benevolent and Protective Order of Elks and a letter granting him permission to photograph Canadian troops issued by the Canadian Minister of Militia, Colonel Sam Hughes. They were to witness the fall of the city.

The French view of the situation was changing. Initially General Joseph Joffre had regarded the attack on Belgium as a preliminary to a strike towards Sedan and the Meuse, but as the German First and Second Armies pushed into the plains beyond Liège it seemed that General Charles Lanrezac's Fifth Army should mount guard on the Meuse from Dinant to Namur and west along the Sambre. The newly arrived British Expeditionary Force (BEF) was sent to take position on Lanrezac's left and push northwards and the Belgians could complete the line. The Belgians, however, were falling back to their redoubt within the ring of forts around Antwerp and had no intention of extending their line southwards to link with their new-found allies. Joffre was still convinced that the action would take place not in the west and the low country between Brussels and the coast but in the hills of the Ardennes, east of the Meuse. On 15 August the French and Germans clashed at Dinant, south of Namur, and the young officer Charles de Gaulle of the 33rd Regiment was wounded. But both sides were cautious, particularly along the line of the Sambre, for the area was one of some large and many small towns, industry, factories and, generally, an urban environment in which armies would be hard to control and fighting would be fragmented and uncertain.

Lanrezac took position on the high ground, south of the Sambre, and placed outposts forward to guard the bridges, in spite of having been ordered by Joffre to advance northwards to join with the BEF and the Belgians; he left the gap on the northern side of the Sambre open. The situation along the river itself was not so straightforward for his troops as Lanrezac supposed. The Sambre meanders through the broad, flat plain, running north and south as much as east and west, so that, as a rule, one bank outflanks another. Moreover, there were more bridges across than the French were aware, so that when, on 21 August, the German 2nd Guard Division found one undefended near Auvelais, midway between Charleroi and Namur, they got across and the 19th Division did the same a little to their west. On the same day the heavy guns reached Namur and the ring of fortresses there came under fire. At 1000 hours the Krupps and Skodas started to shell the four forts on the north and east of the defensive circle. They held out for two days and then two and a half German divisions stormed the gap between Forts Cognelée, north of the town, and Marchevolette to the north-east. Once the ring had been broken the Belgian 4th Division was withdrawn, escaping through France to join the defenders of Antwerp. The German guns were moved to deal with the more westerly forts. The last, Fort de Suarlée, fell at 1700 hours on 25 August. The hinge of the defensive line was now in German hands. To the north the Belgians, whose government had left Brussels on 19 August, had nowhere left to go but Antwerp.

The German advance not only destroyed farms and houses, but also civilians. The Belgian rearguard did what it could to harass the invader, in particular by sniping from concealed positions. Unable to see their attackers, the Germans assumed they were being fired on by guerillas, men fighting as irregulars, *franc-tireurs* as they called them. Reprisals followed. The town of Andenne, east of Namur on the Meuse, was burned to the ground and 110 citizens shot on 20 and 21 August. The graveyard at Tamines has 384 graves marked as those of victims of the Germans.

The National Redoubt, the fortified area around Antwerp, had a perimeter of 58 miles (94 km) made up of old brick-built forts reinforced with concrete, eleven new concrete forts and twelve concrete redoubts. The inner defences consisted of old brick forts and eighteen concrete redoubts. The extent of fortification was beyond the powers of the small Belgian Army's ability to garrison adequately. Moreover, the chief line of supply, the River Scheldt (Escaut), ran through the territory of the Netherlands, a neutral country, and therefore could not be used to transport munitions or men for the war. For the time being, however, the attention of the Germans was concentrated to the south, towards France, and they were content to by-pass Antwerp in expectation of a swift decision against the French.

Alexander Powell wrote of the Belgian preparations for the defence of the city:

The loveliest suburbs in Europe had been wiped from the earth as a sponge wipes figures from a slate. Every house and church and windmill, every tree and hedge and wall, in a zone some two or three miles [3/5 km] wide by twenty [32 km] long, was literally levelled to the ground. For mile after mile the splendid trees which lined the highroads were ruthlessly cut down; mansions which could fittingly have housed a king were dynamited; churches whose walls had echoed to the tramp of the Duke of Alba's mail-clad men-at-arms were levelled; villages whose picturesqueness was the joy of artist and travellers were given over to the flames. Certainly not since the burning of Moscow has there been witnessed such a scene of self-inflicted desolation. When the work of the engineers was finished a jack-rabbit could not have approached the forts without being seen.

Trenches, barbed wire and booby-traps were added to the obstacles, he reports. What Powell omits is the observation that the forts themselves now stood out as clear and easy targets for the heavy guns that would soon be arrayed against them. He continues:

> Stretching across the fields and meadows were what looked at first glance like enormous red-brown serpents but which proved, upon closer inspection, to be trenches for infantry. The region south of Antwerp is a net-work of canals, and on the bank of every canal rose, as through magic, parapets of sand-bags. Charges of dynamite were placed under every bridge and viaduct and tunnel. Barricades of paving-stones and mattresses and sometimes farm carts were built across the highways.

As yet these defences were untested for the fighting was on the southern border at Charleroi and Mons. The first brush the BEF had with the Germans took place on the morning of 22 August when C Squadron of the 4th Irish Dragoon Guards were on patrol north of the canal and engaged a troop of 4th Cuirassiers, killing an officer and capturing five men. The main British force arrived that night and was ordered to dig in. On the left, between Condé and Mons, was IInd Corps under General Sir Horace Smith-Dorrien and on the right, astride the Bavay–Binche road between Mons and the River Sambre at the French border to the south-east, Ist Corps under Lieutenant-General Sir Douglas Haig. Each had two divisions comprising three brigades of infantry with mounted troops, artillery and engineers. In addition the BEF had the Cavalry Corps under Lieutenant-General Edmund Allenby with one cavalry division to the rear of IInd Corps' positions on the canal, close to the Mons–Valenciennes railway. In all about 72,000 troops with some 300 guns to hold against von Kluck's First Army's 135,000 or so men now arriving with 480 guns.

At Nimy, north of Mons itself, four bridges crossed the canal. These were defended by 4th Royal Fusiliers, 9th Brigade on the left of the Brussels road and 4th Middlesex, 8th Brigade on the right. The canal bulged northwards at this point and fell away south-east on the Middlesex's front, while west of Mons it ran straight to Condé and the myriad channels into which the River Escaut, as the Scheldt was called here, divided in the man-made landscape of embanked streams and canals. The Fusiliers set up two machine-gun posts by the railway bridge and the Royal Engineers placed charges to blow the bridges if retreat became necessary.

In the clearing mist of the morning of Sunday 23 August a German cavalry patrol rode cautiously towards the canal at Nimy. The Fusiliers opened fire. The scouts retreated and at 0900 hours the German artillery opened up, to be followed by the massed, grey ranks of the 84th Infantry Regiment advancing at the canal bridges and the 31st Infantry near the railway station a little to the east where 4th Middlesex awaited them. British training had raised the standard of musketry of the regular soldier to aimed firing of fifteen rounds a minute and this rifle fire with the added power of the machine-guns cut the German infantry down with a terrible efficiency; they believed themselves to be facing a British force largely equipped with machine-guns. Undaunted, the Germans returned and returned again to the attack. As more German batteries came up the gunnery front widened westwards.

At Nimy the machine-gun positions of C Company were exposed to, and suffered from, heavy fire from the Germans and the steady pressure from von Kluck's men slowly wore them down. The massed advances were abandoned in favour of sharp rushes by smaller groups and the closer they came the more cover was afforded by the embankments of the waterway. At the railway station B Company of the 4th Middlesex had fortified the platform with sacks of cement. Here they held until nearly noon, reinforced by two companies from 2nd Royal Irish Regiment, and as they fell back a single soldier positioned himself on the roof to give covering fire. He was killed when the Germans finally took the position. All along the line German pressure was telling. On the east, beyond Obourg station, a party had found an undefended crossing. At Nimy a German soldier set the drawbridge machinery in motion and closed it for his comrades to cross. At 1310 hours the order was given to withdraw to the second line of defence to the south. Back down the Brussels road

The St Symphorien cemetery was first created by the Germans after the Battle of Mons in an old potash mining works and was subsequently taken over by the Commonwealth War Graves Commission. It contains both German and Commonwealth graves, including that of Private J.L. Price, a Canadian, killed at 1058 hours on 11 November 1918. *(MME)*

they went, firing on the approaching enemy, through the main square once more towards higher ground. The invaders set fire to more than a hundred houses as they came, killing twenty-two civilians.

To the west, along the straight section of the canal, the 1st Queen's Own Royal West Kent faced the 12th Brandenburg Grenadiers. The Grenadiers had come up near St Ghislain on the evening of 22 August and looked across the flat, marshy meadow to see a peaceful scene in which the cows were grazing. The next day it seemed that every innocent building held a British rifleman and the Grenadiers lost some 500 killed or wounded. Once a crossing had been made at Nimy and another further east, this line became untenable for the British and attempts were made to blow the bridges. As evening came on the British were pulling back and the exhausted Germans looked to get some rest. The BEF had suffered 1,600 casualties, killed, wounded and made prisoner. The battle was accorded an exaggerated importance back in Britain, but it was in fact only an encounter action which gave some minor delay to the German advance.

The French and British retreated southwards, pursued by the Germans. The British fought a delaying action at Le Cateau on 26 August and the French slowed the invaders' progress at Guise on 29 August. The fortified town of Maubeuge drew off a part of the German force with its resistance, just as the Belgian enclave around Antwerp was keeping more of their army tied up further north. Paris itself was threatened until the Germans were eventually halted and pushed back in the Battle of the Marne on 6 September.

Alexander Powell saw his first action on 25 August. He had been in his room at the Hotel St Antoine reading some recently delivered newspapers when, shortly after 0110 hours, he turned off the light and opened his window as he prepared for bed:

> As I did so my attention was attracted by a curious humming overhead, like a million bumble-bees. I leaned far out of the window, and as I did so an indistinct mass, which gradually resolved itself into something resembling a gigantic black cigar, became plainly apparent against the purple-velvet sky. . . . It was a German Zeppelin.
>
> Even as I looked something resembling a falling star curved across the sky. An instant later came a rending, shattering crash that shook the hotel to its foundations, the walls of my room rocked and reeled about me, and for a breathless moment I thought the building was going to collapse. Perhaps thirty seconds later came another splitting explosion, and another, and then another – ten in all. . . .

Powell dressed hastily and clambered up to the roof. The night was ablaze with anti-aircraft and small-arms fire; anyone with a gun was firing it. The destruction of buildings and the loss of civilian lives shocked the American.

The Belgians continued to resist as they fell back on Antwerp. Prince Henri de Ligne was mortally wounded in a raid on Herenthals, east of Antwerp on the canal, when attempting to blow the bridges. As a result of this, efforts were made to protect the armoured cars on which machine-guns were mounted by adding a domed turret. Powell wrote of them in glowing terms that stretch belief:

> . . . a moveable steel dome, with an opening for the muzzle of a machine-gun, was superimposed on the turret. These grim vehicles, which jeered at bullets, and were proof even against shrapnel, quickly became a nightmare to the Germans. Driven by the most reckless racing drivers in Belgium, manned by crews of dare-devil youngsters, and armed with machine-guns which poured out lead at the rate of a thousand shots a minute, these wheeled fortresses would tear at will into the

German lines, cut up an outpost or wipe out a cavalry patrol, dynamite a bridge or a tunnel or a culvert, and be back in the Belgian lines again almost before the enemy realized what had happened.

The doubling of the guns' performance and the rosy view of the effectiveness of the cars was, no doubt, encouraged by Powell's understandable admiration for their crews. In the retreat from Malines an armoured car covering the infantry was isolated when it ran out of fuel, but the crew filled the tank from cans they had aboard and the driver made to withdraw, Powell wrote, 'as cool as though he were turning a limousine in the width of Piccadilly'.

The Belgian Army also inspired Powell to the following observations:

As I stood one day in the Place de Meir in Antwerp and watched a regiment of mud-bespattered guides clatter past, it was hard to believe I was living in the twentieth century and not in the beginning of the nineteenth, for instead of the serviceable uniforms of grey or drab or khaki, these men wore the befrogged green jackets, the cherry-coloured breeches, and the huge fur busbies which characterized the soldiers of Napoleon. The carabineers, for example, wore uniforms of bottle-green and queer sugar-loaf hats of patent leather which resembled headgear of the Directoire period. Both grenadiers and the infantry of

Officers of the Guides pause for a portrait.

the line marched and fought and slept in uniforms of heavy blue cloth piped with scarlet and small, round visorless fatigue-caps which afforded no protection from either sun or rain. . . . The gendarmes – who, by the way, were always to be found where the fighting was hottest – were the most unsuitably uniformed of all, for the blue coats and silver aiguillettes and towering bearskins which served to impress the simple country-folk made splendid targets for the German marksmen.

In order to maintain pressure on the Germans in the north of Belgium and thus make things easier for the Allies in the south, the Belgians mounted a sortie from Antwerp on 25 August. A total of 4 divisions, comprising some 60,000 men, took part in the attack with the Cavalry Division and the 3rd Division held in reserve. The axis of the principal thrust, by the 6th Division, was along the Brussels railway line southwards through Malines to Elewyt where the German IXth Reserve Corps stood on a line that ran east to Aerschot. On their right 5th and 1st Divisions advanced in the area bounded by the River Senne to the east and the Willebroek Canal to the west and on the other flank 2nd Division covered any threat along the line of the River Dyle. Across the flat land the railway enbankments form formidable barriers. On the first day encouraging progress was made. The Germans were ejected from Malines and Hofstade and the 6th Division advanced almost as far as Elewyt. On their right their comrades reached Eppeghem, where the Senne and the railway come together, but the Germans were quickly reinforced and on 26 August the Belgians were driven back once more.

Powell had taken up position on the embankment of a railway branch line at Sempst and watched as the invaders regained the initiative.

By noon the Germans had gotten the range and a rain of shrapnel was bursting about the Belgian batteries, which limbered up and retired at a trot in perfect order. After the guns were out of range I could see the dark blue masses of the supporting Belgian infantry slowly falling back, cool as a winter's morning. Through an oversight, however, two battalions of carabineers did not receive the order to retire and were in imminent danger of being cut off and destroyed. Then occurred one of the bravest acts I have ever seen. To reach them a messenger would have to traverse a mile of open road, swept by shrieking shrapnel and raked by rifle-fire. There was about one chance in a thousand of a man getting to the end of that road alive. A colonel standing beside me under a railway-culvert summoned a gendarme, gave him the necessary orders, and added, '*Bonne chance, mon brave.*' The man, a fierce-moustached fellow who would have gladdened the heart of Napoleon, knew he was being sent into the jaws of death, but he merely saluted, set spurs to his horse, and tore down the road, an archaic figure in his towering bearskin. He reached the troops uninjured and gave the order for them to retreat, but as they fell back the Germans got the range and with marvellous accuracy dropped shell after shell into the running column. Soon road and fields were dotted with corpses in Belgian blue.

The American reporter E. Alexander Powell, in a car decked out with his national flag, among the ruins of Aerschot.

The embankment became the fighting line, assaulted by waves of bayonet-wielding Germans and defended by Belgian riflemen. By 1600 hours only a thin screen of defenders were left covering the withdrawal and Powell remained in his position above the scene, confident he could regain his automobile and run for Antwerp with time to spare when the moment arrived.

> Suddenly a soldier crouching beside me cried, 'Les Allemands! Les Allemands!' and from the woods which screened the railway-embankment burst a long line of figures, hoarsely cheering. At almost the same moment I heard a sudden splutter of shots in the village street behind me and my driver screamed, 'Hurry for your life, monsieur! The Uhlans are upon us!'

Powell surprised himself with the speed he achieved across a ploughed field to reach his car. As he was driven north at speed the German cavalry entered the village. The troops marching wearily back to Antwerp were joined by the greater part of the population of Malines, carrying what they could or pushing their possessions on hand carts.

A dire consequence of the fighting was experienced in Louvain. At nightfall a riderless horse is said to have galloped into the city, fleeing from the action further north. In the dark a soldier panicked, a shot was fired and rumour had it that the

Belgians were on the outskirts of the town. Germans later asserted that an uprising had been attempted by the citizens. In reprisal Louvain was sacked, houses set on fire and the ancient library, founded in 1426 and custodian of more than 600 medieval manuscripts as well as some 200,000 books, was destroyed. Powell, as a neutral, American newspaperman, was able to make his way into German-held territory in his car, flying the 'Stars and Stripes', accompanied by the photographer Donald Thompson. They went to Aerschot first.

> A few days before Aerschot had been a prosperous and happy town of ten-thousand people. When we saw it it was a heap of smoking ruins, garrisoned by a battalion of German soldiers, and with its population consisting of half a hundred white-faced women. . . . Quite two-thirds of the houses had been burned and showed unmistakable signs of having been sacked by a maddened soldiery before they were burned. . . . Doors had been smashed in by rifle-butts and boot-heels; windows had been broken; furniture had been wantonly destroyed; pictures had been torn from the walls; mattresses had been ripped open with bayonets. . . .

In Louvain they found yet greater destruction: 'Here we came upon another scene of destruction and desolation. Nearly half the city was in ashes. . . . The fronts of many of the houses were smeared with crimson stains. . . . And the amazing feature

An armoured train, later photographed in action on the Nieuport–Dixmude railway.

of it all was that among the Germans there seemed to be no feeling of regret, no sense of shame.'

Another attack was mounted on 9 September. The fighting on the Marne had succeeded in driving the Germans back to the River Aisne and there were hopes of another blow here in the north preventing reinforcement of the retreating invaders of France. The significance of the attack was given a somewhat exaggerated standing by Powell, who wrote: '. . . the success of the Allies on the Aisne was in great measure due to the sacrifices made on this occasion by the Belgian army. Every available man which the Germans could put into the field was used to hold a line running through Sempst, Weerde, Campenhout, Wespelaer, Rotselaer and Holsbeek.'

The German IXth Reserve Corps had begun to move south, leaving the line to the IIIrd Reserve Corps, when the attack started. The action took place along the line of the canal between Malines and Louvain, further east than the August battle and threatening the German right wing. The Belgian 3rd Division advanced southwards leaving Malines on its right and struck towards Over de Vaart, beyond the River Dyle and the canal. Alongside the 6th Division moved on Thildonck and to the east again the 2nd Division thrust towards Louvain. On the extreme left the Cavalry Division swept towards Aerschot before turning south-west to Louvain. British support for the Belgians was now given in practical form with the arrival of a Royal Navy armoured train. It carried 4.7-in guns and was used in support of the Belgian infantry in the sortie from Antwerp. Powell reported of it:

No small part in the defence of the city was played by the much-talked-about armoured train, which was built under the supervision of Lieutenant-Commander Littlejohn in the yards of the Antwerp Engineering Company at Hoboken. The train consisted of four large coal-trucks with sides of armour plate sufficiently high to afford protection to the crews of the 4.7-inch naval guns – six of which were brought from England for the purpose, though there was only time to mount four of them – and between each gun-truck was a heavily armoured goods van for ammunition. . . . The guns were served by Belgian artillerymen commanded by British gunners. . . . Personally I am inclined to believe that the chief value of this novel contrivance lay in the moral encouragement it lent the defence. . . .

For three days progress was made, but the Germans pulled IXth Reserve Corps back to oppose the incursion and on 13 September the Belgians were forced to withdraw. Powell witnessed the action near Weerde that day, driving out with Thompson and leaving the car near a convent flying the Red Cross; a location they assumed would be secure. They went forward on foot to a farmhouse from which they could see the little town on the other side of the Brussels–Antwerp road, using the trenches where they could and running across the open spaces in between. They climbed up to the attic and broke a hole through the tiles to look out: 'Lying in the deep ditch which bordered our side of the highway was a Belgian infantry brigade, composed of two regiments of

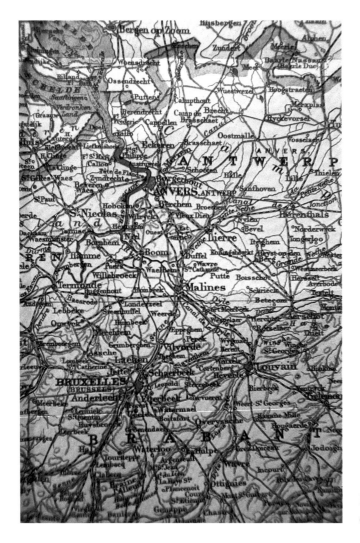

Detail of the Antwerp, Brussels and Louvain area from a contemporary map.

carabineers and two regiments of *chasseurs à pied*, the men all crouching in the ditch or lying prone on the ground.' Beyond, in the town of Weerde, its woods and its château, tell-tale smoke showed the origin of the fire from rifle and machine-gun that swept the position. There they stayed, under small-arms fire but convinced that the enemy artillery had been silenced. Orders arrived for an attack to be carried out at 1730 hours. Powell continued:

> Under cover of artillery fire so continuous that it sounded like thunder in the mountains, the Belgian infantry climbed out of the trenches and, throwing aside their knapsacks, formed up behind the road preparatory to the grand assault. A moment later a dozen dog batteries came trotting up and took position on the left of the infantry. At 5.30 [1730 hours] to the minute the whistles of the officers sounded shrilly and the mile-long line of men swept forward cheering. They

crossed the roadway, they scrambled over ditches, they climbed fences, they pushed through hedges, until they were within a hundred yards [90 m] of the line of buildings which formed the outskirts of the town. Then hell itself broke loose. The whole of the German front, which for several hours past had replied but feebly to the Belgian fire, spat a continuous stream of lead and flame. The rolling crash of musketry and the ripping snarl of machine-guns were stabbed by the vicious *pom-pom-pom-pom-pom* of the quick-firers.

The dog batteries were the first to pass Powell, racing back towards Antwerp. They were followed by a sorry stream of shattered Belgian infantry, wounded and unwounded alike, many falling to German fire as they attempted to get away. Powell and Thompson also fled, bullets falling around them and the howl of shrapnel hurrying them on their way. They regained the car, but now the road to Malines was held by the Germans, so a long diversion in the dark, without lights, was required to bring them safe again within the barbed wire boundaries of Antwerp.

On the evening of 14 September Erich von Falkenhayn replaced Helmuth von Moltke as the commander of the German armies. The immediate problem was the resolution of the situation in Belgium, an open front north of the First Army's positions along the Aisne and south of the Antwerp enclave. Von Falkenhayn decided to bring his Sixth Army from Alsace, but that would take a week so it would be necessary to have

The ruins of Fort Kessel, showing the damage caused by shelling from 420-mm guns, still stand to the south-east of Antwerp. *(Rudy van Nunen)*

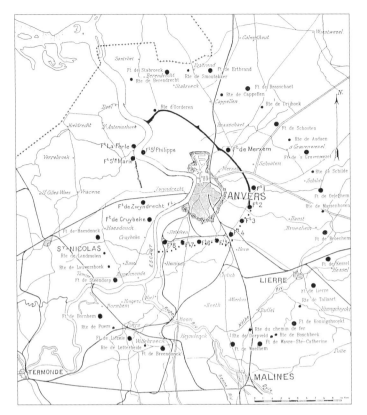

The fortifications of Antwerp in 1914. Note the crosses indicating the border with the Netherlands, which was a neutral country through which the River Scheldt (Escaut) passes. *(Robert Gils/Simon Stevinstichting)*

the forces in France fall back. The commander's staff disagreed and argued for an attack in France. The compromise was the transfer of the Sixth Army but no retreat in France. Supplies were a problem as the railway crossing the Meuse at Namur was out until the bridge there could be repaired, leaving only the line through Brussels to convey material to northern France, and that was still threatened by the stubborn Belgians in Antwerp. On 28 September Hans von Beseler's IIIrd Reserve Corps, reinforced with 173 heavy guns, began the reduction of the Belgian National Redoubt.

The British had also arrived in Antwerp some days earlier in the form of the Royal Navy Air Service. Commander Charles Samson had allocated a flight to the place to attack the Zeppelin sheds at Cologne and Dusseldorf and on 17 September he went there to check progress. There were two B.E. Biplanes and a Sopwith Biplane there at the time, with two Sopwith Tabloids expected shortly. On 22 September a strike was attempted but it was foiled by fog over the River Roer; only Lieutenant Collet managing to get through to Dusseldorf. His bombs were dropped from too low an altitude for the safety device to be disengaged and the one bomb that did explode missed the sheds but killed a couple of soldiers.

The forts to the south-east of Antwerp first came under fire on 27 September. Fort Wavre St Catherine was attacked by a 42-cm mortar of 2 Kurze Marine Kanonen Batterie from a distance of 10.1 km (6¼ miles) and by a 30.5-cm gun of 1 Schwere

Küsten Mörser Batterie 7.5 km (4½ miles) away. The former fired 171 rounds and the latter 327, denying the Belgians the chance to reply and, when the magazine exploded on 29 September, the wherewithal as well. The fort surrendered on 2 October. On 28 September 2 30.5-cm mortars engaged Fort Waelhem and had smashed it utterly by the next day. Fort Lierre suffered the loss of a 5.7-in gun cupola on 30 September and, on the same day, Antwerp's water supply was jeopardized with the shelling of the waterworks and the destruction of a reservoir; the artesian wells could not produce a sufficient supply. The village of Lierre (Lier) was burning on 1 October. Powell wrote:

> Against a livid sky rose pillars of smoke from burning villages. The air was filled with shrieking shell and bursting shrapnel. . . . While we were watching the bombardment from a rise in the Waelhem road a shell burst in the hamlet of Waterloos, whose red-brick houses were clustered almost at our feet. A few minutes later a procession of fugitive villagers came plodding up the cobble-paved highway. It was headed by an ashen-faced peasant pushing a wheelbarrow with a weeping woman clinging to his arm. In the wheelbarrow, atop a pile of hastily collected household goods, was sprawled the body of a little boy. He could not have been more than seven . . .

The destruction of the forts to the south-east of Antwerp was followed by a German advance to threaten a crossing of the River Nethe. The Belgian government concluded that the city was no longer secure and preparations were made to move the government to Ostend, but these arrangements were suspended when news came of the intention of the British First Sea Lord, Winston Churchill, to visit the city himself. The Royal Marine Brigade, the first of a force including two naval brigades under Major-General Archibald Paris, was sent from Dunkirk and Churchill himself arrived on 4 October. Powell reported:

> At one o'clock that afternoon a big drab-coloured touring-car filled with British naval officers tore up the Place de Meir, its horn sounding a hoarse warning, took the turn into the narrow Marché aux Souliers on two wheels, and drew up in front of the hotel. Before the car had fairly come to a stop the door of the tonneau was thrown violently open and out jumped a smooth-faced, sandy-haired, stoop-shouldered, youthful-looking man in the undress Trinity House uniform. There was no mistaking who it was. It was the Right Hon. Winston Churchill. . . . It was a most spectacular entrance and reminded me for all the world of a scene in a melodrama where the hero dashes up, bare-headed, on a foam-flecked horse, and saves the heroine or the old homestead or the family fortune, as the case may be. . . . An hour later I was standing in the lobby talking to M. de Vos, the Burgomaster of Antwerp . . . when Mr Churchill rushed past us on his way to his room. . . . The Burgomaster stopped him, introduced himself, and expressed his anxiety regarding the fate of the city. Before he had finished Churchill was part-way up

the stairs. 'I think everything will be all right now . . .' he called. . . . 'You needn't worry. We're going to save the city.'

The civilians were clearly comforted, but Powell, the hard-bitten journalist, was less optimistic, remarking that the German guns could be heard quite clearly.

The German 37th Landwehr Brigade, reinforced by 1st Reserve Ersatz Brigade, attacked the line of the River Scheldt that day, Sunday, at Schoonarde, west of Termonde, but the Belgian 4th Division held it. As the 6,000 men of the Royal Naval Division arrived on Monday the German blow fell on the River Nethe at Duffel where the redoubt, its ammunition exhausted, had been evacuated. The Royal Marines had arrived near Lierre on Sunday to take over what trivial defensive positions there were. Commander Samson had come up from Dunkirk over the previous two days in command of a convoy of London motor buses and armoured cars, and in the early hours of 5 October he was asked to get a machine-gun to a battalion of Royal Marines in Lierre. He recalled:

> As it was still dark there was a good chance of getting the gun into position before daylight. We set off in the [armoured] car with Captain Richards, the Adjutant; and leaving the car hidden behind some houses, Osmond, Bateman, Captain Richards, his orderly, and myself, crept along the empty streets through the piles of broken glass and rubbish carrying the Lewis gun belonging to the car and a dozen charges of ammunition. We arrived at the head of the bridge, which had been partially demolished, and got into the end house overlooking the river. . . . We got upstairs and found an attic window which gave a good field of fire.

They then began filling pillowcases with earth from the garden, unmindful of the dawn. Suddenly they came under rifle fire and shot back into the house. The only way back to the car was along the street and fortunately they managed to go that way without being seen. Osmond and Bateman returned that night, having expended their ammunition and claimed to have 'got some Huns'.

On 5 October four battalions succeeded in crossing between Duffel and Lierre and held on in the face of Allied artillery fire. Orders for a counter-attack were issued early in the morning of 6 October, but they did not reach the Royal Naval Division in time and only a few Belgian units attempted the action. In spite of some success the instruction to withdraw to the next defensive line was given and the 1st Naval Brigade was deployed between Forts 1 to 5 of the inner ring, while the 2nd took up positions between 5 and 8. The Germany artillery, however, could now be brought forward sufficiently to start on the city itself. Samson took a dim view of the prospects.

> The Belgian Infantry were worn out, and required a rest and refit. The Marines, splendid as we knew them to be and as they proved, were too few and too old to be able to hold out for long. The Naval Division . . . did not impress us as a

German infantry observe the shelling of the Antwerp defences.

A preserved gun turret at Fort Liezele. *(Bart van Bulck)*

fighting unit of much value, being badly equipped, and with very little training. The armoured train, with its 4.7-inch guns, was our only heavy artillery which was of any use. . . . On October 6th it was decided that the evacuation of Antwerp would take place as soon as possible. I received orders to get the aeroplanes and cars away by dawn on the 7th. Certain aeroplanes were to be left to the last in order to carry out an attack on the Zeppelin sheds at Dusseldorf and Cologne.

The air raid was nearly thwarted by the start of the German bombardment at 1130 hours on 8 October. Lieutenant Spencer-Grey, in command of the little party, had the aircraft pulled out of their sheds and positioned in the middle of the aerodrome in the hope they would run less risk of being damaged. The misty weather prevented any flying that day so it was not until 1330 hours on 9 October that the Sopwith Tabloids of Spencer-Grey and Lieutenant Reggie Marix took off. Spencer-Grey made for Cologne, but mist obscured his view of the Zeppelin sheds so he dropped his bombs on the railway station and returned to Antwerp. At 2030 hours shelling destroyed his and the only other aircraft there so the RNAS men left for Ostend.

Reggie Marix was more fortunate. He found the Dusseldorf shed and released his bombs from 600 ft (180 m); both hit the target. The roof fell in and the Zeppelin within, inflated with hydrogen, burst into flames. The updraught threw Marix's Tabloid up in the air but did not damage it, so he turned for base. The return flight was hazardous and, some 20 miles (30 km) short of Antwerp, he was forced to make an emergency landing having evaded small-arms fire but running out of fuel. The journey was completed in part on a borrowed bicycle and in part on a railway engine. He arrived in time to make the car journey to Ostend.

At 1600 hours on 6 October a meeting had taken place in Antwerp to consider what should be done. It was attended by Churchill and by the commander of the British 7th Division (a unit being sent to reinforce the Belgian front), Lieutenant-General Sir Henry Rawlinson. It was decided to hold the inner ring of forts and to withdraw all forces not required for that purpose west of the Scheldt, the Belgian fortress troops with the the two naval brigades and the 4th and 7th Fortress Regiments holding the line and the Marine Brigade and the Belgian 2nd Division in reserve. That night the remainder crossed the river. Rawlinson set off for the coast to meet the incoming 7th Division. Early on 7 October two battalions of the German 37th Landwehr Brigade managed to cross the Scheldt at Schoonaarde and by the end of the day were supported by a completed temporary bridge and the rest of the brigade. From there only the River Durme, through the town of Lokeren, separated them from the main road west from Antwerp along which withdrawal was taking place. The Belgian 3rd and 6th Divisions were to keep this vital route open for the retreating armies and for those civilians now hastening to leave their doomed city.

The news of the coming abandonment of Antwerp came as a shock to its citizens. They had placed confidence in the assurances given to them and they had been cheered by the arrival of British troops. Powell portrayed their reactions to the change in the situation.

Imagine what happened, then, when they awoke on Wednesday morning, October 7, to learn that the Government had stolen away between two days without issuing so much as a word of warning. . . . It was like waiting until the entire first floor of a house was in flames and the occupants' means of escape was almost cut off, before shouting 'Fire!'

No one who witnessed the exodus of the population from Antwerp will ever forget it. . . . It was not a flight; it was a stampede. . . . So complete was the German enveloping movement that only three avenues of escape remained open: westward, through St Nicolas and Lokeren, to Ghent; north-eastward across the frontier into Holland; down the Scheldt toward Flushing. Of the half million fugitives – for the exodus was not confined to the citizens of Antwerp but included the entire population of the countryside for twenty miles around – probably fully a quarter of a million escaped by river. Anything that could float was pressed into service: merchant steamers, dredgers, ferry-boats, scows, barges, canal-boats, tugs, fishing craft, yachts, rowing-boats, launches, even extemporized rafts.

The roads were a solid mass of soldiers and civilians making their way westwards. Every kind of conveyance was to be seen and even more people made their way on foot. Powell continues:

Dutch officials take British Royal Naval Brigade members and others into custody as internees.

I saw sturdy young peasants carrying their parents in their arms. I saw women of fashion in fur coats and high-heeled shoes staggering along clinging to the rails of the caissons or to the ends of wagons. I saw white-haired men and women grasping the harness of the gun-teams or the stirrup-leathers of the troopers, who, themselves exhausted from many days of fighting, slept in their saddles as they rode.

The German heavy guns sent their massive shells into the emptying city at about midnight on 7/8 October and continued until late the following day when a pause permitted people to creep from their cellars and seek food and drink. Warehouses and shops were looted. Before daylight General Paris had news that Forts 1, 2 and 4 had fallen and at a conference held at 0900 hours it was agreed with the Military Governor of Antwerp, General Deguise, that the line could not be held and that the Naval Division should be withdrawn at dusk. The order was given at 1730, but it was not fully communicated to the 1st Brigade; only Drake Battalion received it. As a result the rest of that brigade started their withdrawal late and, after numerous further problems, found themselves cut off from the rest of Paris's men by the German advance. They therefore marched north, across the Dutch frontier, where some 1,500 of them gave up their weapons and were interned for the remaining period of the war. Other groups of British seamen were cut off during the retreat and about 900 of them, together with some 400 Belgians, were obliged to surrender.

Powell had been downriver to telegraph his reports to the USA from Dutch soil, as communications from Antwerp were severed, and returned by launch on 10 October, just before the city was surrendered and in time to see the Germans enter. The American consul being absent, he assumed that duty, rather to the surprise of career diplomats elsewhere, and witnessed the triumphal march-past with which the Germans celebrated their conquest. He and the photographer, Thompson, were, he thought, the sole civilian observers. It took some 5 hours for all the units to parade through the streets. Military police were followed by infantry and field artillery, then horse artillery and finally the cavalry:

> . . . cuirassiers with their steel helmets and breastplates covered with grey linen, hussars in befrogged grey jackets and fur busbies, also linen-covered, and finally Uhlans, riding amid a forest of lances under a cloud of fluttering pennons. But this was not all, nor nearly all, for after the Uhlans came the sailors of the naval division, brown-faced, bewiskered fellows with their round, flat caps tilted rakishly and the roll of the sea in their gait; then the Bavarians in dark blue, the Saxons in light blue, and the Austrians – the same who handled the big guns so effectively – in uniforms of a beautiful silver grey. . . .

> As that great fighting machine swung past, remorseless as a trip-hammer, efficient as a steam-roller, I could not but marvel how the gallant, chivalrous, and heroic but ill-prepared little army of Belgium had held it back so long.

TWO

RETREAT TO THE YSER

By 8 October it had become clear to General Joffre that the operations in the north-east, in Artois, Flanders and Belgium, required the close attention of a coordinating commander. He therefore put General Ferdinand Foch in command of what would become known as 'The Race to the Sea'. It was not, of course, a competition to get to the coast, but a series of attempts made by each side to outflank the other, complicated by the existence of opposing forces in northern Belgium and a lack of forces of either side in Flanders. The British and French entertained hopes of establishing a front from Ghent to Lille and then southwards from there. The Belgians, however, were concerned to rest and

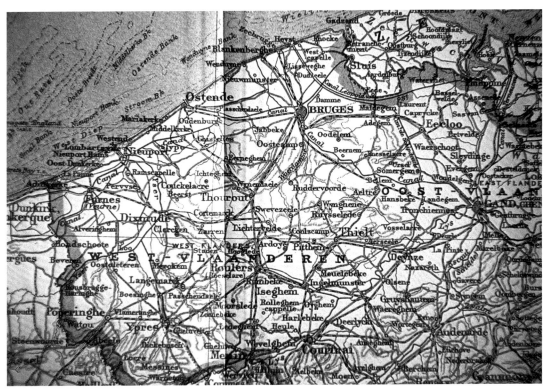

Detail from a contemporary map of the West and East Flanders regions of Belgium. Ghent (Gand) is on the far right and Dixmude left with Nieuport to its north and Ypres to its south. The borders with the Netherlands to the north and France to the south are shown in red.

French Marines leave for the front.

preserve what forces they had as well as to hold at least a portion of their country against the Germans. After the fall of Antwerp the Ghent line quickly became an impossibility. The Belgians had, however, already made plans for a final line along the River Yser which runs from Ypres (or Ieper in Flemish) by way of Dixmude (Diksmuide) to the sea at Nieuport (Niewpoort).

The British 7th Division and 3rd Cavalry Division, 21,942 men, 9,580 horses and 69 guns, had come ashore at Ostend and Zeebrugge on 6 October, only four days before Antwerp fell and too late to influence events there. They were rather over-titled as IVth Corps and were under the command of General Rawlinson who, from 9 October, reported to Field Marshal Sir John French, the commander of the British Expeditionary Force. After its participation in the Battle of the Marne, the BEF was sent north, and closer to home, to take position on the extreme left

of Foch's line with the intention that IVth Corps should be united with it. Meanwhile, IIIrd Corps was directed to Ypres, I Corps to Hazebrouck and IInd Corps to Béthune. On 4 October a French Marine Brigade, Fusiliers Marins, under Rear Admiral Pierre Ronarc'h, was sent to Dunkirk. The unit was, in fact, only partly made up of fully trained fusiliers; they numbered 1,450 petty officers and seamen out of a total force of 170 officers and 6,500 other ranks, including a machine-gun company with 16 guns. They were organized in 6 battalions, each with 4 more machine-guns.

On reaching Dunkirk the Marine Brigade's trains were ordered onward, towards Belgium. The Marines were pleased to be given the chance to get into the fight. One of their medical officers observed: 'At every station the inhabitants were massed on the platforms. Loud cheers were raised, and our compartments were literally filled with fruit, sandwiches, cigars, cigarettes, etc. Beer, tea and coffee flowed freely. You can picture the delight of our Marines, who imagined themselves in the Land of Promise.' The first train, carrying the Admiral, reached Ghent on 8 October, and there he found that their task was now to cooperate with the British and Belgian forces in a retreat.

Ghent is situated on a wide, flat plain at the confluence of the rivers Lys, coming from Armentières and Menin to the south-west, and Scheldt, flowing from Valenciennes and Oudenaarde in the south and turning east to Antwerp. A canal runs

Belgian troops prepare to defend the approaches to Ghent south-east of Melle.

due north of the city to the coast at Terneuzen and another, the Schipodinck Canal, crosses the road to the west at right angles. The Belgians held the canal north of Ghent and the French were sent forward on 9 October to the little town of Melle where the Scheldt runs north–south for a short distance.

The Marines were struck by how pleasant the scene was as they marched towards their positions; flowers grew in profusion. Commander Varney's 2nd Regiment was positioned south of the river on a line through Gontrode, Belgians on their right and Commander Delage's 1st Regiment north of the river on a line through Heusden. The remaining two regiments and the machine-gun company were in support. That evening the Germans advanced south of the river and were repulsed by Varney's men. By 1800 hours the fighting had ceased and a thin mist was creeping over the fields. The Marines remained at their stations. At 2100 hours a shower of star-shell lit up the night and the Germans attacked again. Their own illuminations betrayed them. A fusilier recalled: 'We saw the Boches by the light of the shells, creeping along the hedges and houses like rats. We fired into the mass, and brought them down in heaps, but they kept on advancing. The Commander was unwilling for us to expose ourselves further; he gave orders to abandon Gontrode and fall back a little further upon Melle, behind the railway bank.'

The Marines' new position on the embankment was better and they had no difficulty in holding it, in the words of a sailor from Audierne: '. . . keeping the Boches employed, sending volleys into them when they came too near and charging them with the bayonet. It was fine to see them falling on the plain at every volley. We ceased firing on the 10th, about 4 a.m.' The Germans, fortunately, did not know how close they had been to breaking the line. Second Lieutenant de Blois wrote: '. . . our positions were far from solid; we were on the railway embankment, and the trenches consisted of a few holes dug between the rails; the bridge had not even been barricaded by the Belgian engineers and nothing would have been simpler than to have passed under it . . . the Germans were about 20 metres from the bridge, but they made no attempt to pass!'

The pressure to which the Allies had been subjected at Ghent up to this time had been alleviated by the German error in, after they had crossed the Scheldt, turning east, not realizing that Antwerp had been evacuated. Now, on Sunday 11 October, the mass of the German Army that was not strutting in the parade through the streets of Antwerp was turning west. The Marines were once more obliged to use the railway embankment as their defensive line and once more drove off their attackers. A withdrawal had been ordered and the bulk of the Belgian forces began to pull back at 1500 hours, followed by the French Marines at about 1930 and the British at 2200. The French buried their dead in the graveyard at Melle and marched away, through Ghent and on towards Aeltre (Aalter), on the Bruges road, which they reached at dawn. After a brief rest they turned south-west for Thielt. By evening both the French and the British reached Thielt where their ways parted, the 7th Division for Roulers and the Marines for Dixmude.

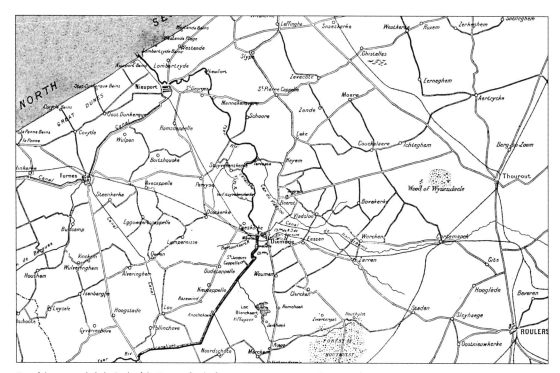

Map of the area in which the Battle of the Yser was fought, from a contemporary account. The course of the Yser, in part canalized, is marked in bold and the l'Yperlee Canal from Ypres joins it at Knochehoek (Knokke-Brug). The road south from Dixmude through Woumen runs to Ypres. *(C. le Goffic, 1916)*

The German commander, von Falkenhayn, was aware of the rate at which the Allies were building their strength on their left wing, for his cavalry corps had encountered resistance in southern Flanders. He therefore disbanded his Fourth Army in the east and brought into being a new Fourth Army, under the same general, the Duke of Württemberg, in the north. The troops of IIIrd Reserve Corps, already on the ground after their victory at Antwerp, were supplemented with units moved from the eastern front at Metz and from the centre around Reims and Soissons, as well as with reserves from Germany. These last were not, as in popular legend, units made up of student volunteers, although there were a few such men in their ranks. By far the greater part of them were older men who, having done their military service, had been put on the reserve list, or men who had been excused service for one reason or another. The Fourth Army was thus a mixture of experienced formations, which, although tired and perhaps in need of rest, were still formidable opponents, and newly created corps with inexperienced officers and incomplete equipment. This army was intended to advance

The road between Ramscapelle and Pervyse crossing one of the many canals that characterize the landscape. *(Alex Deseyne)*

The embankment of the disused railway between Dixmude and Nieuport is still the site of Belgian shelters, now roofless, from the First World War. It is a preserved area and may be visited. *(Alex Deseyne)*

southwards from Belgium, along the coast, to outflank the Allies. Meanwhile, the Sixth Army was to engage the Allies in Artois between La Bassée and Menin. This could only work if the defensive line on the Yser was overcome, that is, if the Belgians could be beaten or by-passed by overthrowing Rawlinson's two divisions west of Roulers.

On 13 October the French Marines were assigned the defence of a line between the railway station of Kortemark (Cortemark), halfway between Dixmude and Thielt, and the wood of Wijendale, to the north. It soon became apparent they could not hold here and, the next day, the order to fall back on Dixmude came. In the early hours of Thursday, 15 October, and in steady rain the final retreat began. The German IIIrd Corps occupied Ostend and Zeebrugge later that day. The French trudged west through Zarren and Esen (Eessen) towards Dixmude, past throngs of bewildered refugees. Just west of Esen the 2nd Battalion, 1st Regiment under Commander de Kerros took position to hold the roads running north–east, south–east and south while the 3rd Battalion, 2nd Regiment made for Woumen to cover the southern side of Dixmude. The remaining four battalions and the machine-gun company went through Dixmude and occupied positions west of the Yser before joining Belgian engineers in fortifying the perimeter of the town itself.

The terrain between Boesinghe, just north of Ypres, and Nieuport is low-lying and water-filled. Innumerable ditches and dykes drain the soil and sluices at Nieuport allow the water out at low tide and prevent the sea rushing in at high water. The roads were raised above the level of the fields and the railway to Nieuport ran on an embankment about 6 ft (1.8 m) high. The River Yser was also raised above the land, flowing between embankments in a canalized channel. Crossing-places were few, only eight bridges existed between Boesinghe and the sea. Dixmude itself is on the tip of higher land intruding from the south-east which rises to the Houthulst Forest and the ridges through Passchendaele and Wytschate, embracing Ypres, leaving the rest of this land low and liable to flood.

The Belgians deployed their forces with the 2nd Division around Nieuport with forward positions at Lomartzyde and Westende and the 2nd Cavalry Division in reserve there. To their right the 1st Division, mainly behind the Yser, held forward positions at Schoore while the 4th Division held the line between the 1st and Dixmude, with outposts at Keyem and Beerst. Ronarc'h's men held Dixmude and to their right the 5th and 6th Divisions stood on the Yser and the Ypres Canal down to Boesinghe.

Admiral Ronarc'h had reconsidered his positions in Dixmude and withdrew to the outskirts of the town itself, putting Delage's 1st Regiment on the north and Varney's 2nd on the south with his own headquarters at Caeskerke railway station. At 1600 hours on 16 October the Germans attacked under an artillery barrage, coming on in solid masses which the Marines had little difficulty in shooting down. The fighting persisted into the morning of 17 October, and did not slacken until 1100 hours. The pause enabled the French to repair their trenches and to begin new ones. Reinforcement arrived during the day in the form of the 3rd Belgian Artillery Regiment, bringing the total of guns to seventy-two. On Sunday 18 October, while the

Marines were left alone, the German IIIrd Reserve Corps struck with full force on the Belgian sector. They dented the Belgian 1st and 2nd Divisions' advance posts, taking Keyem and Schoore, but could not cross the river. The Germans had the advantage of heavy guns used against Antwerp while the Belgians were limited to their 75-mm field artillery, but support was soon to come from the sea. That evening the Belgian 4th Division regained Keyem with a bayonet charge.

At the outbreak of war three monitors, *Javary*, *Madera* and *Solimoes*, were under construction for the Brazilian government. These ships were designed for river or inshore operations and drew a mere 5 ft 8 in (1.72 m) of water. They were immediately purchased by the British and renamed *Humber*, *Mersey* and *Severn*. They were armed with three 6-in guns and two 4.7-in howitzers as well as four 3-pounders and one anti-aircraft gun of similar calibre. The 1919 edition of *Jane's Fighting Ships* classified these vessels as armoured gunboats and noted that the third 6-in gun on HMS *Humber* was salvaged from the wreck of the *Montagu* and mounted on the quarterdeck. These ships formed part of a British Navy flotilla commanded by Admiral Horace Hood and, with the light cruisers *Attentive* and *Foresight* and four Tribal class destroyers, put to sea from Dover on 18 October.

The attack of 19 October was extended a little further south, against a line from Lombartzyde to Beerst, close to Dixmude. Ronarc'h reacted swiftly, sending two reserve battalions against Beerst and another two towards Vladslo to turn and approach Beerst from the south-east. However, the situation in Beerst itself was not known and they refrained from shelling the village lest their own side were still in possession. As the 5th Company, under Lieutenant de Mauisson de Candé, approached Beerst they were met with a hail of machine-gun fire. In the flat land only the drainage ditches afforded any cover and every head raised to observe the enemy became a target. To their left the company heading for Keyem also ran into trouble but Lieutenant Hébert's company penetrated between the two villages. They were ousted by German artillery fire, but not before they had done damage to their enemies. Commander Varney abandoned his command post to lead a charge into Beerst where they became embroiled in house-to-house fighting. The Marines and the Belgian 5th Division took Vladslo and by 1700 hours they were consolidating their positions. The Germans were not slow to react. The XXIInd Reserve Corps inclined north from its advance on Roulers to come into line on IIIrd Reserve Corp's left, giving some relief to the French and British further south around Ypres. The little salient held by the French and Belgians was too vulnerable to leave exposed and the order was given to withdraw. That night the villages were back in German hands. Allied casualties ran into the hundreds.

A priest, the Abbé le Helloco, chaplain of the 2nd Regiment, wrote of the courage of a young Marine:

It was at Beerst. A quartermaster had his leg broken by a bullet in the temporary trench he was occupying with his company. He went on fighting. His comrades were obliged to fall back under a tremendous fire . . . a . . . Marine, who had been trained by him at Lorient, could not make up his mind to abandon the quartermaster. By dint of extraordinary efforts, he managed to reach him and succeeded in dragging him some three hundred yards [275 m] to a house, where he left him under shelter.

The Marine was himself wounded as he went back and met the priest at the dressing station where he told the story. The chaplain continues the story, describing the actions of the Marine when a rescue party was suggested: '. . . he set out in front of us, heedless of the very real danger . . . we were lucky enough to find the quartermaster and bring him back into our lines. I notified the conduct of these two brave fellows to the commanding officer that same evening, and I hope they received the reward they deserved.'

Further north, on the coast at Lombartzyde, the Belgian 2nd Division took the full force of the German assault. A total of three successive attacks were thrown back before, out of the mist, the grey forms of the British Navy's flotilla could be seen. The monitors shelled German positions on the coast and as far to the east as Middelkeerke, some 5 miles (8 km) from Nieuport. The naval shells were not really suitable for such use as they were designed for action against armoured ships and did not fragment in the same way as army rounds, but even given that limitation, they made a real contribution to the fight. German artillery batteries in particular suffered significant damage. The Belgian High Command was later to state that the Germans decided not to attempt a crossing of the Yser at Nieuport by their 4th Ersatz Division because of the threat of the British ships.

On 20 October the weight of the fighting was to the south, in what would become the Ypres salient, and the Yser front was, officially, comparatively quiet, if the continuous artillery bombardment mounted by the Germans is set aside. Infantry attacked a Belgian outpost on the coast and a counter-attack regained it only to be counter-attacked in its turn. The matter was settled when the farm at the centre of the action was flattened by naval gunnery. The first heavy shells fell on Dixmude at 1100 hours. A captain of Marines wrote: 'Up to this date 77 shrapnel, with their queer caterwaulings, were the only presents the enemy had sent us. But during the course of the 20th the big shells began to rain on us, and their first objective was, of course, the church. At the fifth or sixth the beautiful building was on fire.' The Belgian positions south of the town had to be reinforced and as the Marines manoeuvred the Germans attacked. Confident of the success of their barrage, they came on in solid lines and offered easy targets and the assault petered out against the barbed wire. As darkness fell the attempt was abandoned. Another attack at 0300 hours the next day also failed.

On 21 October the pressure continued with persistent artillery fire. At 1600 hours the Germans were reported as having broken into the trenches south of the town. Three companies of Marines were sent to rectify the matter. One wrote:

We tried our hands as marksmen and while the Boches were trying to re-form, before they had recovered from their surprise, we fired into them at 50 metres, and then charged them with the bayonet. You should have seen them run like hares, throwing away their arms and equipment. What a raid it was, five to six hundred dead and wounded and forty prisoners, among them three officers! We reoccupied the trenches, and I spent the night in the company of a dead Belgian and a wounded German, who, when he woke up, exclaimed: 'Long live France!' lest we should run him through. When day came, and we could behold our work . . . (Here an interval. A shell burst just over my head, smashed a rifle, and threw a handful of earth in my face. It was slightly unpleasant. I continue.) It was a pretty sight. All day long stretcher-bearers were picking up the dead and wounded, while we continued to fire from time to time. All the wounded we have picked up are young men, sixteen to twenty years old, of the last levy.

On 22 October the Germans gave their attention to the line to the north of Dixmude, at the village of Tervate. The Yser runs in a wide loop bulging towards the east halfway between Dixmude and Nieuport, and Tervate is on the southern side of the meander. The Germans managed to cross there but were thrown back during the day. However, two battalions of the Belgian 1st Division were badly mauled in the action and were withdrawn to Furnes late in the day. As the 9th Infantry and the 2nd Chasseurs marched into the town to the rear at about 1900 hours they were given a heroes' welcome. That night the Germans attacked at Tervate once more,

French infantry reinforcements approach the Yser front. *(In Flanders Fields archive)*

crossing the Yser and establishing a bridgehead which they linked with entrenchments to their position at Schoorbakke, to the north-west. The Belgians were forced to fall back to a line through Pervyse on the railway line from Nieuport to Dixmude. On the coast the Belgian 2nd Division was exhausted, having thrown back successive assaults on Lombartzyde, and was due to be relieved by the French 42nd Division.

Geoffrey Malins was, in his own word, a 'kinematographer', a cameraman and maker of moving pictures, in the employ of the Gaumont Company when war broke out. He wrote about his experiences, taking care to conceal exact locations, times and the names of the regiments he filmed as must have been his habit, for security reasons, during the conflict. It was during the early autumn of 1914 that he was asked to go to Belgium and he did not hesitate to accept the commission. He took an Aeroscope camera, powered by compressed air taken from a cylinder that required pumping up from time to time. He travelled to Furnes and persuaded a Belgian unit to take him to the front.

> It was still raining, and, as we crossed the fields of mud, I began to feel the weight of my equipment pressing on my shoulders, which with my camera and spare films made my progress very slow. Many a time during that march the men offered to help me, but, knowing that they had quite enough to do in carrying their own load, I stubbornly refused. On we went, the roar of the guns getting nearer; over field after field, fully eighteen inches [46 cm] deep in mud, and keeping as close to hedges as possible, to escape detection from hostile aeroplanes. . . .

A German observation balloon sent them to cover for fear of enemy artillery and they huddled in the rain under a hedge until night and then resumed their trek to the front.

> Ye gods! what a night and what a sight! Raining hard, a strong wind blowing, and the thick, black, inky darkness every now and then illuminated by the flash of the guns. Death was certainly in evidence tonight. One felt it. The creative genius of the wierdest, imaginative artist could not have painted a scene of death so truthfully. The odour arising from decaying bodies in the ground was at times almost overwhelming.

They were ordered to keep silent and hold on to the man in front. This soaking conga of soldiery then made its way into and along a trench knee-deep in water.

> 'Halt!' came the command to the section I was with. 'This is our shelter, monsieur,' said a voice. Gropingly, I followed the speaker on hands and knees. The shelter was about 12 feet [3.65 m] long, 3 feet 6 inches [1 m] high, the same in width, and made of old boards. On the top, outside, was about 9 inches [23 cm] of earth, to render it as far as possible shrapnel-proof. On the floor were some boards, placed on bricks and covered with soddened straw. There was just room for four of us.

They were in the line forward of Ramscapelle. Malins shot various scenes of the fighting and shelling the next day, learning to take cover but forced to take risks to get the images he needed.

> Then I cautiously made my way back, and filmed a section being served with hot coffee while under fire. Coming upon some men warming themselves round a bucket-stove, I joined the circle for a little warmth. How comforting it was in that veritable morass. Even as we chatted we were subjected to a heavy shrapnel attack, and the way we all scuttled to the trench huts was a sight for the gods.

After three days at the front Malins made his way back to Furnes and to London.

The French Marines at Dixmude were, on 23 October, under unremitting bombardment and threatened with a flanking movement on their north by German troops now able to enter Stuivekenskerke. Ronarc'h moved to protect his left and also sent Commander Jeanniot with his battalion towards Oud Stuivekenskerke, south of the principal village. One of the Marines wrote:

> On October 24 we spent a day and a night in the first line. That night we had two men killed in our trench and four wounded by a shell, and we were going to the rear for a little well-earned rest. Scarcely had we swallowed our coffee, when the order came to clear decks, as we say on board ship, and shoulder our knapsacks. When we got nearer, the bullets began to whistle. We crawled on all fours over the exposed ground, without a shred of cover. Those who ventured to raise their heads were at once wounded, though we could see nothing of the Germans. We got so accustomed to the bullets whizzing past our ears that we lost all fear and advanced steadily.

This Marine's confidence was ill-founded, for he was shot in the leg later that day. French and Belgian losses were numerous, but they managed to establish a line facing north against the German incursion and to hold it. A notebook found on the body of a German officer of the 202nd Regiment killed that day contained the following entry:

> We are losing men on every hand, and our losses are out of all proportion to the results obtained. Our guns do not succeed in silencing the enemy's batteries; our infantry attacks are ineffectual; they only lead to useless butchery. Our losses must be enormous. My colonel, my major, and many other officers are dead or wounded. All our regiments are mixed up together; the enemy's merciless fire enfilades us.

He then complained about the number of *francs-tireurs* arrayed against them, a fixation with the Germans who were convinced that concealed guerillas rather than regular soldiers were somehow taking a fearful toll. Clearly both sides were suffering severely.

Ramscapelle station. Later in the war the observation tower was built and from it the area of the inundated front line can still be overseen. *(Alex Deseyne)*

The attacks on Dixmude continued. A Marine of the 3rd Battalion recorded: 'During the night of Sunday the 25th we were obliged to evacuate the houses in which we were, as they fell in upon us.' The main thrust of the German effort then turned to the new Belgian line in the centre, at Pervijze and Ramscapelle where the Belgian 1st Division had the support of the 42nd, under General Grosetti, which had arrived on 23 October, on their left. Two battalions of Senegalese troops were on their way to reinforce the Marines and would arrive on 26 October, but the front as a whole now faced the German 4th Ersatz Division between Nieuport and the sea, IIIrd Reserve Corps to their left as far as Keyem, then XXIInd Reserve Corps and, finally, south of Dixmude, XXIIIrd Reserve Corps; seven divisions against the remnants of the Belgian Army's seven, which had sustained losses of about 25 per cent, and the French forces. It was clear that they were at the extreme limits of their endurance and that, without further reinforcement, this front would fall to the Germans. Further south, at Ypres, the French and British were clinging on and had no men to spare. The Belgians had no alternative to using the elements as their ally.

Belgian civilians, allegedly *francs-tireurs*, being gathered up by German troops. Many such were executed.

Sluices at Nieuport, with the King Albert Memorial beyond. The Belgian *Sapeurs-pontonniers*, engineers, controlled the sluices to maintain the inundation until the end of the war. (*Alex Deseyne*)

In 1795 Nieuport had been defended by flooding the surrounding land and, under the direction of the *Garde Wateringue* M. Charles Louis Kogge, the same scheme was now to be put into action. It was a complicated task depending on the height of the tides and the direction of the wind. In principle the sluice gates had to be open to admit the water at high tide and shut to prevent drainage at low tide, but the waters had also to be confined to form a protective moat in front of a defensible Allied line without disrupting their access to their own positions. The Nieuport–Dixmude railway had twenty-two culverts in its embankment to allow roads and field access paths across the line. Belgian engineers hastened to block them up, turning the railway and its embankment into a long dam. Around Nieuport there were more than ten water-carrying channels and over half a dozen sluices, siphons and overflows; the flooding could not be achieved just by opening a single door. The first attempt was made by opening the overflow of the Old Yser while the Noord Vaart/Old Yser siphon was closed to prevent the inundation of the Belgian 2nd Division's positions. The results were trivial. General Foch considered flooding the country east of Dunkirk, but Kogge persisted in his efforts. On 26 October attempts to open the Old Sluice of Furnes failed but a second effort two days later succeeded and water began to creep across the land.

German assaults had not ceased during this time. At dawn on 26 October they mounted a massive attack along the Mannekensvere road against Nieuport's eastern flank and managed to take three pontoon bridges over the river and canal just as the Allies were pulling back behind the railway. Belgian troops deservedly resting at Furnes were hurried back to the front and the line was restored, the pontoons smashed by artillery. The Germans wheeled to the south-east and struck towards Ramscapelle and Pervijze. German heavy artillery fire fell on Furnes and the townspeople and hospital patients were evacuated. The French 42nd Division and the Belgian 1st Division stubbornly held the line of the railway embankment.

At Dixmude the Germans had attacked at 0200 hours when firing had broken out near Kasskerke station. The French thought it was some mistake, that their own men were firing on each other. However, it soon became evident that the enemy had infiltrated their lines and that somewhere their perimeter had been breached. There had been a skirmish on the southern flank at 1900 hours the evening before and the Abbé le Helloco and the chief medical officer, Dr Duguet, had retired to the latter's billet at about 0130 hours after doing their duty by those involved. However, soon they were roused by gunfire and rushed out of the door, falling at once to rifle fire. The doctor died and the priest fell unconscious. Commander Jeanniot also ran out and, seeing a group of men in the gloom, assumed they were French and ran to lead them against the enemy. They were German and eagerly seized the unarmed officer and, with him and others taken prisoner herded before them, continued towards the Yser where they ran into the guard on the bridge and came under fire. Now isolated within French lines and with no alternative to capture other than seeking hiding places for the day, the intruders turned their guns on their captives. M. Charles Thomas Couture gave an account of the events.

Commander Jeanniot was struck by several bullets, the whole of the front of his skull being blown off. Several of the Belgians fell. My comrade, Bonnet, if I understood him aright, made the movement of a child who dodges a box on the ear. That saved him; the bullet aimed at his head went into his right shoulder. At this moment he saw our sailors and the Belgians coming up, and running as fast as he could lay legs to the ground, he called up to them: 'Go at them; there are only about forty of them left.' The rest had made off across the fields. At 7 a.m. they were all prisoners.

The Admiral at once decided that the murderers should be shot there and then. But as Frenchmen are not given to wholesale executions, the prisoners who had been rescued were called upon to point out the ringleaders. A few seconds later four volleys told me that military justice had taken its rapid course. . . .

The rest of the morning was quiet. A German effort was being made further to the north, where we heard furious fighting. As we were drinking our coffee the Senegalese riflemen arrived to support the sailors. They were received with joy, for the brigade was much exhausted.

The opening of the sluices on 28 October went well and, the next day, when the spring tide was at its full, the gates of Noord Vaart were opened. The inundation

A flooded, shell-damaged farmhouse at Roedesterkte, east of Ramscapelle. *(Provinciale Biblioteek en Cultuurarchief, St Andries)*

Even today, as here on the Ypres–Dixmude road, the land floods readily. *(Alex Deseyne)*

spread across the land; the Nieuport lock-keeper Mr Geraert was doing his job well. On 30 October the process was repeated. As the waters rose the Germans redoubled their efforts to breach the centre of the line. At 0630 hours on 30 October the assault on Ramscapelle was led by two Württemberger brigades. The Belgian 2nd Division on the railway embankment could not hold and the enemy poured into Ramscapelle and Pervijze. The French 42nd and the Belgian 3rd Divisions came to the 2nd's support and street fighting in the ruins of the villages left the issue in the balance. High tide was at 1930 hours and as the water pressure increased the dykes containing the Yser began to fail. The flood quickened and deepened and the Germans realized that if they did not retreat they would soon be isolated on the wrong side of the inundations. Through waist-high water they struggled back.

The French Marines at Dixmude were at the southern end of the newly protected area and had still to guard the line. The rain fell steadily and the major problem was the want of socks; many men had bare feet inside their sodden boots. One of them wrote home:

Dear Mother,
You say my brother is still drinking, and this is very wrong of him, but he took the socks off his own feet to send them to me. I thank him very much, for I did want them badly.

To the south, near Ypres, the British were desperately fighting to save Gheluvelt and the next day, 1 November, Messines fell to the Germans. Here in the north the Allies were planning to attack. On 3 November four battalions of the French 42nd Division and one of Marines struck to the south of Dixmude towards the château at Woumen on the road to Ypres. The artillery preparation began at 0800, but it was not until 1130 that the infantry made a move. They advanced a mere 220 yd (200 m). A further attempt by night did no better. The next day pontoon bridges were brought to span the Yser south of Dixmude and fog facilitated their construction. Two more battalions of Marines and the rest of the 42nd Division were to take part. On this day and the next the French attacks failed to take the château, though they reached its very gates. The pressure elsewhere on this front demanded reinforcement and the assault was abandoned.

Lieutenant-Colonel E.D. Swinton and Captain the Earl Percy wrote of the fronts they had seen in 1915 and described the flooded area:

War has added desolation and horror to the natural melancholy of the country-side, which at all times is of the most dreary character. A dead, wind-swept flat, its only features are the villages, with their tall church steeples, and a few trees, chiefly willows, all bent and twisted by the prevailing winds from the sea. . . .

In front of the line is a waste of water melting into the sky, and the further bank obscured in mist. The grey expanse is here and there intersected by a road running for some distance on an embankment, and broken by a few trees and hedgerows or the remains of a farm rising up out of the flood, on which islands the advance posts of each side are established. The corpses of long dead German soldiers and the swollen carcasses of cattle and sheep with legs sticking stiffly into the air, drift aimlessly about, while large flocks of wild fowl give the one visible touch of life to the desolate scene. . . .

Nothing could present a stronger contrast to this comparative inaction than the nature of the fighting in progress along the sand dunes farther to the north. Here a desperate struggle at short range continues from day to day, the opposing trenches being situated within a few yards of one another. Here, instead of mud and water, the troops have to endure the wind which blows the sand about in stinging clouds so trying to the eyes as to necessitate the wearing of motor-goggles. Under the restless drifting sand the configuration of the landscape is continually altering, fresh dunes being formed at one point, while they melt away at another. Perhaps the best description of this area of soft-looking shapeless white mounds is that given by a French officer, who compared it to a land of whipped cream.

Malins made more visits to this front but the precise dates are not recorded. On one of these trips he heard, when in Furnes, that the French forces at Nieuport included Goumiers, men from Morocco, and he thought they would look well on film. He went forward with an officer to seek them out, braving the shell-fire and chatting as they went. Malins reported the officer's remark and what followed it:

'Our Goumiers are doing splendid work here on the dunes. It is, of course, like home to them among the sand-heaps.' Our conversation was cut short by the shriek of a shell coming in our direction. Simultaneously we fell flat on the sand, and only just in time, for on the other side of the dune the shell fell and exploded, shaking the ground like a miniature earthquake and throwing clouds of sand in our direction.

With the way pointed out to him, Malins went on alone until he came across an interpreter attached to a troop about to go scouting. He continues: 'What a magnificent picture they made, sitting on their horses. They seemed to be part of them . . . as they wound in and out of the sand-hills, I managed to get into a splendid point of vantage, and filmed them coming towards me. Their wild savage huzzas, as they passed, were thrilling in the extreme.' Later Malins followed a party probing forward, crawling after them with his camera strapped to his back:

One may think crawling on the sand is easy . . . I soon found it was not so easy as it looked, especially under conditions where the raising of one's body two or three inches above the top of a dune might possibly be asking for a bullet through it . . . I had crawled in this fashion for about 150 yards [137 m], when I heard a shell come shrieking in my direction. With a plunk it fell, and exploded about forty feet [12 m] away, choking me with sand and half blinding me for about five minutes. . . . Deciding that if I continued by myself I had everything to lose and nothing to gain, I concluded that discretion was the better part of valour. Possibly the buzzing sensation in my throat, and the smarting of my eyes, helped me in coming to that decision, so I retraced my steps, or rather crawled. Getting back to the encampment, I bathed my eyes in water, which quickly soothed them . . . news came in the scouts were returning. . . . The exultant look on their faces told me that they had done good work.

The Belgian front north of Ypres had now been reduced to the theatre of sand-dune fighting around Nieuport and the water frontier along the Yser and the canal to the south of the new, great lake, with only the Dixmude salient projecting into German lines. It was not to remain there for long, but the position was no longer of importance. On 10 November the Germans mounted the final assault. At 0930 hours an attack was made on the 9th and 10th companies of the 1st Regiment on the northern side of the Dixmude defences, but it was beaten off. Artillery fire on the Marine, Senegalese and Belgian positions was intense from 1000 hours, in the words of an officer who was present, 'Impossible to lift one's nose above the ground, so thick and fast came the shells.' Then a mass assault took place. The eastern line collapsed.

A German unit managed to infiltrate along the Handzaeme Canal into the centre of the ruined town. With their force cut in two, the French and Belgians fought hard but the numbers in which the Germans poured into Dixmude could not be countered. Innumerable, small, fierce actions were contested throughout the day, but by 1800 hours all Rear Admiral Ronarc'h could do was withdraw behind the Yser and blow the bridges.

The war did not cease on this front, but it became one of siege conditions along the Yser, the occasional foray by boat over the floods adding to the toll of lives lost. On the seashore, among the dunes, both sides entertained hopes of a break-out. Another of Malins's expeditions to witness Allied forces in action, again undated, gives some idea of the conditions:

> . . . the advance guard came hurrying up in the distance; the attack was about to begin. Suddenly the French guns opened fire; they were concealed some distance in the rear. Shells then went at it thick and fast, shrieking one after another overhead.
>
> The advance guard opened out, clambered up the dunes and disappeared over the top, I filming them. I waited until the supporting column came up, and filmed them also. I followed them up and over the dunes. Deploying along the top they spread out about six metres apart, with the object of deceiving the Germans as to

Trenchless warfare: Belgian troops patrol the inundations on a raft.

The Trench of Death, *Boyau de la Mort*: a preserved position at Stuivenskerke, near Dixmude. *(Alex Deseyne)*

their numbers, until the supporting column reached them. The battle of musketry then rang out. Cautiously advancing with a company, I filmed them take the offensive and make for a dune forty yards [37 m] ahead.

Malins saw French shells hitting the ruins of a village further ahead and observed a series of skirmishes between French and Germans in which, in his opinion, the enemy came off worst. By that time the German gunners had the range of the group Malins was with and shells started to fall near them.

. . . an explosion occurred just behind me, which sounded as if the earth itself had cracked. The concussion threw me with terrific force head over heels into the sand. The explosion seemed to cause a vacuum in the air for some distance around, for try as I would I could not get my breath. I lay gasping and struggling like a drowning man for what seemed an interminable length of time, although it could have only been a few seconds.

  At last I pulled round; my first thought was for my camera. I saw it a short distance away, half buried in the sand. Picking it up, I was greatly relieved to find it uninjured, but chocked with sand round the lens, which I quickly cleared. The impression on my body, caused by the concussion of the exploding shell, seemed as if the whole of one side of me had been struck with something soft, yet with such terrible force that I felt it all over at the same moment.

Malins filmed another column going into the attack and then, in the fading light, made his way back. As his car took him towards Furnes the night was lit with shell-fire: 'What a magnificent sight it was. Magnesium star-shells were continually sent up by the Germans. They hung in the air alight for about thirty seconds, illuminating the ground like day. When they disappeared the guns flashed out; then the French replied; after that more star-shells; then the guns spoke again, and so it continued.'

The British were to have their turn on this front in 1917. On 20 June the 1st and 32nd Divisions relieved French units at Nieuport, taking over the front between St Georges and the sea. To their right the line stretched away along the railway and their right flank rested on the inundated area, but the terrain held was north-east of the Yser, in front of Lombartzyde, and had the function of securing control of the sluices on the north-east of Nieuport that controlled the floods. The front was divided up by waterways; from the Yser itself on the right, then the Plassendale Canal and finally, at right angles to the Yser between Nieuport and the sea, the Geleede Creek which ran just to the left of Lombartzyde. The effect was to cut up the terrain into potentially isolated areas should the bridges between them be destroyed.

Sergeant George Ashurst of the 16th Lancashire Fusiliers, 1st Division, wrote of the forward positions to the right of Geleede Creek which they occupied shortly after their arrival at Nieuport.

A pontoon foot-bridge across the Yser at Nieuport.

. . . we moved into the front line crossing a bridge over the canal on which it was suicide to stay one moment longer than was necessary. My company also had to cross a swamp on duck-boards and then proceed up a communication trench that Fritz [i.e. the Germans] could fire straight into. There were good trenches in the line, however, and also good small concrete pillboxes. This front was fairly hot and one had to be most careful when moving about. Night patrols and listening posts went out every night, and working parties were busy wiring and digging.

After a spell in the line we were relieved and dropped back into the town. We were now living in a tunnel that ran through the middle of the main street, a kind of covered-in communication trench which also carried telephone wires to the different fronts.

Next to the sea a battalion of the King's Royal Rifles held the line some 600 yd (550 m) forward of the Yser and a battalion of the Northamptonshire Regiment were on their right. At the end of the first week of July the weather became rough and the Royal Navy flotilla was obliged to pull away from the coast to avoid shipwreck, thus depriving the British of naval artillery cover. On 8 July the Germans unleashed a bombardment of gas and high-explosive shells. Ashurst reports:

. . . suddenly, without the least warning, Fritz opened a terrific bombardment on the town, also raining shells on the front line, the reserves, and the new gun emplacements . . . the order came along for every man to be ready for the line at once. Quickly and excitedly we strapped on our equipment, fixed our gas masks

Belgian trenches and barbed wire on the seashore.

in position for immediate use, and waited for the order to move. Very soon the order came. . . . Shouting out 'Come on, lads!' off I went. At the end of the tunnel we dashed into the open street. Shells seemed to be falling everywhere; bricks and slates and glass were flying all over the place and the air was thick with dust and powder smoke.

Aeroplanes roared high up in the sky dropping great bombs that seemed to rend whole rows of buildings asunder. . . . Madly we ran for the canal bridge, but awestricken we hesitated as salvo after salvo came screaming about it. However, it had to be crossed, and preparing ourselves for the mad dash we ran like frightened rabbits, not feeling our heavy loads as we pictured in our minds those terrible shells racing for us.

Once over they sheltered under the canal bank and waited for the rest of their little band to come over. Most made it. Ashurst continues: 'Our next move was over that terrible swamp on the duck-boards, right in the open. I glanced over the bank to see how the land lay in that direction. Shells were falling fast, churning up the muddy swamp; the duck-board track was broken up in places, and shrapnel balls were pit-patting into it like hailstones.' Ashurst decided to take a longer route by way of a communication trench, slower but much less exposed; it saved most of their lives:

The front line was having a nasty time of it. Trenches had been blown up in places and one had to dash across the open, risking the sniper's bullet. Fritz kept up the bombardment and we crouched in the low pillboxes. Some shells hit the top of them but the two feet [60 cm] of reinforced concrete held and we just received a nasty, dull thud in our heads, or when a shell burst near the entrance we felt the mighty draught through our shelter.

Bridges over the Yser and the Geleede Creek were smashed and the barbed wire in front of the defenders was cut. At 1945 hours on 10 July the 1st German Marine Division attacked, their crescent-shaped line hitting the King's Royal Rifles first and most heavily. Sergeant Benjamin Cope of the Northamptons swam the Yser to warn the troops on their right, of whom Ashurst was one, of the nature of the assault, enabling them to take position to enfilade the attackers. Meanwhile, the Rifles and Northamptons fought on, suffering great losses. Captain Aylett, C Company, 1st Northamptons, had taken the precaution of ordering the Lewis gunners to button their tunics around their weapons to keep out the sand, so these machine-guns were able to function. The 16th Lancashire Fusiliers, to the right of the creek, were not attacked at all; Ashurst kept looking out to see a German advance behind the barrage, but on his front none came. From the Nieuport side, west of the creek, a soldier swam over with a rope and this allowed a number of the British to make their escape, but the majority were killed, wounded or taken prisoner; more than 1,000 of them in all. Of the 2 battalions on the extreme left only 4 officers and 64 men got back over the Yser.

Ramscapelle Road Military Cemetery. These are the graves of men of the Royal Sussex Regiment who died in July 1917. *(Alex Deseyne)*

The memorial to the civilians killed in Nieuport stands near the church. *(Alex Deseyne)*

In just over an hour a section of front about 1,400 yd (1,280 m) wide between the creek and the sea had been taken by the Germans.

East of Geleede Creek German progress had been less impressive. What ground they gained was soon lost again and the crucial locks controlling the water levels inland remained in Allied hands. Another attack on 13 July failed once more. Two weeks later all attention turned south as the Third Battle of Ypres, also known as Passchendaele, began.

On another Belgian front, and at the end of the war, the USA took part. The American 91st Division was switched from the Meuse–Argonne campaign to Belgium in October 1918 to serve, as did the US 37th Division, under the command of the King of the Belgians. The Americans were attached to the French Army of Belgium under Major-General de Boissoudy in the centre of the line while the Belgian Army was on the left and the British Second Army was on the right.

On 18 October the 91st arrived by rail at four different points near Ypres. They found the town utterly destroyed and were obliged to march on at once towards Roulers (Roeselare). They crossed the Passchendaele Ridge and pushed on through the desolate landscape. There were virtually no buildings standing. On arrival few houses could be occupied so they camped as best they could and applied themselves to their first task, the burial of the dead.

The Americans' next job was made clear in the field order of 30 October: 'The French Army of Belgium will attack the enemy and drive him east of the Scheldt River.' For the attack of 31 October the 91st was given an objective west of Audenarde (Oudenaarde), Spitaals Boschen from a front between Waregem (Waereghem) and Steenbrugge. The 182nd Brigade of the 91st (363rd and 364th Infantry Regiments and 348th Machine-Gun Battalion) was assigned the northern sector and the 181st (361st and 362nd Infantry and 347th Machine-Gun) the southern, while a battalion of 364th Infantry and two machine-gun companies were detached to mop up the wood. A significant problem was that civilians were still in the area, farmers and their families who sheltered in their cellars from the fighting.

At 0530 hours on 31 October the attack began. The infantry tackling the northern side of the wood, 363rd, made quite good progress against determined resistance and had gained some 3,000 yd (2.75 km) in 3 hours, but shelling from Anzegem (Anseghem) slowed the 362nd on the south considerably. The mopping-up force set out as ordered at 0650 hours but, instead of gathering prisoners among positions already gained, found itself in front-line fighting. It was only at great cost that, by the end of the day, the wood was taken, but as the Germans still held Anzegem it was necessary to pull back on the right and consolidate for the night. The Germans, however, had been outflanked to their south by the British, so the French 41st Division might, it was hoped, be able to overcome them next day. In the meantime the 361st Infantry was switched to the northern side of the wood to take part in the continuing advance.

At 0630 hours on 1 November the attack resumed, but the 361st did not get to the start line until 0800 hours and had to race to attain contact with their comrades.

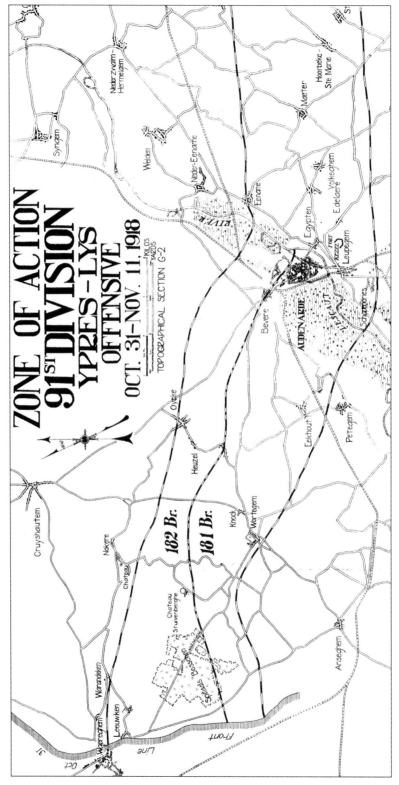

The map of the area attacked by the US 91st Division between 31 October and 11 November 1918. *(from The Story of the 91st Division)*

By 1000 they had caught up and swept forward, with only artillery fire from east of the river to delay them. By evening it was learned that the three bridges in Audenarde had been blown up and the ruins had partially blocked the waterway, flooding the western side. The nearest place that a pontoon might be constructed was now Eine, a short distance to the north. The outskirts of the city had been reached by 361st Infantry and one of the canals had been crossed, but the prospects for a further advance were not clear.

That night an officer from Utah, Captain John H. Leavell of the 316th Engineers, took a party of four men forward to see what conditions were like. He confirmed that the bridges had, indeed, been destroyed and reported the locations of machine-gun posts covering them. Leavell tried again before morning to see if there was a way to make use of the wreckage in fashioning some kind of crossing, but ran into a group of Germans leaving a cellar near the cathedral, Sint Walburgakerk. Five of them died in the subsequent fire-fight and a Belgian helping them escape from the city was captured.

Downstream, between Eine and Heurne, the American 37th Division found they could get over on fallen trees and makeshift foot-bridges and they established a

Company A, 316th Engineers, US 91st Division, crossing the Scheldt near Audenarde (Oudenaarde) by pontoon bridge.

The German Military Cemetery at Vladslo, north-east of Dixmude. Peter Kollwitz was killed on 23 October 1914 and is buried here. The sculpture in front of his grave is by his mother, Käthe Kollwitz, and is entitled 'The Parents'. *(Alex Deseyne)*

foothold on the eastern bank on 2 November. By daylight the next morning the 364th Infantry, which had been waiting impatiently to get clearance to enter the 37th Division's sector, arrived on the bank of the Scheldt and was ready to begin bridging operations after dark. To their surprise they were withdrawn, and remained in reserve for six days. Orders came to renew the assault, attacking on the evening of 10 November, but, as they moved up the day before, intelligence came that the Germans were pulling back from the Scheldt. The timing was brought forward and at 0630 hours on 10 November over they went, both here and in Audenarde itself where improvised bridges had been completed on the remains of the peacetime crossings. The Americans prepared themselves for what they anticipated would be the toughest phase of the action, the attack of 11 November. Then came an order to pause; ammunition supplies had failed to arrive. There would be no attack that morning. At 0830 another, unexpected but entirely welcome, message arrived. Hostilities were to cease at 1100 hours. The war was over. In this sector the 91st had lost 215 men killed and 714 wounded.

THREE

THE COAST

The Western Front ran across meadow, marsh and mountain to the Swiss border and the fighting took place beneath the earth, over its surface and in the air for almost the entire length of it. Belgium was unique in having a frontage on the sea. The Germans built numerous emplacements for heavy guns to defend their acquisition from assault by the Royal Navy and from invasion. They also made use of the territory as a base for operations against the Allies and in particular against shipping. The submarine, *Unterseeboot*, abbreviated to U-boat, was the principal weapon used in the confined waters of the North Sea, the English Channel and the Western Approaches. It could move, largely undetected, underwater running on electricity provided by huge batteries, but these needed regular recharging on the surface and long distances were best traversed on the surface, using diesel power.

German fortifications on the Belgian coast near Ostend.

The range of these boats was limited and the availability of harbours in Belgium was eagerly exploited by the Germans.

As early as 1914 the British were taking a lively interest in the potential of the ports of Ostend and Zeebrugge as outlets for enemy boats. Commander Samson wrote to the Admiralty on 1 December to propose an attack on Zeebrugge where, he said, he had information that there were three lock gates or caissons in the canal there, the operation of which could be compromised by blowing up the outer one. For this he suggested they use a specially modified motor boat carrying a 14-in torpedo which was to be launched on a foggy night within the harbour. It was turned down. Undeterred, four days later he sent another message to propose a programme of work to bomb the submarine depot south of Bruges as well as Zeppelins at Brussels and Antwerp. Reggie Marix was hot to bomb Essen using a new Breguet machine, but, luckily for him, it was not ready before the RNAS was posted to the Dardanelles. It proved to be a difficult machine and would probably have cost Marix his life.

The attack on the submarine base at Bruges was made on 14 December. Lieutenant R.B. Davies carried nine 16-lb bombs in his Maurice Farman, Lieutenant Rainey in a similar aircraft had six 16-lb bombs and Captain Collet, in an Avro, had four such bombs. The weather was windy and scarcely suitable for these early aircraft, but the Admiralty was keen to have the raid carried out so off they went. Davies saw no submarines but, almost hovering as he flew against the headwind, dropped six bombs through the fog. Collet could not see Bruges at all in the fog and instead bombed the railway between Bruges and Ostend, hitting a train and killing about twenty German Marines. Rainey reached Bruges and two of his bombs hit the submarine shed, but then his engine failed and he was forced to land in the Netherlands where he was interned. Samson recorded: 'I was not too downcast over his absence, as I felt certain he would turn up sooner or later, as he was such a redoubtable fellow, competent to get out of any trouble. . . . The Dutch had a terrible time with him, and they must have been glad when he escaped again, as he did in a coal bunker of a ship.'

A week later Samson himself made a night flight, the first, he claimed, to attack Ostend. He was in a Maurice Farman aircraft, a 'Pusher', in which the engine was behind the pilot, giving him an excellent view. No lights were carried and Samson's only equipment was an electric pocket lamp and a Very-light pistol. His bombs were mounted in a specially constructed rack that held eighteen 16-lb missiles which could be released either one by one, three by three or all at once. He set off at about 2200 hours and flew out to sea for 4 miles (6.4 km) before turning parallel with the coast at about 6,000 ft (1,830 m). He then throttled the engine back and glided towards his objective.

When I got over the harbour I could see no signs of any submarine; I therefore determined to bomb the batteries just to the south of the town, where there would be little risk of killing civilians. The lights of the town were all lit, and the view was splendid. The flash of the guns and the glare of the bursting shells was a wonderful sight all along our line through Dixmude to Ypres. . . . As soon as the noise of my engine was heard pandemonium started. Star shells, rockets, and searchlights played into the sky, and the lights of the town went out in about two minutes, but they stayed on long enough for me to pick out my objective.

Samson released his bombs in threes and saw them explode. He then turned out to sea, leaving the searchlights sweeping the sky and the anti-aircraft fire popping uselessly behind him. He landed on the beach directly outside his headquarters at Malo-les-Bains, close to Dunkirk.

On 22 January 1915 Lieutenant Peirse bombed a pair of submarines alongside the mole, the protective sea wall covering the canal entrance, at Zeebrugge and reported one hit. Another, but unsuccessful, raid was made on 1 February. More aircraft were arriving at Dunkirk and for 10 February an organized air raid using twenty-two aeroplanes and twelve seaplanes was planned. The weather was terrible and the command was attempted from Dover, with the result that the operation was ill-controlled. With Samson given command, more raids were made through the month with some small success, demonstrating that the aeroplane had a contribution to make to the war against the submarine threat.

The most severe situation for Allied shipping was brought into being by the German decision to resume unrestricted submarine warfare. American lives had been lost with the sinking of merchant vessels and on 16 April 1916 American President Woodrow Wilson had issued an ultimatum: diplomatic relations with Germany would be severed if submarine warfare against their merchant vessels continued. Germany complied, but by the end of the year the British blockade of Germany was causing serious suffering in the civilian population as well as shortages of vital material for the pursuit of the war. As the USA's army was so small the Germans calculated that they could win before the Americans could put a force of significance in the field. On 31 January 1917 the German Ambassador called on American Secretary of State Robert Lansing and handed him a note stating that, as from 1 February, unrestricted submarine warfare would begin again. The American ship *Housatanic* was torpedoed off the Scilly Isles the next day. By April the tonnage of sinkings exceeded the half-million, an increase of more than four times the January total. The introduction of a convoy system from then on steadily reduced the losses, but the incentive to attack at least part of the problem at its root, Bruges, was immense.

The submarine pens at that inland town were roofed with thick concrete to protect them against aerial attack, but the vessels themselves, as well as the motor-torpedo boats, had to put to sea by way of Zeebrugge and Ostend. Something curiously like Samson's plan emerged: not the destruction of the locks, but the blocking of the outlets with sunken ships.

The canal at Zeebrugge opened into the shallow harbour through a lock and an entrance channel with a curved wall on either side to slow the rate at which it silted up. The idea was to sink three ships in the entrance channel. The harbour itself was shallow and subject to severe silting. It was protected by a curved mole, a concrete

The Raversijde Museum at Ostend includes the site of the Aachen Battery, the only one remaining from the First World War. Trenches still wind through the sand dunes overlooking the seashore. *(Alex Deseyne)*

The remains of a 150-mm gun emplacement of the Aachen Battery at the Raversijde Museum. *(Alex Deseyne)*

structure forming a long jetty, open entirely to the east and with a smaller opening to the west, bridged with a railway viaduct, and intended to allow the tides and currents to move silt away from the canal entrance. It was only partially effective. The shape of the railway and the mole is reflected in the inner arrangement of the port today. The approach to the entrance channel from the east passed between a line of barges at right angles to the mole and a boom of entanglement nets further inshore. At the extreme eastern end of the mole there was a lighthouse on a long, narrow extension of the main structure and all along this finger of wall were about six or seven defensive guns of, it was thought, 3.5-in calibre. The wider part of the mole was 243 ft (74 m) across and on the outer edge there was a parapet about 16 ft (4.9 m) high with a 4-ft (1.2 m) external wall on top. This wide part of the mole was used to dock the fighting ships and as a seaplane base, with sheds for supplies and troops, barbed wire defences and rail access over the viaduct. There were more guns at the channel entrance on the mainland as well as trenches, barbed wire and machine-gun nests. The Germans had evidently taken care to fortify the place as thoroughly as they deemed necessary for complete security.

Up and down the coast the heavy gun batteries were capable of providing a shielding barrage and out to sea minefields limited the scope of manoeuvre of an attacking force. Ostend was equally set about with hazards for the assailant. Altogether this was a formidable target and the plan to overcome it was detailed and complex.

The huge concrete submarine shelters at Bruges.

The Admiralty chart of the Port of Zeebrugge, February 1918. The rail access to the mole from the land, bottom left, goes over the viaduct to the sheds and seaplane base on the mole itself. Within the curve of the mole the dots on the chart are all that can be seen of the figures giving the depth on the original. From the barges at the end of the mole, top right, the larger dots showing depths in double figures trace the route to the entrance channel. *(Ordnance Survey, Crown Copyright, 1918)*

Barbed wire entanglements at the mole at Zeebrugge.

The Zeebrugge and Ostend raids were made under the command of Vice-Admiral Roger Keyes. He, with the rank of Rear Admiral, had been director of the plans department of the Admiralty and had submitted a scheme on 3 December 1917 for such an operation but the commander of the Dover Patrol at that time, Admiral Sir Reginald Bacon, had made various changes. Keyes set about finding the men. They were all to be volunteers, but clearly could not be told for what they were offering themselves other than a hazardous undertaking. The practical problem that arose was an excess of men wanting to take part in anything that meant having a chance to fight. On 24 December Admiral Lord Jellicoe, the First Sea Lord, resigned and Admiral Sir Rosslyn Wemyss succeeded him. Wemyss replaced Bacon with Keyes at Dover and the operation he had originally designed thus came under his command.

The essentials of the plan were simple. The raid was to be made in darkness with additional cover in the form of artificial fog to avoid the fire of the shore batteries. The appearance of a vanguard for an invasion or an assault on the port as such was to be created. At Zeebrugge the mole would therefore be attacked in spectacular style as a diversion from the true objective, the placing of blockships in the canal entrance. At Ostend a similar storming of the port was not thought necessary. The actions would include long-distance shelling of shore installations and batteries by monitors. The blockships were old light cruisers. For Zeebrugge the *Thetis*, *Intrepid* and the *Iphigenia* were chosen, while *Brilliant* and *Sirius* were destined for Ostend. Concrete was placed in the ships to make it more difficult to cut up the hulls and clear them from the channel and explosives were arranged to enable the commander to blow the bottom out of his ship and sink it once it had been swung into position across the waterway.

The attack on the mole at Zeebrugge presented particular challenges. First, it would be necessary to place a ship or ships alongside the mole and then to enable men to get onto the structure to destroy the German guns which would otherwise prevent the blockships even getting close to their destination. There was no provision, such as bollards, for mooring on the seaward side of the mole, so grappling irons were to be used much as in the Napoleonic wars. Even then the deck of a ship would be well below the top of the wall on the parapet, so special gang-planks would be needed.

HMS *Vindictive*, another cruiser, was the principal vessel chosen and she was supported by two Mersey ferries, *Iris* and *Daffodil*. They had the advantage of being able to carry some 1,500 men each, but suffered from the disadvantages of being slow at sea and having little freeboard, so long ladders would be needed to get their men into action. As there was no time to modify or build alternatives, their faults had to be tolerated. On the cruiser eighteen gangways were fitted along the port side, howitzers were added to her gunnery provision, two flame-thrower installations were fitted and Stokes mortars, more commonly seen in the trenches of the Western Front, were put in place. As her

The blockships chosen for the Zeebrugge raid.

HMS *Vindictive* in Dover harbour after the Zeebrugge raid. The gangways fitted to allow the troops ashore can be seen as well as the specially built fighting positions, including the flame-thrower hut, high to the left. Massive fenders to prevent her hull being smashed against the mole hang alongside.

ordinary armament, which remained for conventional use, would be unable to bear on any targets once she was alongside the 29-ft (8.8-m) high wall of the mole, quick-firing guns were installed in the fighting top of the foremast. By the time all this was done the ship appeared very odd indeed to her captain, Commander Alfred Carpenter.

There were many other vessels involved in the expedition. There were two old submarines, C1 and C3, filled with explosives which were to blow up the viaduct between the shore and the mole to prevent reinforcements coming in action. The artificial fog was to be laid by motor launches while the crews of the blockships, assuming they survived, were to be rescued from their sinking craft by yet more launches. In all the Royal Navy committed the following forces to the Zeebrugge enterprise: the inshore forces, comprising the flagship of Vice-Admiral Keyes, the destroyer *Warwick*, the 3 blockships, the 3 storming vessels, the 2 submarines with a picket boat to rescue survivors, 65th Wing, RAF to bomb shore installations, and 10 destroyers, 31 motor launches and 16 coastal motor boats for various other duties; the offshore forces, consisting of an outer patrol, 1 scout and 4 destroyers, and a long-range bombardment flotilla of 2 monitors, *Erebus* and *Terror*, and 3 destroyers. Ostend called for bombarding forces of 7 monitors, 3 destroyers, 6 motor launches, 3 French destroyers, 4 French torpedo boats and 4 French motor launches. The army's heavy guns in Flanders would also join in. Inshore there were the 2 blockships,

7 destroyers, 18 motor launches and 8 coastal motor boats. The whole operation was given cover by forces from Harwich numbering 7 light cruisers, 14 destroyers, 2 leaders, the special service vessel *Lingfield*, 2 motor launches and 61st Wing RAF. There were 162 ships and 2 wings of the air force. The term 'raid' scarcely covers such a massive effort, in which every ship and boat had a precise role to play.

The date of the operation had to remain unfixed as so much depended on an appropriate conjunction of high tide and night. The first chance came on 11 April 1918. HMS *Vindictive* took the two Mersey ferries in tow as they could not match her speed and off they went, followed by the blockships, across a calm sea for Rendezvous A, where they were to meet with those starting from Dover. They passed numerous incoming merchant ships of which Alfred Carpenter wrote:

> Each of these merchant ships was just completing a successful operation, namely, that of bringing the necessities of life to this country after running the gauntlet of the enemy submarines and mines . . . these mercantile mariners had risked their lives over and over again without ostentation, with small hope of glory, with practically no reward. . . . Some of them, doubtless, had been torpedoed three and four times, losing all their effects each time, but here they were again with yet another voyage to their credit.

HMS *Vindictive* and her flotilla soon met up with the rest of the force, which Carpenter described:

> The Vice-Admiral with his flag flying in the destroyer *Warwick* took up a position of advantage. Destroyers and blockships took small motor craft in tow. Other vessels acted as tugs for the submarines. Motor launches, puffing for all the world as if they lacked training, thus acting an untruth, assembled according to their ultimate duties. Somebody remarked that we resembled a sea-circus, there were so many turns taking place simultaneously. One hardly knew which to admire most. The destroyers throbbing with latent energy, some of them shouting through their safety valves that they were in a hurry to get to business. The motor launches, pretending the sea was rough and often rolling heavily in their pretence. . . . The CMBs [Coastal Motor Boats] were tearing through the water and almost leaping into the other element as if to emulate the flying fish.

As soon as they were sailing eastward innumerable checks and preparations were undertaken aboard each vessel. Guns were made ready, flame-throwers prepared, explosives placed. The medical staff and damage-limitation parties put their equipment at the ready. Carpenter mentions seeing the courses and navigational instructions for the return voyage painted on the interior of the conning tower in case charts and navigation officers became casualties. They reached the further rendezvous and check points B, C and D without mishap. The wind became uncertain and they feared that, if it set in the wrong direction, their smoke and fog screen would be blown away and the attack cancelled. Day gave way to twilight and then, in the darkness, searchlights, explosion flashes and gunfire lit the distance. The RAF had begun their work. The convoy halted to take the passage crews off the blockships; many men contrived to go unnoticed, failed to disembark and thus put themselves in the attacking force. As this took place the wind fell off and then resumed, but from the south.

Keyes now had a serious problem on his hands. If the wind stayed southerly the covering smoke and fog would be blown away, revealing the exact positions of the approaching fleet to the German guns. They were well over halfway there, but Keyes gave the order 'Course West' to the seventy-eight ships in close formation ready to strike the ports. That no serious casualties were sustained in reversing the mighty armada is a tribute to their detailed contingency provisions. One Coastal Motor Boat was holed near the bow and her skipper had one of his men sit in the orifice until enough speed had been worked up to lift the forepart of the boat clear of the water. As she was then doing 27 knots to the convoy's 10, she went home speeding round and round her comrades in a series of loops.

On 13 April the flotilla set off once more, but after going a mere 20 miles (32 km) the sea had become so rough that they would never have been able to set themselves alongside the mole. For a second time the attack was called off. As it would be some time before tide and dark were in harmony again they fell to refining their plans. The first day of the next suitable period was 22 April. The day dawned calm but misty. By 0800 hours the mist had cleared and visibility was excellent. High tide would be soon after midnight at Ostend and Zeebrugge, so the voyage over the North Sea would have to take place in full daylight, with all the risks of being seen by enemy air patrols, submarines or patrol boats. However, every other factor was favourable. The decision to go was taken.

Once more the force gathered and set off to the east. Before darkness fell the Vice-Admiral made the signal 'St George for England' – the next day, 23 April, being the patron saint's day. Carpenter gave orders for the response 'May we give the Dragon's tail a damned good twist!' to be sent. His signalman put 'darned' in place of 'damned' and when told to restore the original word indulged his sensibilities by spelling it 'dammed'.

As the night passed they approached Position G, the point at which the Zeebrugge and Ostend forces would part. Before then the launch intended to take the passage crew off the blockship *Intrepid* failed to turn up, delayed by some technical problem. The men assigned to sailing *Intrepid* this far and then leaving had been particularly keen to follow the operation through, even sending a delegation to their commanding officer to plead to be allowed to stay. The absence of their relief boat must have pleased them a great deal. As the ships approached Position G rain began to fall, limiting visibility and thus checks on the precision of their navigation, and also making aerial operations difficult. On they went, a screen of destroyers before them. At 1030 hours hot soup was served to *Vindictive*'s men and there was a rum issue an hour later.

At about 1110 hours the hawser towing the ferries parted and there was no time to fix it so they proceeded at a slightly slower speed. A light-buoy was seen off Blankenberghe, the small port a little west of Zeebrugge, confirming their position. Then star-shell and searchlights lit the sky, again aiding navigation, but as it was directed against possible aircraft, the assault force went unseen. Between *Vindictive* and the shore the artificial fog was laid. The wind died and the rain fell more heavily. Then they were among the smoke as the wind blew it off shore. A few seconds before midnight the smoke cleared. The mole and its lighthouse were a mere 300 yd (274 m) ahead. *Vindictive* made a curving course westwards to come alongside and as she did so the mole battery was at 250 yd as she passed the eastern gun and down to 50 yd by the time the western gun was reached. The firing from both ship and shore was intense and the damage inflicted was great.

Carpenter recorded his observations:

Looked at from the view of a naval officer it was little short of criminal, on the part of the Mole battery, that the ship was allowed to reach her destination. . . . The petty officer at one of our 6-inch guns, when asked afterwards what ranges he fired at, said that he reckoned he opened fire at about 200 yards and he continued till close to the Mole. 'How close?' he was asked. 'Reckoning from the gun muzzle,' he replied, 'I should say it was about 3 feet!'

It appears that the German gunners, taken by surprise, poured fire at the closing warship as quickly as they could without taking too much trouble over their aim. While the damage to the ship was heavy but not serious, the loss to her men was significant. While almost all the storming force were below decks, their commanders were ready to lead them ashore and much more exposed. Lieutenant-Colonel Bertram Elliot of the Marines and his second-in-command, Major A.A. Cordner, were both killed as were Captain H.C. Halahan, commanding the naval force, and Commander Edwards.

At 0001 hours, 23 April, St George's Day, HMS *Vindictive* made gentle contact with the mole. Carpenter, in the flame-thrower hut, was about 5 ft (1.5 m) higher than the wall and could see that they had over-shot so the engines were kept in reverse. Although aerial photographs had been studied repeatedly and in detail, the situation looked very different by gunlight. There were only 20 minutes before the blockships were due and precision in mooring was the smallest of their objectives. Carpenter ordered the starboard anchor to be let go. Nothing happened. The order was repeated. Still nothing. An officer went to investigate. It had jammed, so the port, the inshore, anchor was lowered. The cruiser swung away from the mole. Everything now depended on the *Daffodil*, detailed to act as a tugboat and nudge the larger ship snug to the wall. Out of the darkness came *Iris*, under Commander Valentine Gibbs, and, as planned, came alongside the mole forward of the cruiser. Then Lieutenant H.G. Campbell brought *Daffodil* up against *Vindictive*'s side and shoved her gently but firmly against the wall, precisely as required.

Only two gangways had survived the gunfire during the approach, and with a heavy swell running which made the ship roll horribly, they were lifting on and off the deck at the lower end and sliding about at the upper end, with a nasty drop to the gap between ship and shore below. None the less, Lieutenant-Commander B.F. Adams stormed up with a party of seamen at once. Neither flame-thrower worked. One had its pipe severed and poured oil all over the deck while the other had been deprived of the igniting device by shell-fire and hosed oil, not flame. The grappling irons gave trouble. The rolling of the ship made the heavy hooks hard to handle; one of the davits broke sending the uncooperative object into the sea. Seeing that they were useless, Carpenter ordered Campbell to keep *Daffodil* in place to push rather than put her alongside *Vindictive* to send her men over to the mole.

The damaged funnel and ventilators of HMS *Vindictive* after the Zeebrugge raid.

Tucked in under the mole, the hulls of the vessels were safe from enemy gunfire while the cruiser's fighting top projected high enough to shell not only the German battery but also a destroyer moored within the harbour. Lieutenant Charles Rigby and his men kept up continuous fire until struck by a shell which left only three men alive. Sergeant Finch and Gunner Sutton of the Royal Marine Artillery maintained the fire. Meanwhile, the Marine gunners under Captain Reginald Dallas-Brooks brought the howitzers into action against German shore batteries.

One of the submarines intended to attack the viaduct, C3, under the command of Lieutenant Richard Sandford, approached the target soon after midnight. Her sister boat, C1, had been delayed by a parting tow hawser and held off lest she get in the way. C3 was seen and fired on briefly, but got away from that inconvenience and then sighted the viaduct. Sandford ran his vessel at the space between two of the vertical struts at about 10 knots. She struck with such force that she became wedged between the girders as deep as her conning tower and lifted partly out of the water. The Germans opened fire with machine-guns as the men struggled to get their escape boat into the water. Stanford set the fuse of the explosives and they abandoned ship. The engine was useless as the propeller had been smashed. They rowed madly away with gunfire pouring down on them. Stanford and two of his men were wounded and the boat was holed, but luckily the pump worked and they managed to stay afloat. Suddenly a huge explosion removed the submarine, a great section of the viaduct and the men shooting at them in a single, welcome burst of noise and light and out of the dark the skipper saw his brother, Lieutenant-Commander F.H. Sandford, guiding a picket boat to their rescue. They found refuge on board the destroyer *Phoebe*. C1, commanded by Lieutenant Aubrey Newbold, withdrew; a difficult decision but prudent. Less wise was the cycle unit pedalling vigorously to the support of the Germans on the mole. Unaware of the gap in the viaduct, it is said, they raced into space and the cold sea below.

An aerial photograph of Zeebrugge after the raid. The gap in the railway viaduct can be seen clearly and close examination reveals two of the three blockships in place in the curving jaws of the entrance channel. *Intrepid* lies diagonally, level with the two pale areas of beach on either side of the channel. *Iphigenia*, left or further inland, is almost along the line of the channel and the third dark form is a German vessel moored to a jetty.

On the parapet above the mole Lieutenant-Commander Adams put men to hold the top of a ladder, west of his ship, leading down to the floor of the mole and then investigated what was happening to the east. There he saw a machine-gun firing from the wire-guarded trenches and, beyond, the three-gun battery at the end of the wide part of the mole. The parapet was exposed to fire from the floor of the mole and something had to be done to suppress it. Lieutenant-Commander A.L. Harrison, in command of the seaman storming parties, had been wounded during the approach and suffered a broken jaw. He gathered men and charged the machine-gun. He and all but two of his party were killed, but Able Seaman McKenzie, though wounded, made good use of his Lewis gun. The Marines, now led by Major B.G. Weller, turned east and dealt with one group who were firing on the parapet as well as hurling grenades onto a destroyer. On the other flank they went to the assistance of the seamen and a further force of Marines under Captain E. Bamford soon joined them.

Meanwhile, the men from *Iris* were striving to get ashore. The little ferry had come alongside at about 0015 hours but as she bounced about in the swell the efforts to moor her were frustrated. Lieutenant Claude Hawkings had some men hold up one of the scaling ladders without resting it against the wall, swarmed up it and jumped ashore. Astride the wall he was attacked and tried to defend himself with his revolver, but was killed. Lieutenant-Commander George Bradford used a derrick to climb high enough to leap to the wall, taking a grappling iron with him. As he put the mooring device in place he was shot and fell into the sea. The mooring failed, so Commander Gibbs moved to send his men across *Vindictive*. She got alongside at about 0055 hours, but was ordered off and came under fire from a German battery. Gibbs was killed as was the commander of the Marines, Major C.E.E. Eagles, together with some fifty of his men. A motor boat laid smoke and the battered vessel withdrew with seventy-seven dead and more than a hundred wounded on board.

As this action was in progress the blockships were making their thrust. In the van was *Thetis*, under Commander Ralph Sneyd, followed by *Intrepid*, Lieutenant Stuart Bonham-Carter, and *Iphigenia*, Lieutenant Edward Billyard-Leake. They saw the mole at 0020 hours and *Thetis* increased speed, rounded the lighthouse and steered for the end of the barge boom. She fired on and sank the barge nearest the shore but then, caught by the tide, ran over the end of the net boom, fouling her propellers and stopping her engines. She had grounded about 300 yd (274 m) from the canal channel entrance and was heavily engaged with batteries both ashore and on the mole. She signalled to her fellow blockships, which were comparatively unscathed, and they took advantage of the wider gap created by *Thetis* to enter the channel. Bonham-Carter took *Intrepid* within the shore-line before turning her across the channel and blowing the charges to sink her. The crew were in part picked up from their boats by Motor Launch 526 while some rowed out past the mole to be rescued by the destroyer *Whirlwind*. The captain and his officers launched a raft and, under machine-gun fire, managed to reach Motor Launch 282.

Both German and British servicemen lie in Zeebrugge Military Cemetery. The mass grave is that of the crews of Torpedoboote *S15* and *S20* and beyond the characteristic shapes of Commonwealth War Graves Commission headstones outline the area. *(Alex Deseyne)*

The present St George's Day Memorial at Zeebrugge includes plaques from a number of other memorials. The originals were destroyed by the Germans in the Second World War. *(Alex Deseyne)*

As *Iphigenia* passed *Thetis* Sneyd decided to sink his ship where she was, but engineer Lieutenant-Commander Boddie managed to get the starboard engine going at that moment, dragging the injured ship into the channel leading to the opening of the entrance. There they blew the charges and were picked up by Motor Launch 526 which was coming up astern and then went on to retrieve men from *Intrepid*. Billyard-Leake had problems when a shell severed a steam pipe and steam shrouded the forepart of the ship. Then smoke obscured the entrance. Suddenly he was on the point of ramming the western pier. Engines were put hard astern as she ran between a dredger and a barge. The barge got pushed ahead of him and then, alternating the engines between forward and astern, he turned his ship across the waterway and sank her. Motor Launch 282 picked up many of the men and took the cutter with the rest in tow. Her skipper, Lieutenant Percy Deane, found he could steer only by using unequal power on his engines and in this fashion made it close under the mole and out of the harbour to deliver the seamen to safety aboard *Warwick*.

The retirement order was initiated at 0050 hours, but *Vindictive*'s sirens were no more and *Daffodil* attempted to sound hers. It eventually groaned into life and sounded a number of times through the din of battle. The landing parties started to come back almost at once, bringing what wounded they could. By 0105 those who were able to return had done so, but Carpenter hesitated to leave because he had

At Ostend the bow of HMS *Vindictive* stands as a memorial to the ship and those who fought in her. *(Alex Deseyne)*

stated that 20 minutes would elapse between the signal and sailing. Repeatedly assured that there were none left, he gave the order to leave. The conning tower had been shot to pieces and the telegraphs were gone, but the telephone to the engine room remained in operation. Only one, unreliable, compass was left. At 0111 *Daffodil* pulled *Vindictive* away from the wall, breaking the hawser but doing the job. The gangways fell into the sea and away she went, still seaworthy after more than an hour at an enemy's harbour wall. After 20 minutes the Blankenberghe buoy was seen again and then the destroyer *Moorsom* was sighted. Lacking both compass and proper signalling equipment, a pocket torch was used to signal for guidance homewards. The raid had cost 170 killed, some 400 wounded and 45 missing, probably killed, and the loss of the destroyer *North Star*.

The raid on Ostend was not successful. The smoke screen blew back on the attacking force and a relocated buoy misled them. The Navy came under heavy fire from shore batteries, the Aachen Battery among them, and, as a result, the blockships sank outside the channel. The cost here was 188 killed, 384 wounded and 16 missing. Another attempt was made on the night of 9–10 May, using *Vindictive*, now under Commander A.E. Godsall. He was killed as the cruiser was sunk only partially blocking the entrance to Ostend harbour with another forty-seven casualties, of which eight were fatal.

In closing the exit from Bruges to the sea the raids did not achieve all that had been intended. A channel viable at high water had been dredged at Zeebrugge within a day and the entire blockage removed by mid-May. Ostend was open to destroyers, with some difficulty, within a week. The rewards were in another quarter. In March the Germans had launched their mighty attack Operation Michael, driving the Allies back from St Quentin to Amiens. A feat of arms of which the British could be proud was a vital ingredient to the maintenance of morale. The award of 8 Victoria Crosses and 209 other decorations bears witness not solely to the undoubted courage of the men, but also to the need for heroes.

THE VOSGES

'. . . *men coming from the Hartsmannsweiler Kopf wandered through the streets of Soultz during the night, with mutilated limbs and bloody heads. We only get half a pound of bread a day now. I should like to know how long it will be before we get nothing at all.*'

An extract from a letter written by a German soldier on the Western Front

Overleaf: Tired German soldiers, 1918.

FOUR

THE FIGHT FOR THE SUMMITS

France had lost her provinces of Alsace and Lorraine in the north-east of the country as a result of the Franco–Prussian War of 1870–1. In 1875 General Séré de Rivières planned a series of fortifications to prevent another incursion. The works included the forts around Verdun and major defensive areas at Toul and Nancy together with a string of forts between them. The Germans had no intention of hurling themselves against this line in 1914, but the French were prepared to launch themselves eastwards from it to recover their lost lands.

The forts sat on the circumference of a circle centred on Metz, in what was then German territory, covering the line between the mountains of the Vosges in the south and the forests of the Ardennes in the north. Much of the terrain within this segment was the open, rolling country of the Woevre Plain and the River Moselle cut north from Nancy to Metz through it. On the east the Rhine ran north from the Swiss border, bounded to its west by the Vosges, a north–south feature ending at the Belfort gap where the city of that name defended the space between the Vosges and the Jura mountains. In case of war the French intended to secure their hold on the Vosges, penetrate the Haut-Rin, Upper Rhine, region from Belfort and make the major effort passing east of Metz and thrusting towards the Saarland, in Germany to the north-east.

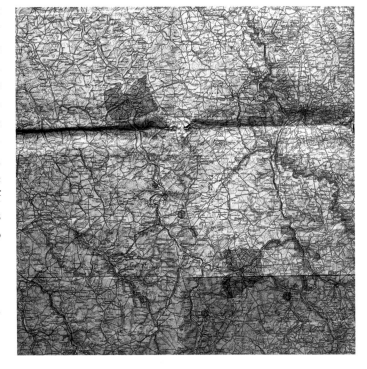

A German map, pre-1914, showing the French frontier in purple and, highlighted in red, the principal French fortifications facing Metz. *(Brian Kibby Collection)*

The French commander-in-chief, General Joseph Joffre, made his Plan XVII in the belief that violation of Belgian neutrality could not be contemplated. He therefore devised a scheme to hold a line along the River Meuse, south of Namur, with the British Expeditionary Force operating further west while the main effort would be the north-eastward advance from Sedan, Verdun and Nancy. The plan depended on the greatly increased efficiency of the railway system running to the east from Paris; a set-up that was to prove its worth in moving troops the other way when Germany failed to conform with French forecasts and attacked through Belgium.

The French, from south to north, had the First Army facing the Vosges mountains from Belfort to Lunéville, 256,000 men under General Auguste Dubail, and the Second Army, 200,000 men under General Noël de Castlenau, based on Nancy. General Pierre Ruffey's Third Army of 168,000 men covered the front to the north-east of Verdun, while the area west to Sedan was held by the Fourth Army, 193,000 men under General Fernand de Langle de Cary. South of their Second Army, which was poised to attack Liège, the Germans had their Third Army, 180,000 men under General Max von Hausen, and to occupy Luxembourg the Fourth Army, 180,000 men under Albrecht, Grand Duke of Württemberg. Just north of Metz the Fifth Army of 200,000 men was under the command of Crown Prince Wilhelm of Prussia, and to their south the Sixth Army of Crown Prince Rupprecht of Bavaria with 220,000 men. On the Rhine front in Alsace was the Seventh Army, 125,000 men under General August von Heeringen.

On 2 August 1914 the Germans moved not only against Belgium but also against Luxembourg. Joffre had modified his plan by putting the Fourth Army into the line instead of holding it in reserve. On 7 August the French VIIth Corps under General Bonneau advanced rather languidly, although unopposed, into Mulhouse, but the Germans soon moved forces against them from Strasbourg and by 10 August they had fallen back towards Belfort without offering a fight. Joffre's reaction was to dismiss Bonneau, increase the strength by creating the Army of Alsace and summon General Paul Marie Pau out of retirement to command it. He wanted flair and determination from his generals and sacked those who fell short of this.

German strategy on the Lorraine front was to draw the French into a trap, allowing them to advance, at a cost, until they had stretched their supply lines and exposed their flanks enough to be vulnerable. In so doing French attention was to be drawn from the decisive sector – Belgium. For four days the advance of the First and Second Armies continued and by 17 August General Ferdinand Foch's XXth Corps, Second Army, had taken Château Salins and threatened Morhange. Sarrebourg fell to the First Army the next day. In the south Pau retook Mulhouse and from the heights of the Vosges the French advanced to the very gates of Colmar. The German commander-in-chief, Field Marshal Helmuth von Moltke, became concerned about his left wing and Prince Rupprecht harried headquarters with arguments for an attack. As the German Sixth and Seventh Armies had been brought under a single staff for this operation they had a significant advantage over the divided French force, no matter how meticulously the latter might liaise. On 20 August the blow fell; all eight German corps assaulted

THE FIGHT FOR THE SUMMITS 79

the six French. Heavy artillery inflicted the first of many massacres on the French and only Foch's XXth Corps on the Second Army's left held firm. By 23 August the French were back where they had started, on the River Meurthe and the Grand Couronné de Nancy. Rupprecht's pleas to be allowed to continue his offensive were acceded to by von Moltke, but by 7 September it had become clear that the French were not going to break here. In the mountains Pau's men had to fall back to create a link with their comrades to their north and concentrated on the occupation of the high ground.

Where they did fail was in the Ardennes. On 22 August, having been assured that no serious opposition was to be expected, the French Third and Fourth Armies pushed forward towards southern Belgium through the wooded, hilly country north-east of Sedan. They ran directly into the advancing Germans. All except the Fourth Army's Colonial Corps, a regular army unit, were stopped. The Colonial Corps fought stubbornly on, mounting repeated bayonet charges through the woods, outflanked both left and right. In that single day they suffered 11,000 casualties out of a strength of 15,000 men. On 24 August the French pulled back across the Meuse. Plan XVII had failed entirely.

In the Vosges the line was still changing. The key features each side sought to control were the west-to-east routes, running over high passes, but offering access to

East of Épinal, the Franco–German border ran along the heights of the Vosges, through which only a few, difficult routes passed. (*The Times* History of the War)

The Route des Crêtes, the Crest Road, built to supply positions on the heights of the Vosges. *(MME)*

From the Château de Freundstein, on the Crest Road, the dominant position of the Hartmannswillerkopf over the plain to the east can be appreciated. *(MME)*

enemy territory. From north to south these are the road east from St Dié by way of the Col de Ste Marie to Ste Marie-aux-Mines and Sélestat (Schlettstadt), the route from St Dié to Colmar over the Col du Bonhomme and down the valley of the Weiss, the Gérardmer to Colmar road over the Col de la Schlucht to Münster and the valley of the River Fecht and, finally, the Remiremont to Mulhouse (Mülhausen) route through Thann.

Thann and the valleys of the rivers Doller and Thur, west of Mulhouse, remained in French hands but further north the situation was fluid. The front from Lapoutrie, east of Bonhomme, to Soultzbach, east of Münster in the Fecht valley, was held by the Schlucht Brigade and the 81st Brigade. It was attacked by the Germans on 27 August and on 2 September the villages of Lapoutrie and Orbey together with the Weiss valley were evacuated, pulling the line back to the high ground from Le Bonhomme to Le Linge and the Wettstein Pass and thence to the Fecht valley front which was unchanged. Then an order was received suggesting that the Fecht valley could be yielded if the loss of the Weiss valley to its north now threatened the flank. It was treated as a direct order to pull out of the Fecht and back up to the heights, where the Route des Crêtes, the Crest Road, would be constructed to provide a lateral supply line to the French front.

General Dubail was annoyed and ordered the reoccupation of the ground, but this was only partly achieved, leaving the Germans in possession of Orbey, the Wettstein Pass and the Fecht valley east of Metzeral. To the south the French held the high road, the Hartmannswillerkopf and Thann. Here things settled down for the time being as both sides devoted their energies to the war in Flanders.

The Hartmannswillerkopf is a mountain some 3,000 ft (915 m) high that stands to the east of the Crest Road and was not considered of very much importance early in the war. In November a unit of the Chasseurs Alpins, French light infantry mountain troops, occupied it mainly to set up an observation post for artillery to their rear on Molkenrain mountain. The French knew the feature as the Vieil-Armand; the Germans called it HWK.

As November drew to a close General Putz, commanding the new Army of the Vosges, was forming plans for an advance down the valley of the Fecht and along a front as far south as Thann so as to swarm off the hills and into the valley to threaten a line from Colmar to Mulhouse with his artillery. Cernay, between Thann and Mulhouse, would be taken as would Pont d'Aspach on the Mulhouse–Belfort road. It was an ambitious undertaking. It was to be carried out by 115th Brigade and the 57th and 66th Infantry Divisions with the 10th Cavalry Division and Alpine unit in reserve. The assaults began on 25 December 1914, the snow heavy on the hills. Pushing south-east with the 57th on the right of the Thann–Mulhouse road and the 66th on the left, progress was slow. Steinbach, north-east of Thann, was taken, lost and, on 4 January, taken again. On 26 December 123rd Landwehr Regiment attacked the Hartmannswillerkopf and was thrown back. On 7 January the height above Cernay, Hill 425, was taken but had to be abandoned because the

German infantry throng about a mobile shop in the Vosges, 1914.

trenches were filled with water and rotting corpses. All along this front the offensive slowed as the difficulty of taking up supplies became more severe.

The Col du Bonhomme and the road to Colmar were overlooked from the east and south by a rocky outcrop called La Tête des Faux, or the Buchenkopf. It was held by the Germans who used it as an observation post for their artillery, thus commanding the access to the pass. A plan to take this viewpoint and the Brézouard to the north of the road had been formed and approved on 8 November. The attack by 28th and 30th Battalions of the Chasseurs Alpins and a battalion of the 215th Infantry of 66th Division on 2 December took the Germans entirely by surprise and the 3rd Bavarian Landwehr counter-attacked to no good purpose. On Christmas Day the 14th Mecklenburgs gained some ground and another German attack on 21 February was to establish them on the eastern slope while the French would hold the summit for the rest of the war.

Geoffrey Malins, having delivered the film he shot in Belgium to his chief in London, was then asked to go to the Vosges to make a record of mountain fighting. He travelled by way of Basel, in Switzerland, not without a number of adventures resulting from being thought a spy, and made his way to St Dié, using skis for the first time in his life on the way. There he managed to get accepted by some French officers who advised him on where to go to see some action. He set out with his skis and found a position of vantage to which he crawled having abandoned the skis.

The attack was beginning. The snow-covered hillside became suddenly black with moving figures sweeping in irregular formation up towards the crest. Big gun and rifle fire mingled like strophe and antistrophe of an anthem of death. There was a certain massiveness about the noise that was awful. Yet there was none of the traditional air of battle about the engagement. There was no hand to hand fighting, for the opponents were several hundred yards apart. It was just now and then when one saw a little distant figure pitch forward and lie still on the snow that one realized there was real fighting going on, and that it was not manoeuvres. The gallant French swept on up the hill, and I think I was the only man in all that district who noted the black trail of spent human life they left behind them.

The next wave of attackers came through and Malins moved into a wood to follow their progress, finally filming them in pursuit of a retreating enemy down the snow-covered slopes. His film exhausted, he then set off homewards. From St Dié to Besançon and from there to Dijon and Paris he made his way over a number of days, only to be forced to wait in Dieppe until German submarines had been cleared from the Channel before getting back to London: '. . . my trip to the fighting line ended in a prosaic taxi-cab through London streets that seemed to know nothing of war'.

Between 8 and 13 January the Army of the Vosges was reinforced by ten battalions of Chasseurs Alpins formed into the 47th Alpine Division under

The French cemetery below the Tête des Faux. *(MME)*

General Blazer. This strengthened army was to attack once more but this time north of the previous battle area and past the Hartmannswillerkopf. Snow hampered operations as supplies could only be brought up by mule train, which were supplied by motor convoys coming as far as possible up the valleys to the west. The attack was planned for 19 January 1915.

The French had dug in on the Hartmannswillerkopf and on 4 January it had been assaulted again, this time by four regiments of Jäger, Uhlans and Grenadiers. The attack was renewed on 19 January and the Germans fought around the

A rock-cut trench, dug-out, barbed wire and shelters still in position on the Hartmannswillerkopf. *(MME)*

southern flank of the mountain, cut the Chasseurs Alpins off from support, then proceeded to plaster the height with shell-fire . By 22 January resistance was over; one report telling a story of the last forty defenders attempting a break-out on their skis, only to fall to German small-arms fire. The Germans then began a methodical fortification of the mountain and its summit.

The loss of this position and the terrain immediately to the south of it looked like the start of a movement intended to roll up the French position on the height running northwards, so Putz determined to take the mountain back. On 27 January the 41st and 57th Divisions made some small progress but the units charged with

Robert Wolfsohn, the author's great-uncle, in the uniform of the Chasseurs Alpins. This picture was sent to his family in Paris. *(J-PRME)*

A postcard photograph sent by Robert Wolfsohn to a friend on 14 September 1916 after he had been ill and in hospital. He claimed to be the bearded figure sitting in the centre, but is actually standing on the left. The full name of the restaurant is, no doubt, obscured. (*J-PRME*)

the task of taking the Hartmannswillerkopf, 47th and 66th Divisions, fared badly in the snow.

General Joffre now asked Putz to put the pressure on further north, around the valley of the Fecht and on the western approaches to Colmar. The task of making detailed plans for attacking the ridges north of the Fecht and south of the Weiss, that is, Le Linge and the Hohnack, was given to General Blazer of the 47th Division. Before the French attack could be brought to fruition the Germans struck at the Schlucht Pass and the Reichackerkopf, west of Münster, and along the ridge Blazer had intended to secure to the north, so that between 17 and 21 February the front was disputed all the way from the Ferme Sudel, near the Sudelkopf, just north of the Hartmannswillerkopf, to Le Linge. German heavy artillery laid down a formidable barrage but with the usual problems for gunners in the mountains; in steep terrain a near miss is a complete miss. On the night of 23 February an attempt by the Germans to push northwards in a furious snowstorm from the road just west of Münster was repulsed and the next day the offensive collapsed. The holding of this northern sector had cost the Chasseurs Alpins casualties of 33 officers and over 1,500 men.

Joffre's reaction was to demand renewed efforts both on the mountain crests and in the Fecht valley, as well as the taking of the Hartmannswillerkopf. The offensives further south were cancelled to conserve ammunition. On 27 February the

66th Division again threw itself against the HWK defences. Despite the fact that twenty-seven heavy guns and twenty-six field guns supported the attack, the Münster Bavarian Division was unshaken. The French gathered their energies and on 23 March the 1st Chasseur Brigade struck once more. The first two lines on the Siberloch flank of the HWK fell quickly, were secured and then held in the face of determined counter-attacks. On 26 March 152nd Infantry, with the Chasseurs, assaulted and took the summit. There are two ridges that lead from it north-east and south-east. These, too, were taken, establishing the French on the Hartmannswillerkopf for the time being. A letter captured on the Western Front gave some insight into the German view.

> 28th March.
> Nothing changed here, but it must be terrible on the Hartmannsweiler Kopf. Men are continually being sent forward, and none return. Last week men coming from the Hartmannsweiler Kopf wandered through the streets of Soultz during the night, with mutilated limbs and bloody heads. We only get half a pound of bread a day now. I should like to know how long it will be before we get nothing at all.

A heavy artillery bombardment preceded the German attack of 25 April and the summit fell to them again. On the evening of 26 April a fresh French assault regained it. It is not clear what either side hoped to gain by the occupation of this mountain top, but by this time military advantage had been subordinated to military pride.

The French attempts to eject the Germans from their positions on the slopes of the Fecht valley at this time were not successful. Blazer was removed from command and replaced with General de Pouydraguin. His enthusiasm for securing the Le Linge position was decidedly muted, but his chiefs insisted. Meanwhile, the winter persisted, snow continued to fall and the winds whipped it into blizzards. Frostbite was as much a danger as enemy fire. On 4 April the Army of the Vosges was designated the Seventh Army and General Louis Comte de Maud'huy was put in command. He had been born in Metz in 1857 and had taken an oath not to enter a place of public entertainment until the city was back in French hands. He was also an advocate of the doctrine of attack as the best method of defence. The force he took over had, by the end of April, suffered casualties of some 300 officers and 20,000 men in 1915 alone for no significant gain.

While fighting on the heights went doggedly on, new plans were laid for an attack both north and south of the Fecht valley. General Serret's 66th Division was to advance in the south, taking the Petit Ballon and the valley below while de Pouydraguin's 47th was to seize Le Linge and push east along the ridge tops north of the Münster–Colmar road, forcing the Germans to withdraw from the valley. De Maud'huy demanded reinforcements. He contended that a fresh division would be needed just to take Le Linge; what he got was two regiments and another brigade of Chasseurs Alpins, the 5th, under Colonel Trouchard, which joined the 47th Division. The orders for this campaign were issued on 7 June. The attack was scheduled

A German map of 1915. French trenches are shown in red while, for security, German trenches are omitted, and only their front line is marked. The German 'Sulzern' lines ran across the Soultzeren–Münster road, at Stosswihr to Le Linge, top right, where the French trenches are packed tight up the hillside. The road on the left climbs to the Col de Wettstein and was the French supply route. The Fecht valley runs south-west of Münster. *(Brian Kibby Collection)*

for 1630 hours on 15 June after an artillery barrage from over 100 guns, starting at noon. The German 19th Reserve Division, elements of 6th and 12th Bavarian Landwehr Divisions and 187th Brigade fought fiercely to hold their positions but were slowly pushed back. They set fire to Metzeral, on the Fecht south-west of Münster, on 17 June and withdrew. The Germans were now forced to fight from positions less well prepared; indeed, an officer of the 8th Chasseurs reported that in front of Muhlbach there were no trench lines as such, just individual fox-holes and the occasional trench only knee-deep. The road to the mountains to the south, through Ober-Brietenbach was, he said, overlooked by the French and was, in any case, almost too steep to get supplies up. Even so, they held on.

Sondernach, south of Metzeral, fell to the French 66th Division on 21 June. With the 47th making progress on their left, the opportunity to thrust on towards Münster, now under fire from their artillery, seemed open to the French. The view was not shared by GHQ; the Münster valley, it was ordered, was to be outflanked in order to take it. Le Linge and the Barrenkopf to its south were to be taken first. Even continued pressure towards Muhlbach was to be suspended if the assault in the mountains to the north might be jeopardized. The commanders on the ground did not support the strategy. Indeed, the hill of Le Linge, at the northern end of a ridge, overlooked a valley of no relevance to supporting or denying communications through the mountains and stood

The Col du Bonhomme from German positions at Le Linge. *(MME)*

above a hill-top route of no importance at all. As the French had prepared to assault the line in the Fecht valley in the spring, the Germans had fortified the hills to the north with well-cut rock trenches and secure shelters against shell-fire. The French 3rd Brigade had reported the movement of trucks, the evidence of tree-felling and the sound of explosions quarrying out the rock. By the time the decision was taken to attack, the German defences, concealed among the trees, were formidable.

General de Pouydraguin carried out a personal reconnaissance and reported to General Maud'huy that the offensive would be extremely risky and uncertain of outcome. The ground, he pointed out, was steep and the wood-covered hills would make it difficult for artillery support to be effective. The Fecht valley advance, on the other hand, held great promise. Given the consistent and logical opposition of the commander of the 47th Division, Maud'huy brought in 129th Infantry from General Dubail's force and delayed the attack so that the commander of the fresh division, General Nollet, would have time to familiarize himself with the terrain. The assault began on 20 July at 1400 hours.

What the Germans termed the 'Sulzern Line', because they faced Soultzeren on the Münster–Gérardmer road, began from the high spur of Le Linge in the north, dipped to the Collet de Linge, the saddle between the northerly hill and the next height, the Schratzmännele. It then continued south-west over the Barrenkopf and the Kleinkopf

The French in action in the wooded hills of the Vosges.

Trenches shattered by mortar fire in the Vosges.

before running down to the road at Stosswihr, just to the west of Münster. West of Le Linge the land dips away towards the Col de Wettstein and, north of that pass, Les Hautes Huttes and the Col du Bonhomme, an area that was to remain relatively peaceful. The 3rd Brigade under Colonel Brissaud-Desmaillet used its five battalions of Chasseurs Alpins to assault the German positions. The 14th and 54th Battalions were on the left, against Le Linge and the Schratz, the 30th and 70th in the centre and the 22nd on the right, against the Barrenkopf. On the Schratzmännele the Germans had used the quarries to establish machine-gun positions and from these and the trenches of the Barrenkopf the 22nd came under heavy fire. As a result, 6 officers and 186 men were killed with roughly another 400 wounded. The Chasseurs fell back, bringing with them a sign that had been hung on the German barbed wire. It read, 'Le Linge will be the Chasseurs' Grave.' On the other wing the 14th and 54th gained the saddle of the Collet and pushed left and right respectively. The 54th reached the top of the Schratz, but then ran into solid resistance and were forced to give ground. On their left the 14th, once within the woods, could make no further progress and did not reach the summit. In the centre, with both wings stalled, the attack was cancelled.

In order to draw off any possible reinforcements the Germans might have sent north, the French 47th Division renewed its offensive in the Fecht valley, attacking the

Reichackerkopf south of the road west of Münster. Here they ran into 8th Bavarian Ersatz Division which, over two days, threw them back and then mounted ferocious attacks against them. The decision was taken to go on the defensive and to support the 129th instead. The Germans also strengthened their forces on the Sulzern Line, sending a Guard and the 14th Mecklenburger Battalions to join 1st Bavarian Landwehr Brigade.

At 1030 hours on 22 July the French tried again. This time General Trouchard's 5th Brigade was to attack the southern end of the line at the Barrenkopf while the 3rd resumed its efforts on Le Linge and the Schratz. The 106th and 120th Battalions of the 5th managed to gain the shelf of La Courtine but when they went on to attempt the summit of the Barrenkopf they came up against the superbly prepared positions of the Germans and were cut down by machine-gun fire. Back they came. On the other wing the result was much the same. Lacking accurate artillery fire to keep the enemy's heads down and struggling to rush forward in a maze of fallen trees, loose rocks and barbed wire, they failed against the concrete blockhouses and rock-cut trenches held by the Germans. They, too, retreated to their start lines.

Maud'huy paused to regroup and rest the exhausted troops. The weather was foul, wet and misty, and remained so for days, including the day of the next attack, 26 July. This time the artillery barrage was more effective; so many trees had been cut down by shell-fire in the preceding battles that, at last, artillery spotters could see what was going on. At 1800 hours 30th Battalion swarmed over Le Linge and 14th seized the Collet. The cost was high, especially among officers. Only twelve survived in these two battalions. The shelling forced the defenders from their positions on the Schratz but as the 30th approached along the ridge they regained their trenches and stopped the attack. The German reaction to their loss of the stronghold of Le Linge was immediate. Their artillery poured fire onto their own works and onto the approaches to the west.

All night long the shell-fire continued. At 0300 hours on 27 July the first counter-attack was beaten off. At 0800 hours Le Linge and the Collet were counter-attacked again, with the same result. At 0830 the artillery barrage started once more. At 1000 hours, the 14th Mecklenburgers and the Guards attempted to oust the Chasseurs but were again repulsed. The French plan to assault the Barrenkopf front was delayed by the action on the left until 1310 when the 15th Battalion took the Barrenkopf and the 115th and 120th Battalions gained a hold, tenuous though it was, on the Schratz. By evening the 115th had been pushed off the hill and, believing the 15th to be dangerously isolated on the Barrenkopf to the right, General Nollet ordered them to withdraw. Commandant Dussauge could not believe it and queried the instruction. It was confirmed and, at 2100 hours in the steady rain, back they came, never to regain the position.

At GHQ Joffre considered the situation and came to the conclusion that the hoped-for breakthrough was not going to take place. He decided that the 129th Division would be withdrawn on 20 August and would not be replaced; the Seventh Army would then have to hold as best it could. On the ground the obvious temptation was to get as much use out of the 129th as possible while it was still there. A fresh attack on

A German blockhouse with access by a communication trench cut into the rock on Le Linge. *(MME)*

Preserved at Le Linge are look-out shields. One, a simple plate, is set into stone while the other, an evil-looking dome, gives standing room to a sentinel. *(MME)*

the Schratz and the Barrenkopf was mounted on 29 July and while it had a certain success in approaching the top of the former, it was stopped, literally, dead on the latter. The action on 31 July was entirely an artillery battle. Thousands of rounds fell on French lines, both here and in the Fecht valley and the hills flanking it. On 1 August the French replied with their own barrage and another attack. At 1930 hours 5th Battalion went into action against the Linge–Schratz ridge and by 2100 hours it was in their hands and they were threatening the last strongpoint of the Schratz itself. The 12th Battalion was making progress on the Barrenkopf and the next day they inched forward a little more.

On 3 August the day was rent with an unprecedented artillery assault on the French lines. It began at 1000 hours and went on until 1600. The 106th and 121st Battalions suffered severely. At 1630 the German attack came, sweeping the shattered French out of their positions on Le Linge and the Collet. De Maud'huy exhorted Nollet to hold on and promised fresh troops. On 4 August the German artillery intensified its shelling yet further; over 40,000 rounds poured into French positions. One of the men of 4th Company, Chasseurs Alpins, marked his twentieth birthday with the remark that it felt as if his eyes were melting – tear gas was being used. New men were committed to the struggle. Sergeant J.A. Bernadin wrote to his family:

> For the first time I go like an animal to the slaughterhouse. . . . In a little while the impression is strengthened: we meet wounded, Chasseurs Alpins, almost all with head wounds. . . . They come in an endless line with haggard appearance. 'Oh! You're going up there,' they say 'A fine butcher's shop!'
>
> A little further on a wounded man is sitting, naked to the waist, in the icy rain. 'I'm cold!' he groans, with chattering teeth. 'Please, friends, get my tunic on me.' Already two sections have gone by and no one has stepped aside. As we climb the bodies become more numerous. In a gap through the wire, cut by hand, I count a cluster of six dead men. Getting near the top, here are two officers of the 14th Chasseurs Alpins, recognisable by their fine, black tunics garnished with silver, smartly gloved. . . . Everywhere the dead and now more wounded. Most of the dead are covered in tent canvas, waiting to be fetched by the stretcher bearers when there is time to pick them up and bury them. One of these sad parcels leans on the parados of the trench we are taking over. But the cloth trembles and a sort of groan comes from it. 'But he's not dead!' I say to a soldier who is peering through a loophole. 'No, not yet. But the major said it was useless to evacuate him, that he's had it. That was forty-eight hours ago. . . .'

On 7 August the Germans attacked all along the line and again at 1730 the next day. A 420-mm railway gun was brought up on the Colmar–Münster line and thirty shells from it fell on the road to the Col de la Schlucht, closing the Altenburg tunnel, forcing the French to use the Bichstein Pass. At Joffre's instigation Dubail asked Nollet for one last effort. Nollet, de Maud'huy and de Pouydraguin met at the Lac Noir command post on 16 August to discuss the attack as well as the difficult business of the relief of the 129th by the 47th Division. French artillery shelled the objectives, the same Le Linge–Schratz line, the German Sulzern Line, that was first attempted weeks before. By 22 August 23rd Battalion, 47th Division had got the summit of the Schratz, while 23rd held a trench just below the crowning blockhouse on the Barrenkopf. The cost since 20 July had been 176 officers and 9,485 men. On 26 August de Pouydraguin and the 47th took the front over from what was left of 129th Division.

At 1300 hours on 31 August the Germans unleashed a new horror on the French – poison-gas shells. Their infantry attacked at 1700 and gained ground on the Collet. On 9 September a major assault took place not only on Le Linge but on the Hartmannswillerkopf as well, using flame-throwers. The positions of vantage on the high ground fell once more into German hands, but over the next few weeks counter-attacks and attacks in response to them did little to alter the position. A final flurry of slaughter on the Hartmannswillerkopf in December spelt the end of the offensives in the Vosges. On 21 December the French 152nd Regiment, with Chasseurs Alpins on either flank, struck after a massive artillery barrage and took the summit together with 1,500 prisoners. That night, in silence, fresh German troops gathered and many who had hidden in the deep shelters the French had overrun emerged behind the attackers' line. With the dawn a blistering counter-attack was launched and while fighting continued into the New Year, the position remained in German hands. At last, both sides recognized that there was no gain to be had and infinite cost to be incurred; 30,000 French and German lives had been lost in the contest to possess just this unimportant mountain.

The Vosges became relatively quiet for the rest of the war, the conflict being pursued by artillery duels, sniping and the occasional raid. The principal use of the front made by the Allies was in training new troops and it was here that the Americans gained their first taste of modern warfare after entering the war in April 1917. The 1st Division, a regular unit, was sent to Europe almost at once and a squad from the 16th Infantry marched through Paris on 4 July to honour the Frenchman who had played a significant part in the Americans' fight for independence, the Marquis de Lafayette. Private Donald Drake Kyler wrote a memoir of his experiences that day and then of the training they received at Gondrecourt-le-Château, south-west of Nancy.

After we had been in Gondrecourt several days, orders were received outlining the training programs to be followed. The 11th Regiment, Chasseurs Alpins, of the French Army, was assigned to our brigade for demonstrations and joint training purposes. They were one of the best infantry units in the French Army, and it was intended that we should absorb as quickly as possible the latest technique in the kind of fighting that we would soon be engaged in. We did not march back to quarters for noon meals. Instead, sandwiches were brought to us in the training area.

As soon as enough tools arrived we spent some of the time digging a practice trench system. It was a complete typical defense position, with communicating

The Chasseurs Cemetery at the Col du Wettstein. *(MME)*

trenches, strong points, wire entanglements, redoubts, etc. An obstacle course was built and a rifle range was started.

The obstacle course consisted of ditches to be jumped over, obstructions to be crawled under, barriers to be climbed over, wire entanglements to be gotten out of, and other impediments to progress. Many of the men had trouble getting through the maze and had to try over and over again.

Nearby was a bayonet training course, where straw stuffed dummies were suspended on wires, around corners, and holes in the ground. By the use of concealed wires the instructor could cause the dummies to move. The trainee who was going through the course was supposed to react to the surprise of their movement, and stab them as nearly as possible in the spot marked with red paint. The dummies were soon worn out by the onslaughts, and had to be replaced.

Once they had received what was considered sufficient training in the rear, the 16th Infantry entered a quiet part of the line on 21 September 1917. That it was quiet did not mean it was at all safe.

The trench system that we entered was known as the Sommerviller Sector of the Lorraine Front. It had been stable since 1915, and both sides were deeply dug in, with extensive communication trenches, second line trenches, belts of barbed wire entanglements, dug outs, and protected gun emplacements. A series of strong

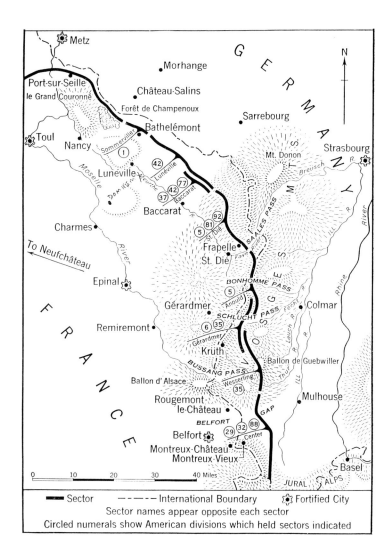

Sectors held by American divisions in the Vosges. Divisional numbers are shown in circles. *(from* American Armies and Battlefields in Europe*)*

points were placed so as to support each other, with lightly held areas between. The land was undulating, with a few hills, and was partly wooded. Many of the trees had been broken by shell bursts in the past and the land was pitted with shell holes, partly eroded, and overgrown with weeds.

My platoon was the last one of the company to enter the trench. We followed along a constantly curving and gradually deepening one for perhaps a mile before we came to the position we were to occupy. The trench at that point was on high ground and about seven feet deep in the middle. On each side was a dirt or board shelf on which to stand to fire one's weapon. The trench curved in a zigzag fashion. That was so that a single shell hit would cause casualties in only one section, or bay, as they were called. The trench led forward to a cross trench where another platoon had taken position.

The descriptions given by Kyler were of commonplace trenches but have the freshness of being a teenager's impression of a new experience:

American soldiers of the 1st Division being trained in the use of hand grenades. *(US Army Military History Institute, WWI Survey)*

My platoon was in the company support position. Slightly to our rear was a large dug out where our company command post was located. It was connected by telephone to all our platoon command posts and to the battalion command post. At several places along our trench there were narrow tunnels leading downward into the earth to our sleeping places. To enter, one had to stoop and descend into a dark, damp, smelly hole. When enough depth had been reached the tunnel widened and became level. Short cross tunnels led off of it. There one could sleep if he was tired enough. The whole place was infested with rats, body lice, and bed bugs. At the far end of the tunnel was a shaft and ladder to escape by in case the entrance was caved in by shell fire. Near the entrance to our dug out, and in the opposite direction, a spur trench led to a trench latrine.

The Germans were well aware of the arrival of these new adversaries and determined to put them to the test.

I think it was about 3: A.M. [on 3 November] when suddenly! – the horizon to the north and east was lit up as by a single flash. It was the muzzle blasts of the enemies' guns. No sound was heard for a few moments until the sound wave hit us, and then with a mighty roar it came. Then the whistling and shrieking of the shells as they hurtled down. So far as I know, none of the shells struck in my company's position, but were concentrated on F Company to our right. Sergeant

Thompson sounded an alarm for our platoon to take position in the fire trench. The bombardment continued so intensely on F Company's position that the explosion of one shell could not be distinguished from any other. It was an inferno of crashing, splintering, rending explosions. We later learned that the enemy had put a box barrage around one of F Company's platoons and followed with a raiding party behind the protection of the barrage. Some F Company men died in their trenches and ten were taken as prisoners by the Germans. Some of our wounded were left, but the Germans carried away all of their wounded. The barrage ceased almost as suddenly as it had started. Our artillery shelled their lines for a while. Soon everything was as quiet as before. Our dead were buried the next day at Bathlemont [Bathelémont].

These were the first Americans to die in the front line. Their names were Corporal James B. Gresham, Private Thomas F. Enright and Private Merle D. Hay.

The accumulation of experience by the Americans continued with standing patrols at night in listening posts in no man's land and with raiding parties. Kyler wrote of these events after the war.

The second night we were there, Private Pinaire and myself were given an assignment to man a listening post in front of our left platoon. We had to crawl out of our front line trench, through a gap in our wire, and to a shallow and camouflaged shelter, which was our post. We were not to fire on enemy patrols except to prevent our

The burial of the first American soldiers to be killed in action. *(US Army Military History Institute, ASC 67149)*

capture but were to observe and listen to all enemy activity. In case an enemy raiding party approached, we were to note its size if possible, and crawl back to our own line with the information. As it was not feasible to make regular reliefs on that post we were to stay out there from soon after dark until almost dawn.

That was a cold and miserable assignment. We could converse only in whispers and could not move around much to keep warm. Also, we always missed the regular feeding time, which while in the trenches, was once every night. Our corporal saved our portions, which we ate after we returned to our trench before dawn. The food and coffee were cold by that time.

The sergeant in charge of the trench behind us sometimes crawled out to our post to see how we were doing. On the third night a French officer came out and questioned us. He did not crawl, but walked. At first we thought that it was all right, since we were more or less under French command. But then he said, 'Wot would you do in case of fug?' That made Pinaire suspicious. He was of French descent and knew the language fairly well. After the officer had left he crawled back to the trench and reported to the sergeant that the officer's accent didn't sound right to him. The sergeant reported it to the officer in charge of our company's forward defenses, who in turn reported to the French commanding officer. An investigation was made, and the same officer who had questioned us, and his orderly, were caught questioning other Americans. They were German spies. Their hands were tied and they were taken away. We heard that the French executed them the next day.

The passive phase of the Americans' first front-line tour of duty eventually came to an end, although they were still not ready to undertake a serious attack. Kyler's account is quoted here in full.

After Pinaire and I had been off the listening post a few days Lieutenant Phipps organized a combat patrol. About twenty of us were selected and given detailed instructions as to what each man was to do. The plan was that we were to crawl out of our front line trench at night and take a position crossing the gully that I mentioned earlier. We would go through a gap in our wire and maintain absolute silence. It was essential that it be done smoothly and without attracting the enemy's attention. If the enemy should know that an ambush was being prepared, our mission would be a failure and we would be the targets for heavy fire from machine guns and mortars. Two of our flank men were to be armed with automatic machine rifles. The rest of us were given daggers and pistols. The pistols were lent to us from others in the company who were armed with them in addition to their rifles. Everything that might rattle or shine was removed from our persons. We also smeared burnt cork and oil on our faces.

When it became dark enough we crept out as planned. The night was damp and chilly. We wore raincoats and belts with pistol holsters and dagger sheaths. Gas masks and helmets were left behind. Each of us had several magazines of pistol cartridges. We took a position with our center astride the gully, with each wing extending out from it at an angle. We settled down to wait as inconspicuously as possible in the brush. We were all apprehensive and scared. It was miserable waiting there. The plan was to let the enemy patrol leader get past our center. Then Lieutenant Phipps was to fire, after which we were all to fire and the wings rush in to cut off the patrol's retreat. The two automatic riflemen were to fire automatic bursts in the direction from which the patrol had come, while the rest of us were to charge in and assault the enemy at close range.

Occasionally, an illumination flare went up from the enemy's line. During the time of its duration we were absolutely still, hardly daring to breathe. The slightest movement might attract attention. After a considerable wait, some of our nervousness had left us and a sort of numbness had come.

We were then just outside the enemy wire and nearer to their trenches than to our own. There was occasional firing up and down the line, as was usual at night, but none in our vicinity. Then – faintly at first, we could hear an enemy patrol approaching. They were entering our trap. Tensions rose. Then someone in our group made a sound like a suppressed cough. The enemy patrol leader stopped and stood still a moment or two, then gave a signal and the patrol retreated rapidly. Lieutenant Phipps fired and we all did likewise with as rapid fire as we were capable of. Some of the enemy were hit and went down. With the exception of a few dead or wounded the enemy patrol escaped. They had not entered our trap far enough for us to cut them off. They probably carried some of their wounded with them. It would have been foolish for us to have pursued them. The lieutenant signaled for a rapid return to our lines.

We knew that as soon as the enemy patrol had gotten into their trench the whole area would be raked by intense fire. We had to get through the gap in our wire, and quickly. Several of our men got snarled in our wire. Some did not seem to realize the urgency of getting to cover quickly. If there ever was the necessity for haste, regardless of noise, it was then. If Sergeant Thompson had taught me anything, it was that now we should expect a hail of bullets at any moment.

I did not want to charge through the gap over or through the other men, though I could have done so. Instead, I kept urging and helping them through the narrow place. In so doing I got caught in some low lying tangled ground wire. While getting free of it an illumination rocket went up from the enemy trench, bathing the area in a bright light. I dived into a nearby shell hole. It was none too soon, because bullets began to hit the rim of that shell hole, and small stones, bits of rusty wire, wooden splinters, and dirt showered down on me from the bullet hits above. They kept sweeping that area for some time. I stayed in the bottom of the shell hole. Our artillery fired a few shells into the area from which their machine guns were firing. The fire then ceased.

I then had the problem of getting back to our own trench without being shot by our men. One does not crawl up to his own trench at night without some sort of an announcement: that is – if he wants to live. Therefore, I crawled through the rest of our wire and again took cover. I whistled several times and called my name. But until I heard a reply I did not go nearer, and even then they had several rifles pointed at me when I got to the trench.

The 42nd Division, known as the Rainbow Division because its men were drawn from all over the United States, arrived in the Lunéville sector, on the north-western slopes of the Vosges, in February 1918. Lieutenant Isaac G. Walker of the 151st Machine-gun Battalion left a brief memoir of his service in France with the 42nd, a document that becomes ever more terse the closer he gets to describing the fighting and pays small attention to the spelling of French place names.

> . . . I was ordered to bring up supplies at dusk the next day, 23d February, which I did, but dusk due to cloudiness on the 22d was later on the 23d. The Germans spotted my wagon train about 3 miles from Ancierville and shelled us with shrapnel. The shelling came close and began to get heavy, so I gave the command to 'trot' and trotted on into Ancierville to find the French officer and Captain Palmer much concerned about my arrival. I received orders in no uncertain terms to unload and clear Ancierville at once. We were fatalist and neither the writer nor his men were aware of the danger they had passed through.
>
> We spend 115 days in the Lunneville sector with Division Headquarters at Baccarat, in the lines 15 to 20 days and out for 10 days at a time our casualties were few, only four. This sector was comparatively quiet when we relieved the Frenchmen, but became a very active one before we were relieved by the 77th Division.
>
> It was in this trench warfare sector we learned to apply our knowledge of machine guns, determine how and when to use them and how to conserve ammunition. Also we determined the cool, level headed officers and men in our organizations. We found that the excitable high strung and the extremely slow, calculating and quiet types broke quicker under stress of battle than officers and men between the two extremes.

It was from this sector that the 42nd moved to the Champagne in early July where, alongside the French, they took part in halting the last great attack of the Germans on the Western Front.

The 32nd Division had their first taste of trench life in the south, at the Belfort Gap. Samuel M. Kent, Company K, 128th Infantry kept a day-by-day journal. It was on 5 June that he first saw the front line at Hirtzbach, just south of Altkirch, east of Belfort.

> After supper, the company was divided into groups and a French guide, who speaks English, took us up to the front line trenches. Every thing seems so peaceful – it is very pretty around here. Our guide is a very nice little corporal

Men of the 42nd Division carrying out a grenade raid under the supervision of a French trainer near Badonviller. *(US Military History Institute, ASC 8362)*

who has fought on the 'Somme' front. He says he learned to speak English in London before the war, very interesting chap. We call him 'Poilu'.

June 6 – Thursday

In the trenches on the front, at last. This is supposed to be a 'quiet sector', a resting place for the French and Boche after a great battle on a very 'active front'. But I am afraid the Yankees won't let it remain that way very long. They are here to fight! The tendency has been, if you don't shoot at me, I won't shoot at you – tit for tat. But you know the Yanks. Do you think they could look across 'No man's land' and see a Boche without taking a shot at him, after coming three thousand miles for that purpose? I am afraid somebody is going to get hurt. We have dug-outs up here, too, to sleep in and for protection when Fritz is shelling us. It is supposed to be bomb-proof – I am a company runner (messenger) and I have it pretty soft – at least, I can sleep at night while the others are on guard.

June 7 – Friday

Still in the trenches. The weather is fine and things are rather quiet, except for a few occasional shots. The Huns' trenches are about 800 yards in front of us, down thru a sloping valley. A town to our right front is called Hirshbach. We have guards posted all along the line of trenches and out in front, we have a

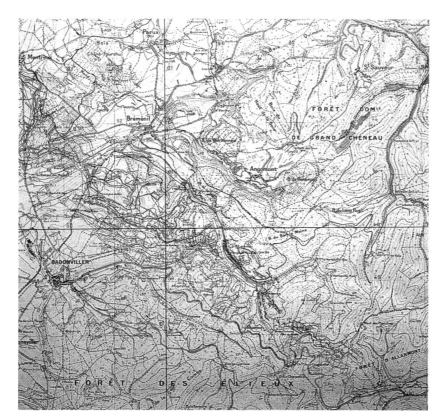

The sector, on the Cirey sheet, held by the 42nd Division near Badonviller. The mapping is dated 13 October 1918, after the 42nd was there, and shows German trenches in blue and the Allies' in red. *(US Army Military History Institute)*

The 42nd Division's trenches survive in the woods east of Badonviller, off the D992, located by using their trench map. *(MME)*

'listening post' or 'P.P.' as the French say. Company headquarters is called a 'P.C.' post of command. A detail of men, who are not in the front line, bring our chow up to us at 5:30 a.m., 12 noon and at 6 p.m. in large 'marmite' cans. Sometimes, it is pushed up on a small narrow-gauge truck and sometimes tied upon the backs of burros [mules]. At 8 p.m. we were relieved from the front line, by the third platoon and have fallen back to the 'line of support'.

June 8 – Saturday

Today, being in 'Support', we have taken our turn of carrying the chow up to the boys in the front lines. The weather is fine and slightly warm. Fritz sends a few shells over and we return the 'compliments'.

June 9 – Sunday

Practically the same program as yesterday. Around this place, the rats abound and in the still of the night they sound like human beings – they are so big. Many a man on guard duty has been scared at their noise and fired his rifle thinking it was a Boche creeping towards our lines. The much heard of 'cooties' [lice] have at last made their appearance and I have felt one upon me, today, for the first time. May it be the first and only one; I wish I could believe that it would. Tonight, some time, the whole company is going to be relieved and go back of the lines a few miles to rest up – so they say. The only time you rest over here, is when they lay you to rest.

After five days, late on Sunday, they were withdrawn to the reserve lines a little to the west.

We left the trenches last night at 10 p.m. and we are now in the town of 'Fullerin' [Fulleren] (Alsace). We arrived here early this morning after a rather long hike. As usual, we are sleeping in barns. It has been raining all day and has been very disagreeable. Because we were up so long last night, we have been excused from drilling, etc. – but I guess we will pay up to-morrow.

June 11 – Tuesday

It is raining, again, today – but we 'fell in' just the same at 6 a.m. We each got a pick or shovel and went out with a Frenchman to learn how to dig trenches and, incidentally, help them to build up a system of trenches at our expense. In building trenches, you reinforce them with tree-boughs inter-twined and we must ask the Frenchman which trees we can cut, because they must conserve forests and everything else and he is responsible in this section. We dug until noon, some job – hard on the back. This afternoon, the Boche shelled the town and a Frenchman and woman were hurt by the exploding shells. We have noticed that the majority of his shells are 'duds' – they don't explode – for which we are thankful, because, often, they come too close for comfort. We have not been drawing full rations and, consequently, the meals have been somewhat skimpy. There is only one store in the town and it hasn't much of a variety in the way of eats.

June 15 – Saturday

The weather is 'magnolious' and most of the day the fellows bask in the glorious sunshine, as long as Fritz behaves himself. I made several trips back to headquarters and the rest of the time I acted as 'gas sentinel', so the rest of the fellows could sleep – and to give the warning in case Heine sent over a gas barrage. While there are shell-holes, barb wire and trenches all around, yet it is a little hard to realize that this is war; because the grass and trees are nice and green and with the warm sunlight beaming it makes you think of home and peace: – then the Boche awakens you from your sweet summer's day dreams by dropping a few 'G.I. Cans' close by which reminds you of what Sherman said – 'War is hell', and so it is.

The next morning Kent was sent to the rear to collect the detail bringing up rations. The support area was scattered with sheds and dug-outs as well as being protected by barbed wire. As the sun started to come up Kent saw a German aircraft slowly circling around far above the lines. Suddenly shells began to fall. At first it looked as if the American guns were the target, then the kitchens, then Kent himself. Frantically he sought a gap in the wire so that he could take shelter in a dug-out and finally he did so. He dived into the first shelter he could find, rousing a sleepy officer who asked what was going on: 'He asked me, all in one breath, what was the matter, what was

The YMCA at Bathelémont. The YMCA, Salvation Army and other charitable institutions played an important part in maintaining the health and morale of the American troops. The sign reads: 'Say it without swearing, thank you.' The separation of the black soldier from the others is no accident. *(US Army Military History Institute, ASC 2353)*

I excited about?, which made me peeved under the circumstances, and without regard for his rank, I told him plainly it was time and there was reason to be excited. Contrast the position of the two of us – he in his bunk, perfectly safe and I out there perfectly unsafe.' Fortunately Kent had no more than a fright and one of his comrades sustained a small wound in his leg, but he had learned that the peace of the scene was an illusion. A week later the 32nd was moved to Château Thierry, where they were soon in action on the right of the 42nd on the River Ourcq.

The 77th Division relieved the 42nd in the Lunéville sector. Paul R. Ostertag was with Battery D, 304th Field Artillery as a telephone sergeant. Their initial training was at Sougé-Champ-de-Tir in Base Section No. 2 which had its headquarters at Bordeaux. There he learned to set up and run a sophisticated communication system for the direction of the guns.

My detail and self attended school for a half day daily except Saturday and learned practical telephone work on all kinds of fones and laying lines under all sorts of conditions. For the other half of the day we used our time doing practical wiring and forming data to become as familiar as possible with the whole game. These were pleasant days for us and the boys 'got to it' in good style.

About two weeks put the 'firing battery' into shape for service firings and we went to the camp range for daily firings from then on till the end of our training. The range was miles in extent, had a wire and central system of tip top class and, while one regiment fired, another manned the centrals, so that all had an opportunity to become familiar with all phases of the work. . . .

On July 7 we pulled out from Souge for a trip across France to Baccarat (south of Toul and Nancy) and took up position on the 12th in a well camouflaged emplacement. The entire regiment moved into positions very near us in the next few days, but we were first in and first to fire a shot at the Germans of our regiment.

Before I go any further I might explain that when a battery goes into position it does so under cover of darkness and only the guns and the men needed to do the work at the emplacement are left there. Horses and the rest of the men are sent to a place previously selected which is called the Echelons. If possible men are sent up to replace those at the guns by a regular relief system, but it frequently happens that the work comes in such a way that there is not the desired regularity to the changes. One gun group may be on duty for several days when they have firing to do at such hours that their rest is interrupted night and day and they have no chance at all to sleep. Their relief may have nothing whatever to do. The men at the Echelon are mostly drivers with few spare cannoneers and these men work by night drawing ammunition and other supplies up to the battery position from a dump or from the Echelon, usually several miles distant. Meals for men at the guns are brought up in a small cart (from the Echelon) to some point nearby that affords concealment and then carried by hand in fireless cookers to the position. You can understand that a camouflaged position would have very little real value so far as

Tired beyond belief, German soldiers pose for the camera in 1918.

concealment goes, if men were allowed to go back and forth and attract attention by their movement.

Our first position was on the reverse slope of a moderate hill and was camouflaged by a large square netting supported on 5 foot poles which represented on the surface, a cultivated patch of a size well suited to match the general plan. The guns had overhead cover of sheet iron, at least splinter proof, and two dugouts, one each side of each gun were used one for ammunition and one for sleeping quarters for men. Both were deep enough and well enough protected by courses to keep out German 77 pills up to direct hits. We continued the digging to connect up our guns and dugouts with a very complete telephone dugout and a Command Post which we built while in that position.

The Frenchmen treated us O.K. plus and we of the Telephone Detail established the best relations imaginable before we finally parted company. One of our number could 'French it' a little and he was automatically appointed interpreter for our lil crowd. As it happened we took the position July 12th and on the 14th we arranged to cooperate with the French for a National Holiday celebration by buying wine for a little party. There were only seven of us but we had no room for more in our little dugout. I, for one, enjoyed it immensely, not because the wine was good but because of the good spirit that was so evident at this little party of ours. Looking back at it all now I realize that many of the things we so strongly hoped for have come to pass and this much more quickly than we hoped, or dared to hope, then. The Château Thierry Drive was just beginning then and, tho we did not realize it, we were scheduled to take part in it. . . .

The 77th relieved the 4th and 32nd Divisions near Fismes in early August, at the end of the great reduction of the Soissons Salient. Almost all of the twelve American divisions which trained here were involved in raids, either as victims or as raiders, between 3 November 1917, when the first men were killed in action, and the end of the war. Their losses were comparatively light as there was no reversion to the fanatical conflict that had marked the contest between the French and Germans in the earlier years. It was, all things considered, a quiet front.

THE
ITALIAN FRONTS

'... *the heavy projectiles began to burst on the roof of the "dug-out" with such terrific force that one expected at any moment the whole place would be blown to atoms.... I never thought that human ears or nerves could stand such an inferno ...*'

Journalist Julius Price's report of his experience of an Austrian
bombardment, 1916

Overleaf: Austrian troops load a heavy mortar. (*Guy Cavallaro*)

FIVE

ITALIA IRREDENTA

As the war spread to the border between France and Switzerland in the west and from the Baltic to Serbia in the east, both sides were concerned to secure the position on the southern flank of Europe – in Italy. This was a country that had only come into being in 1870 and was still indignant that territories peopled by Italians, the Trentino, Tyrol, Venezia Giulia and the Dalmatian coast, were part of the Austro-Hungarian Empire. At the same time a traditional antipathy to France existed, offset by long-established friendly relations with Britain. When, in August 1914, Austria declared war on Serbia and Germany on France, Italy, supposedly in alliance with the Central Powers, declared neutrality in part because there was an escape clause in her Triple Alliance membership; she was not bound if Britain was on the other side in a dispute. The road

The border between Italy and Austria-Hungary, which ran through terrain that presented incredible challenges to military operations. *(from* The Times History of the War*)*

to the abandonment of neutral status was decorated with tempting promises made both by the Allies and by the Central Powers. In essence the final decision was based on hopes of regaining *Italia Irredenta*, the 'lost' lands of the north and east. The Treaty of London, signed secretly by Italy and the Allies on 26 April 1915, guaranteed their restoration as well as the territory of Libya in north Africa.

The lands in question encircle the plains of north-eastern Italy today. From the Swiss frontier at the Stelvio Pass the border ran due south over the Alps to Lake Garda where it turned north-east to place the Asiago plateau within Italian boundaries and the border along the summit of the peaks overlooking the Val Sugana, the headwaters of

the River Brenta which drains to Padua and the Adriatic, and the Dolomites beyond. The border turned east along the Carnic Alps before running south along the heights overlooking the valley of the Isonzo River which lay in Austrian territory to the east. The front that offered, or so it seemed, the best prospect of territorial acquisition by force of arms was this eastern border. In the north the Julian Alps and Monte Nero (now Krn) stood above the river and the small town known as Caporetto to the Italians, or Karfreit to the Austrians, and Kobarid today. This was unpromising but needed to be secured to permit progress over the two plateaux of the Bainsizza, south of Tolmino and the River Idria, and the Carso, between Gorizia and the sea. Between these objectives and the Italians the River Isonzo zig-zagged southwards from mountainous country to broad plains.

The Austrians, on the other hand, were offered opportunities for invasion from the Trentino front, between Lake Garda and Asiago, from which they might debouch onto the plains and thrust towards Padua and Venice, cutting off the armies facing the Isonzo. The Trentino region depended on supplies from Austria coming from Bolzano, in the Tyrol south of Innsbrück and the Brenner Pass, to Trent (Trento). The high mountain frontiers between the two were not areas in which either side could operate aggressively or in numbers.

The town of Tolmino and the Isonzo valley beyond. *(Guy Cavallaro)*

General Luigi Cadorna became commander-in-chief of the Italian Army on 1 July 1914 and within weeks had to undertake the tasks of creating an effective army and of planning an appropriate strategy should war come. The purpose of action in the east was in part to relieve Serbia, in part to regain land and in part to threaten centres of communication and supply in Austrian territory at Laibach (now Ljubljana), Villach and Klagenfurt through which supplies could reach this part of the Austrian front as far south as Trieste. This front was, in comparison with the Trentino and the Cadore, unfortified. Although the Austrian chief-of-staff, Field Marshal Franz, Count Conrad von Hötzendorf, was confident that the Italians would attack on the Isonzo he had not made up his mind whether to establish a strong front there or to draw them east as far as Laibach and then wipe them out. Only on 21 April 1915 was the order given to close the Isonzo crossings below Tolmino and set up defensive positions along the western side of the Carso, but the work proceeded so swiftly that the new commander in this sector, General Svetosar Bor[o]evich von Bojna, with only seven divisions at his disposal, would be able to make an effective defence. As the threat of war on this front grew Austria moved troops onto her borders. On 26 April the arrival of two corps from Serbia and one from the Eastern Front brought the strength to some 81,400 men and 324 guns over and above the fortress garrisons. On 14 May the advance detachments of another three divisions arrived from Poland. On 22 May the Archduke Eugen was given the command of the Austrian South-Western Front with General Krauss as his chief-of-staff. On 23 May Italy declared war.

The Italians had mobilized a force of about 850,000 men and 23,000 officers with some 9,000 civilians in support. On the Isonzo front the sector from Monte Maggiore, north-east of Tolmino, to Gorizia was that of the Second Army of General Frugoni and to his right, between Gorizia and the sea, was the Third Army under General Zuccari, soon to be succeeded by the Duke of Aosta. In the west in the Trentino the First Army under General Brusati held the front from the Swiss border at the Stelvio Pass to Lake Garda and the Fourth Army, General Nava, stood from there to the headwaters of the Piave River. The high mountains of the north between these two fronts were the domain of General Lequoi with nineteen battalions of Alpini, mountain troops, a squadron of cavalry and eight gun batteries. The weakness in artillery was felt throughout the Italian Army, particularly in heavy guns.

The situation in Italy was the latest excitement in London. The editor of the *Illustrated London News* hustled his artist, Julius Price, away on 20 May to observe, draw and report on what was happening while the British fought to hold on around Ypres and the French strove to seize Vimy Ridge and to dominate the heights of the Vosges. On arrival he found his entry barred to the War Zone, but Venice was not, for the time being, part of it so he went there. He soon found he was getting closer to his objective.

At 3.30 on the morning of 24th May the inhabitants [of Venice] were aroused by the loud boom of a signal gun – and this was immediately followed by the screech of all the steam whistles in the City and on the boats. In a very few minutes the batteries of the Aerial-Guard Station and the machine guns and rifles were firing as rapidly as they could at the intruders – several Taubes flying at a great height – without effect, unfortunately, as they managed to drop several bombs and get away unscathed. Two of the bombs fell in the courtyard of the Colonna di Castelpo, one in the Tana near the Rio della Tana, another in the San Lucia and a fourth in the Rio del Carmini.

That same day the Italians took the Plöcken Pass in the Carnic Alps and the next day the Italian 6th Division attempted an attack west of Lake Garda, part of the Italian five-day 'First Offensive Bound'. The Tonale Pass did, however, fall to the First Army and the Fourth Army made similar conquests in the mountains of the Cadore. The Second Army took Caporetto and a number of mountains east of the Isonzo but further south General Vercellana failed to attain his objectives, believing Austrian disinformation about the presence of mines at all crossings, and he was sacked by Cadorna. Indeed, Cadorna got rid of more than 200 generals during his tenure of command.

Price, still in Venice, had met 'a very nice fellow' whom he mistook for a journalist and thus missed an interview with Peppino Garibaldi, who had returned from France to serve his country. What Price did manage was to persuade the British Consul to give him a letter of introduction to the Military Commandant at Udine, the town in which Cadorna had his headquarters, and with a borrowed waiter who spoke English as his interpreter, he set off. The War Zone by now included Venice and apparently it was assumed that those already within it had a right to be there. Certainly Price was in

Italian mountain troops, Alpini, on patrol.

Two men of the Austrian mountain troops. *(Guy Cavallaro)*

anything but disguise – he wore a Norfolk jacket, breeches and leggings and carried a rucksack – and could scarcely be suspected as a spy.

> It was supposed to take three hours to get to Udine, but we were two and a half longer, as we were continually being held up for trains with troops, artillery and every description of *matériel* to pass. It was an endless procession, and the soldiers in them seemed as happy as sand-boys, and cheered lustily as they passed us. . . .
>
>   At one place we passed a long Red Cross train full of badly wounded men just in from the Front. This was the first time there had been any evidence of the fighting that was taking place on ahead. It was almost a startling sight, and came in sharp contrast to the cheering crowds of healthy boys in the troop trains that had gone by a few minutes previously.

Price was impressed by, if not entirely well informed about, the Italian performance. He wrote:

> Everything seemed to go as though by routine in the early operations, and from the moment war was declared and the Italian army made its 'Tiger spring' for the Passes on the night of May 23rd–24th it was manifest that General Cadorna had well matured plans, and that they were being carried out without a hitch anywhere. . . .
>
>   I was in Cormons shortly after the entry of the troops, and it was difficult to realise that the Italians had not always been there. The inhabitants of Italian origin helped to remove as many traces as possible of the Austrian occupancy – the hated names disappeared as if by magic from shop fronts and street corners. . . .
>
>   Everywhere the soldiers were received with open arms by the peasantry of the redeemed province, and many touching scenes were witnessed in the villages through which they passed, villages that had long given up hope of ever being under the Italian tricolour again.

The efforts did not cease there. The gains on the upper Isonzo were vulnerable to the Austrians who still held the height of Monte Nero and an attack failed there on 2 June. Three days later an assault on the Carso and Gorizia failed as a result of insufficient artillery support. The Second Army tried again at Gorizia on 9 June but managed only to cross the river. In the south the Third Army had better fortune in taking Monfalcone, near the coast. The next day the Ravenna Brigade, already over the Isonzo near Gorizia, mounted an attack on Hill 383, but it was another week before the Italians took it having lost over 2,000 men. On the night of 15/16 June the Alpini renewed the assault on Monte Nero.

  The mountaineers were divided up into small units and preceded by scouting parties moving as far as possible in silence. The 35th Company of the Susa Battalion led the way, commanded by Captain Vittorio Varese. Hill 2138 fell to them, as did Hill 2133.

The ridge of Monte Nero taken by the Italians in June 1915.

Then the 84th Company of the Exilles Battalion scaled the Kozliak Ridge to seize the summit against tough resistance. By dawn, when a detachment of Hungarian troops arrived to reinforce the Austrian garrison, the Italians were in place and captured the whole battalion. Julius Price was full of praise.

> The whole story of the capture of Monte Nero is a veritable epic of heroism and courage. It started with a series of stubborn conflicts for the possession of the spurs leading to the summit; these were gradually taken, and then came the crucial moment when only the actual summit remained in the possession of the Austrians. This had been transformed into a veritable fortress. . . .
>
> Many an experienced climber would hesitate to negotiate so precipitous an ascent in daylight. The Alpini, with almost incredible daring, undertook it on a moonless night.
>
> It meant practically scaling a cliff of rock in pitch darkness, encumbered with rifle and munition. . . . In order to lessen the danger of making any noise which might arouse the suspicions of the Austrian sentries, they removed their boots and bound rags round their feet to prevent them being cut on the rocks.
>
> Up they climbed in the Cimmerian gloom of midnight like so many panthers stalking their prey; now and again a rock, dislodged by accident, would disturb

the stillness of the night as it rattled down to the valley below, and instantly the column would halt and remain motionless expecting the next moment the mountain side would be illumined by the enemy's flares and their presence discovered, but their quarry slumbered on in blissful ignorance of their approaching doom, and the sentinels, fortunately, heard nothing.

Half-an-hour before dawn the various detachments reached the summit and found themselves within a few yards of the front line of entrenchments. These were instantly rushed and captured at the point of the bayonet within a few minutes, most of their defenders being killed before they were awake. The second line shared the same fate after a short and stubborn fight, for once aroused the Austrians fought like cornered rats and with the courage of despair. . . .

Price was not, of course, present during the action and his account is an example of 'magic-carpeting' – producing an apparently eyewitness account from what he learned from others. None the less it is probably not too far from the truth, for the action was a remarkable achievement. He numbers the prisoners at 750, approximately a battalion, of Hungarian troops who, they told him, had come from the Serbian front. Many were without boots and were wearing wooden shoes fastened to foot and ankle with leather straps. They appeared to be reconciled to captivity, 'taking it very philosophically'. The Austrians mounted numerous counter-attacks to regain possession of the position on Monte Nero, but did not succeed.

The First Offensive Bound had given the Italians a number of useful positions in what had been Austrian territory, but it could scarcely be considered a greatly damaging blow to the northern Empire. Julius Price went back to Udine to await the next development. There he frequently saw the Italian King's Fiat car going about the streets and he wrote of the monarch: '. . . the King appeared indefatigable and was out and about in all weathers, and was said to have visited all the sectors of the Front and to be never satisfied unless he saw for himself all that was going on amongst the troops'. Price, however, was not to remain in Udine for long. He was suddenly summoned to the office of the

The King of Italy, although excluded from military decision-making, was energetic in visiting his troops.

Military Governor and ordered to leave. Nevertheless, he managed to get agreement that Florence would be his place of banishment and learned that he was not suspected of anything untoward – it was simply that all journalists were being sent away until a new policy about war correspondents was formed and new arrangements for them put in place.

On 23 June the first of many battles of the Isonzo began. There were to be eleven of them in the coming years. The objective was to capture the three major towns in the centre of this front: Tolmino, north of the confluence of the Idria and the Isonzo, Plava, at the western-most curve of the river in this sector, and Gorizia, commanding the entrance to the valley north of the Carso. The artillery bombardment lasted a week, but was delivered by the fairly modest number of 530 guns, few of which were heavy. On 30 June seventy battalions assaulted the Austrian's forty, while on the previous day a preliminary attack had secured a foothold on Monte San Michele and the ridge running southwards, but the efforts of the next couple of days left them with no more than bridgeheads at Plava and at Sagrado, south of Gorizia. A further attack by their Second and Third Armies on 5 July gained nothing of significance and brought total Italian losses to 14,947 men, of whom some 1,900 were killed and more than 11,000 wounded. The effect of shells in this rocky terrain was to hurl fragments of stone at the opposing sides, causing a high incidence of head injuries. Austrian casualties numbered 9,948, also a serious loss.

On 18 July the Second Battle of the Isonzo started. The Italian artillery, with some augmentation of their heavy guns, performed rather better but fierce fighting brought trivial gains. Monte San Michele was taken on 20 July but lost again two days later to a determined Austrian counter-attack. Monte Sei Busi, between Sagrado and Monfalcone on the edge of the Carso, fell to the Italians on 26 July, but their efforts were faltering and by 3 August the battle was over with another 41,866 casualties added to the Italian count.

After using his time of exile in Florence to produce a number of finished drawings for the *Illustrated London News*, Price learned that twenty-six journalists were to be recognized as war correspondents. He was included in this number and they were to make a tour of the various fronts, convening first at Brescia, west of Lake Garda.

Everything for our big journey had been planned out with true Italian thoroughness, even to providing every one of us with a set of large and reliable maps, whilst on the head of giving permission to see all we desired there was no cause for complaint, as we were to be allowed to go everywhere along the Front; the only reason for disappointment being in the information that immediately after the tour was finished we should be obliged to leave the war zone until further orders.

The journalists' reports were to be, naturally, subject to censorship and offices for that purpose, from which the despatches were forwarded to their papers, were set up in key

centres. A banquet marked the recognition of the press corps on the eve of their departure from Brescia. The first sector Price and his companions visited was the east-facing line between Brescia and the Swiss border at the Stelvio Pass. They were amazed at what had been achieved in the few months since spring.

> Trenches and gun emplacements confronted you on all sides. A sort of gigantic furrow wound through the valley and climbed the mountain like some prehistoric serpent, till lost to view away up on the summits more than two thousand metres above; and round about this fantastic thing were numberless little quaint grey

A contemporary map of the Isonzo front west of the Carso. Sagrado is south of Gradisca and south of the river on the left and Monte san Michele is to the north-east, halfway to Merna. Gorizia is top right.

The Stelvio, close to the Swiss border.

shapes dotted here and there on the rocks, and often in positions so steep of access that you wondered how they got up there at all, and for what purpose. These were the encampments of the thousands of Italian soldiers who have accomplished all this marvel of mountain warfare. . . .

As we advanced further into this impressive zone of military activity you realized that all your pre-conceived notions of mountain warfare were upset. Instead of fighting taking place in the valleys and passes as one would have expected, the positions and even the trenches were on the very summits of what one would have taken to be almost inaccessible peaks and crags, and in some places actually above the snow-line.

Price was also surprised by the contribution made by troops normally associated with different activites. For example, the Bersaglieri, light infantry sharpshooters, were undertaking engineers' tasks in the high mountains, commonly the province of the Alpini, the mountain troops, but seemed perfectly content to be doing so.

The cavalcade moved south to Lake Garda, the northern tip of which lay in Austrian territory. Here the Italians had a flotilla of gunboats: 'The officers and crews of these boats are all picked men from the Royal Navy, and I was told that they had taken to their novel duties with the greatest enthusiasm. The *Mincio*, which was of about 150 tons, carried a very useful-looking Nordenfeldt quick-firer, mounted on the foredeck, and also a big searchlight apparatus.'

A few days later, on 20 August, Price and Jules Rateau of the *Echo de Paris* made the journey all the way to the Forcola, at the meeting point of the Swiss, Italian and Austrian borders close to the Stelvio Pass. Having stayed overnight nearby they were placed in the care of a young soldier of the Alpini and set off to climb. Their guide carried their coats and other belongings, but, '. . . we were neither of us as young as we had been. This . . . was irritatingly brought home to me at one time when we were really making splendid progress as we thought. Some Alpini, in full marching order, caught us up and passed us as easily as if we had been standing still.' Then they came under shell-fire from the Austrians and hurried on as best they could.

> The track now became more and more steep and zigzag, till at length the windings terminated, and there appeared to be a long straight stretch, going without a break along the face of the bluff, up to the summit at an angle of at least 60 degrees. Even now when I recall it, it makes me shudder. It was certainly not more than a couple of feet in width, and overhung an abyss hundreds of feet deep. The mere aspect of it almost gave me vertigo.

Having come so far, Price felt obliged to brave the path and, in spite of making the mistake of looking down and so having to cling on with eyes shut for some minutes to regain courage, he made it to the inside of the fort.

> A wonderful spectacle confronted me as I looked round. The Forcola is nearly 10,000 feet [3,050 m] high, and here, right on the summit, was a veritable citadel in course of construction, with armoured trenches, sandbag emplacements for big guns, barbed wire entanglements; in fact, everything that modern military science can contrive to insure impregnability. . . .
>
>   Behind its line of armoured trenches is a deep hollow, which could shelter an army corps if necessary; and here, under complete cover, are well-built, barrack-like buildings, in which the troops can be comfortably quartered during the long winter months when the fort is buried under yards of snow and practically isolated from the outer world.

The visiting journalists were made welcome and shown round. They admired the largest mountain in the area towering before them, the Ortler, remarked on the new-fallen snow and wondered at all the arms and equipment that had been hauled so high. Price continued:

> We gladly accepted the invitation to have some lunch in the mess-room, for the keen air had given both of us healthy appetites, and while we were doing justice to

a well-cooked steak with fried potatoes and a flask of very excellent *Valtellino*,
I had a chat with some of the younger officers and learned to my surprise that
they had not stirred from the place since they had come up nearly three months
before, and they had no hope of getting leave for a long time to come as things
were developing and winter was coming along.

After lunch they went to watch the shelling, much as one might cast a casual eye over a
game of football taking place by chance on a walk through the countryside and then,
to Price's apprehension, they scuttled back down the cliff-side path.

The party of correspondents moved on to the valley of the Adige to view the
Austrian Rovereto positions and then to the Cadore front where the Col di Lana, near
Cortina d'Ampezzo, was held by the Austrians and was under pressure from the
Italians. The best place to see it was from a mountain facing the Col and the best way
to get the journalists up was by mule. Price described their experiences:

The sturdy Alpini who accompanied us treated the excursion as a good sort of
joke apparently, and plodded steadily alongside us in the best of spirits, laughing
now and again at our vain efforts to keep our steeds from walking on the extreme
edge of the precipices.

This ride gave us a splendid opportunity of seeing how the Italians have
surmounted the difficulty of getting heavy artillery up to the very summits of the

Heavy guns were hauled up newly built roads in the mountains.

A restored First-World-War building on Monte Cristallo (Ivano Dibona) near Cortina d'Ampezzo. The possibility of fighting here challenges the imagination. *(Philippa Carling)*

mountains, where no human feet had trodden before the war broke out. Rough and terribly steep in places though the road was, it was still a real roadway and not a mere track as one might have expected to find considering how rapidly it had been made. Men were still at work consolidating it at the turns on scientific principles, and in a few weeks, with the continual traffic passing up and down it, it would present all the appearance of an old established road.

The next visit was from Gemona di Friuli, north of Udine, up towards the Plöcken Pass, the Passo di Monte Croce. The journalists passed through Tolmezzo and Paluzza to a village called Muse where they were mounted on mules and carried on up to the Pal Piccolo. Price reported that on the way they passed a column of

. . . peasant women carrying barbed wire up to the trenches . . . although it was high in the mountains, and the women must have been tramping for some hours, they were all as cheerful as possible, and appeared to regard their job as a sort of

Italian trenches on the Pal Grande.

pleasure jaunt. . . . Many of the girls I saw were distinctly good-looking, and the
bright tones of their picturesque costumes made a cheerful and unexpected note of
colour against the dull grey of the wild mountain pass.

They climbed the Pal Grande and found themselves looking down on Austrian
trenches, made after the Italians had ejected them from this eminence, and across to
the Freikoffel, taken by the Alpini. Price was full of admiration:

How mortal men could be found to scale these giddy heights at all, leave alone
under such awful conditions, baffles me. There are no tracks at all to ascend it by,
so it is a mystery how it was accomplished. The Austrians abandoned all their
positions here so precipitately that they left all their wounded behind, who,
together with those of the Italians, had to be actually lowered by ropes from the
summit, there being no other means of bringing them down to the ambulances.

Price was also warm in his praise for the arrangements made to keep the Italian
troops well fed, although in this, as on other topics, he based his view on what
happened when the situation was peaceful enough to permit him to be there. He had
shared the soldiers' meal of Rancio, a stew of meat and pasta taken with bread and

wine, on a number of occasions: 'In advanced trenches, outposts or similar exposed positions, where culinary operations are, of course, impossible, the *rancio* is taken to the men after dark in special receptacles for keeping it hot, known as *Cassette di Cottura*, which are constructed on the Thermos principle.'

Finally the party descended from the hills to Price's former stamping ground of Udine and made a trip east to Cormons. Price had not been here for three months and noticed many changes. The town had become, as far as appearances went, entirely Italian. They drove on to Mount Quarin and looked out across the Lower Isonzo. The plain below them was heavily cultivated and divided neatly into numerous fields, while immediately beyond was the battlefield.

> There was a good deal of smoke and mist hanging about, and standing out in sharp relief against it was the peculiar hog-backed contour of the blood-soaked ridge of Podgora bristling with the charred and shattered stumps of trees. Even as we gazed, the distant boom of artillery reached our ears, and we saw shells bursting constantly along the summit and we knew that the attack which was costing so many gallant lives, was being vigorously pursued.

Price remarked on the complex of trenches between Cormons and Brazzano at Subida and guessed how, in time to come, it might be visited and studied by researchers of the military arts. In the next few days equally distant views of the front to the north at Caporetto and to the south at Gradisca were presented to the journalists and then, to their great disappointment, they were sent away. Once they had gone the next Italian attack was launched.

Cadorna had been under pressure from the Allies, who had suffered reverses at Ypres and in the Champagne on the Western Front in addition to the failure at Gallipoli and the retreat of the Serbs in the Balkans, to renew his efforts against the Austrians. In spite of an outbreak of cholera among some of his troops who had occupied enemy trenches and the worsening weather, Cadorna gathered 19 divisions and 1,250 guns to launch the Third Battle of the Isonzo. On 18 October they attacked both north and south of Gorizia, but the effect of the artillery on the Austrian trenches and wire was minimal and at Plava no advance was achieved at all. Against the Carso positions some small success came at first, but Austrian counter-attacks repossessed the positions. Against the summit of Monte San Michele the Third Army came close to taking the position but steady machine-gun fire held them off. On 28 October Hill 383 at Plava was assaulted in heavy rain without success as were the attacks further north in the Tolmino sector. On the Carso the results were slightly more satisfactory, but by the time the battle came to an end on 4 November the Italian losses had climbed to more than 67,000 men, of whom 10,733 were killed. The Austrian losses totalled 42,000 men.

Fighting was also taking place in the mountains and on 7 November General Peppino Garibaldi, the man Price had mistaken for a journalist, led the assault on the

Col di Lana. He had a battalion of the 51st Regiment and two of the 59th under his command. In the previous fortnight the Cappello di Napoleone and the Montecolo had been taken and now Garibaldi seized the longed-for objective. His victory was brief. The Austrians shelled their former positions with amazing ferocity and the Italians had no choice but to withdraw, yielding the Col to their enemies once more.

Only three days later the Fourth Battle of the Isonzo started. The Sassari Brigade distinguished themselves on the Carso and some progress was made towards Gorizia, which was now being shelled by the Italians, but by early December, when the fighting stuttered to a halt, another 48,967 Italian and 30,000 Austrian casualties had been sustained without any significant change to the front in dispute. Indeed, the efforts of the entire nine months' fighting had given the Italians only Monte Nero, Caporetto and tiny bridgeheads further south. In the high Alps the Fourth Army had made some gains but still lay under the eyes of the Austrians on the summits. In the Trentino progress had been made, for here the First Army had achieved the objectives given to it, but they were of minor importance in the overall scheme of the Italian war.

Paolo Monelli, a 24-year-old lawyer from Firoano di Modena, joined the Alpini as a private soldier, but was to attain the rank of captain before the end of his service. The decline in fighting that accompanied winter conditions made life no less dangerous for him.

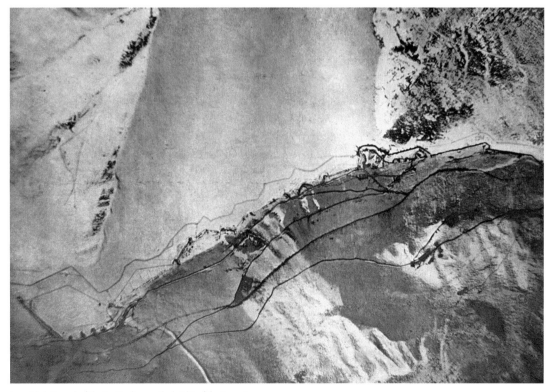

An aerial photograph of the Austrian lines on the heights of the Panarotta.

The Val Sugana between Levico and Borgo, with Panarotta top left, from a contemporary map. The mountain of Cima Dodici is on the rose-coloured border, south of Borgo.

Christmas brought the promise of action and Monelli and his comrades distracted themselves by visiting the inn where the attractive young ladies served the light wine of Salorno. Their destination became known: Panarotta, the source of the enemy's daily shelling. They moved off, up the valley of the River Brenta, the Val Sugana, on the northern front of the Trentino sector. Panarotta is the height dominating the road between Levico and Borgo, and the Alpini made a 6-hour night march along the valley, sunless even in daylight, to reach their new billets. At 2100 hours the next evening they moved off to their first experience of attack, through the snowy woods. Monelli heard rifle fire and saw flares, but no enemy and no target. Dawn came and food was brought up. Finally a brief, incomprehensible burst of action, branches shorn from the trees, the whine of bullets and scream of shells and then silence. On their return they were dazed by the experience of their first combat action. However, Monelli wrote, '. . . the divisional commander . . . greets us at the gap in the wire, hard, cold, and hostile. He says too few of us got killed. He says we ought to have taken the position. He says it is very easy to find, even on the map (and he consults the map that has more mistakes than indications).' The fact that seeing anything at night is extremely difficult, and finding an obscure objective even more so, was ignored. All the commander wanted was success and, lacking it, he had himself driven away to his comfortable quarters. A long, cold winter awaited Monelli and his comrades.

SIX

BATTLES OF THE TRENTINO AND ISONZO

The fighting in Italy during 1915 had changed the frontage only a little, but had demonstrated that the Italian soldier was capable of substantial courage and determination. General Cadorna's policy of concentrating on a breakthrough on the Carso and merely holding the small gains made on the upper Isonzo and in the mountains led to considerable criticism but insignificant proposals of sensible alternatives. What was to have a severe effect on the Italians was the lack of understanding the aristocratic commander-in-chief had of his men. Tensions between front-line troops and bureaucratic staff to the rear increased and the failure to rest, and give home leave to, the fighting men eroded their good spirits here just as it did in the French Army until they had been brought to the point of mutiny. The sensation of neglect experienced by the troops on the front line was increased by the knowledge that men at home, employed in the factories producing the munitions, were not only safe from enemy bullets, but very much better paid.

While winter prevailed the fighting was muted, but none the less lethal for those in action. In February 1916 Monelli's Alpini had captured the village of Marter, halfway between Levico and Borgio on the River Brenta, and, as the Austrian shelling began to fall among them, they took shelter in the cellars of the houses. They were warned that the Austrians had poisoned the wine before withdrawing. They discussed the matter among themselves and decided that an antidote was probably available, so the single brave man who sampled the drink would, if he failed to be in evident good health after an hour, be saved by the medical officer. Fortunately the medical officer was not required and the men on guard duty were suitably fortified. All night they watched and waited. The night was broken by a single shot, but nothing followed. Then a grenade burst and again silence. Rain fell steadily. The guard changed. Ears strained to discern the sound of human movement through the wind and rain. As day dawned the enemy struck in a brief, unsuccessful flurry before the situation lapsed into silent tension once more.

On occasion the Italians were the ones to attack. Monelli and the 265th, now down to a mere fifty-eight men, groped forward in the sodden darkness to reinforce the Feltre Battalion at Marter. A nervous march brought them to an abandoned house where they sheltered. Nothing had happened. Another day, and Monelli's flanking patrol was ambushed. There were a few wounded and a great deal of confusion in the pine forests, but both sides were soon back in what warmth they could contrive in their billets. Meanwhile, the daily paperwork went on. Unanswered messages were explained by claiming an enemy shell had destroyed them. Headquarters demanded to know how many shells were expended in the previous day's action. The officer said, 'Answer as I dictate: "44,252 and three misfires." Don't forget the misfires.'

Sudden snow storms swept the mountains, adding to the men's fear of their enemies and the danger of freezing to death, lost on the mountainside. Snow storms shut out everything, making movement almost impossible. When the wind dropped the silence was incredible, but soon the shriek of the wind resumed, hurling ice crystals into their faces and disorientating and unbalancing the men. Neither side could attack in these conditions; it was a matter of enduring as best one could.

While the Italians fought and hung on through the winter, the Central Powers were making ready to strike. The German chief-of-staff, General Erich von Falkenhayn, decided that he had to grind down the French, for that was the most substantial professional force arrayed against him, before the new British Army raised by Lord Kitchener could be brought to bear. The French, Britain's 'best sword', would be knocked out at Verdun. On 21 February a hurricane of shells fell on the French lines and, as Falkenhayn had predicted, the defenders were augmented relentlessly with fresh troops to die under German assault. The Allies appealed to Cadorna to begin his next attack on the Austrians as soon as possible in order to draw away at least a portion of the resources devoted to Verdun. The Fifth Battle of the Isonzo therefore started on 11 March, when seven corps and two Alpini groups went into action. The weather was abominable. In the north snow fell and in the south fog obscured the scene. Little or nothing was gained and the trivial advance in the south, the costly capture of a part of Monte San Michele, was given up in the face of Austrian gas shelling. In 4 days the battle was over, inflicting 1,882 casualties on the Italians and 1,985 on their enemies.

Apart from the weather, the action failed because of the Italians' lack of heavy guns. Cadorna demanded help from his Allies and was to go on doing so, receiving only grudging allocations in response. Verdun, however, was not the only blow the Central Powers had planned for the Allies. Field Marshal Conrad von Hötzendorf, commanding the Austrian forces, observed that the Serbs were now defeated and the Russians were tottering, so the time had come to crush the Italians and open a southern front in France. It was a logical concept. An attack southwards from the Trentino could cut off the Italian Army on the Isonzo and bring Italy to negotiate a separate peace.

The build-up began while winter still raged. The Tirol Defence Command under General Dankl was upgraded to full army status with the addition of four divisions from the Isonzo front and five from the Russian. This was designated the Eleventh Army and the Third Army, under General Kövess, was moved from the conquered Serbian territories to give 18 divisions in all, together with 60 batteries with more than 1,000 guns, including 262 heavy guns and another 46 massive weapons of

The Adamello range where the Italians attacked in April 1916.

Alpini fighting on the Adamello.

more than 305 mm in calibre. The nominal command of this army group was in the hands of Archduke Eugen but the effective control was that of his chief-of-staff Major-General Alfred Krauss. As March moved towards April the Austrians finished gathering 157,234 men in readiness for their campaign. Cadorna was aware of the increasing Austrian strength in the Trentino, but failed to appreciate its significance. He was later to claim that he had ordered defensive positions to be established to prevent an enemy success here, but he remained distracted by the Isonzo front and the lure of Trieste. General Brusati's Italian First Army had, in theory, five successive lines of defence but only two were manned and armed with any degree of strength. Cadorna transferred the 9th and 10th Divisions, some Alpini and seventy-two guns to the Trentino in early April and a delay in the Austrian attack caused by the bad weather, which Cadorna could not have known about, did give the Italian commander-in-chief the chance to visit later in the month. On 8 May General Brusati, still failing to array his defence in depth, was replaced with General Count Pecori-Giraldi and another sixty-seven battalions and eighty guns were allocated to him, but it was by now perilously late.

On the western flank of the Trentino the Italians had taken the initiative. Undaunted by the blizzards, on 12 April the 5th Division attacked Monte Fuma in the Adamello Range and took their objective. In the Dolomites a mine was exploded under the bitterly contested Col di Lana on 17 April, giving the Italians the position at last. By the end of the month the Italians had seized the Crozzon di Fargorida, west of Lake Garda, and made gains that would endure until the end of the war. However, these triumphs were soon cast into the shade.

On 14 May the Austrians struck at Monfalcone as a feint before attacking in the Trentino the next day. The assault was made over a 21-mile (34-km) front. The Austrian VIIIth Corps thrust east from the Adige valley south of Mori but were halted by the Roma Brigade who resisted until they were finally wiped out two days later when Zugna Toirta fell and the Austrian 10th Mountain Brigade took the summit beyond the next valley to the east, Monte Col Santo. Julius Price

The railway station at Ospedaletto in the Val Sugana with Cima Dodici rising to the south.

was still in London, but was keeping abreast of events in Italy. The impression he had was of an artillery assault with little movement on the ground, the Italians holding firm in the valleys of the Brenta and the Adige, but he reported on 23 May, '. . . the 50 mile [80-km] front from Lake Garda to Val Sugana was ablaze, and the Italians were defending themselves for all they were worth against a heavy and determined Austrian thrust that tried their endurance to the utmost limit'.

The Italians north of the Val Sugana, Monelli among them, were in danger of being cut off as the Austrians took back the peaks along their old, pre-war border. The Austrian thrust was south of the Val Sugana and Monelli was up on the Panarotta, north of it. He envied those who could retreat in good order, their barrage following on wagons and all neat and tidy, though in his imagination the ease enjoyed by other soldiers was largely a fiction. He saw the guns pulled out, first the heavies, then the field guns, and still the Alpini had to stay. Behind them Cima Dodici fell to the enemy. The Italians threw back an attack and held on grimly until dark, when finally they slipped away.

The Alpini were pulled back and thrust into the line once more, now at Monte Cima. It was a Hungarian unit that attacked them there on 26 May. They came on under the cover of fog and, clearly unable to make out the true situation, started to rejoice in their victory when the newly arrived Feltre Battalion, hauled back from their

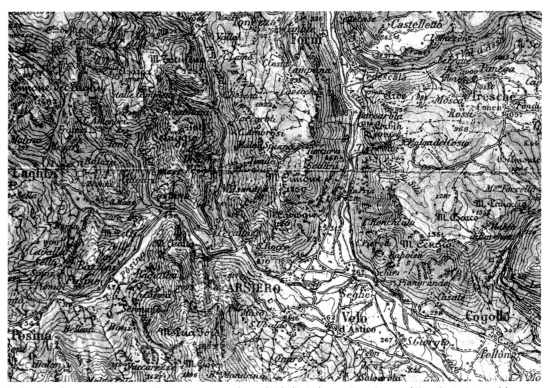

The Val d'Astico from a contemporary map. The River Astico runs south towards Velo d'Astico between Monte Cimone and Monte Cenzio. Arsiero and the River Posina are to the left. The River Assa is top right.

march towards the rear and a much-needed rest, fell upon them. A short, sharp, hand-to-hand fight accounted for many of them while machine-guns looked after those attempting to flee. Monelli wondered if any had escaped to give an account of what had taken place.

The Austrian advance, so impressive at first, slowed, but still struggled forward to reach the Asiago plateau and the Italians were forced to evacuate Asiago itself on 29 May. The next day the Austrian XXth Corps took Monte Pria Fora, south-west of Arsiero and well to the south-west of Asiago. On 31 May the XXth Corps' 59th Salzburg Regiment was attacking Monte Cegnio on the eastern side of the Astico valley but the Granateri Battalion held on stubbornly and the Austrians were pulled back on 1 June. Further west the next day the Austrian attempt to take the Posina valley also failed.

On 4 June General Alexei Brusilov unleashed his great offensive between the Pripet Marshes and the Romanian border on the Russian front. The defending Austrians reeled under the pressure of numerous, simultaneous attacks over so wide a front. On 8 June two divisions were withdrawn from the Trentino to go to the eastern front and, although the Austrians managed to take Monte Castelgomberto, north-east of Asiago and Gallio, their momentum in the Trentino was spent.

Monte Cengio (Cenzio) and Monte Cimon (Cimone) dominate the Val d'Astico.

Now that it appeared the Italians were holding their own and that good news might emerge from a journey, Price was sent back to Italy by his editor. Accredited once more as a war correspondent, he went to Vicenza and then on to Arsiero. At first the countryside presented a familiar image of Italian village life, but suddenly Price found himself beyond an invisible border.

It was like going from daylight into darkness. The smiling villages were deserted, save where some of the cottages were occupied by soldiers. . . . Once inside the radius of the big guns the spectacle was but a repetition of what I had seen on the Western Front; heaps of shapeless rubble and smouldering ruin on all sides bore witness to Hun methods of frightfulness. . . .

Arsiero is situated in the valley of the Astico; behind it is the semi-circle of mountains which form the boundary of the tableland of the Altepiano, so close as to dominate it completely, foremost among these mountains being M. Cenzio and M. Cimone, standing like colossal barriers above the valley. . . . If an enemy were in possession of all these superb heights, then positions below in the valley would be very undesirable, to say the least of it; and without any knowledge of military matters you realised that the valley and all it contained – towns, villages, vineyards and what not – was completely at the mercy of the men who manned the guns up above, and also that under the cover of these guns immense masses of troops could safely be brought down the side of the mountains on to the plains, and established there pending further movements.

Price marvelled at the determination that the Italians had shown in rolling the Austrians back from here. The front lines were now facing each other across Asiago itself and Price went up the valley to see the action. They drove up a road that had the appearance of being long established, although it had only been brought into being by the needs of the war. After passing bleak, rocky hillsides they entered thick pine forest, the forest of Gallio. Gallio lies north-east of Asiago, but from the context it seems possible that he has confused it with the Forest of Sanio, south of Asiago, where the British XIVth Corps would be fighting later in the war. Price writes: 'The forest on either side of the road was a big bivouac. The gloom under the trees was alive with troops as far as one could see. . . . It was probably for this reason that the forest of Gallio was the hottest section of this Front, as it was continually being shelled, and the casualties were always correspondingly heavy.' Price and his companion left the car and walked to the edge of the woods to look out to the white houses of Asiago, which the Italians had retaken on 25 June, and to the bulk of Monte Interotto beyond, to the north, where the Austrian guns were. They went forward to go into the town itself.

It was a typical summer morning, with the birds singing merrily on all sides, so it was somewhat difficult to realize that there was danger in strolling along leisurely, but before we had gone far we met stretcher-bearers coming towards us with their

The Asiago plateau seen from the San Sisto Ridge on the southern side. The white arch is at the Ossario Militare, the Military Ossuary, where the bodies of 33,086 Italians and 18,505 Austrians, gathered from small graveyards in the surrounding mountains, now lie. The rocky outcrops in the foreground were the positions of the forward piquets of the 11th Sherwood Foresters on 15 June 1918. *(John Chester)*

sad burdens, and quite a number of soldiers carrying wounded men on their backs. No big engagement was in progress we learned, but the guns and rifles were taking their steady and relentless daily toll all the time.

They looked around the abandoned town and met the local commander who warned them of a barrage due to be laid down by the Italians. All too soon it began and they ran back to the shelter of the woods and dived into a dug-out as the Austrian guns opened up in turn.

Some soldiers were there, so we sat down with them and had a chat, and it was as well we did, for the firing increased in intensity every moment, and the heavy projectiles began to burst on the roof of the 'dug-out' with such terrific force that one expected at any moment the whole place would be blown to atoms. The very ground trembled under the shock of the explosions. I never thought that human ears or nerves could stand such an inferno as we were in for during the next hour.

   The effect on me personally was at first a sort of atrophy of my senses – a feeling came over me that if this was to be my end, well let it be a quick and complete finish, no blinding or maiming or other drawn-out agony. Next a sensation of extreme hunger, which at the time I felt inclined to pat myself on the back for, as indicating heroic indifference to my surroundings, but which later I learned, to my disappointment, is a well-known manifestation of 'funk', a sort of nervous dyspepsia – 'fringale', the French call it.

As the shelling continued and his nerves steadied, Price looked around him. Some soldiers were in a terrible state of nervousness, calling on God or their mothers for comfort while others sat in a stolid, moody silence. In the end Price and his companions decided to make a run for it. The driver had difficulty in turning the car round, but eventually they were away down the hill, dodging shell craters and diverting through the forest where the road was destroyed, back to safety, leaving the soldiers to face what came.

The Val d'Astico, looking north. Monte Cimone is on the left. *(John Chester)*

On 1 July the British launched their major offensive on the Somme in France and in the Trentino the Austrians withdrew slowly as the demands of the Russian front called men away. By 22 July the Italians were seeking to repossess the heights above Arsiero in an action that drew Price's admiration.

The table-like summit had been in the possession of the Austrians since the latter part of May, and had been transformed by them into a veritable citadel, and was one of the strongest points on their line of defence in this region. The Alpini, as was to be expected from these mountaineering athletes, set out without hesitation to accomplish what must have looked like the impossible to the ordinary soldier. . . . It appeared to me as a layman, incredible that anything but a chamois could clamber up the cliff-like front of Cimone. . . . It looked a sheer impossibility, yet the Alpini did it, and in spite of plunging fire from machine guns on the summit, and the shells from flanking batteries at Settecase further up the valley of the Astico.

After their stubborn defence of Italy up at Monte Cima, Monelli and his comrades were granted a little leave. Monelli made his way down the Castelfranco Veneto to draw stores for his unit. He expected to be greeted with respect, if not, perhaps,

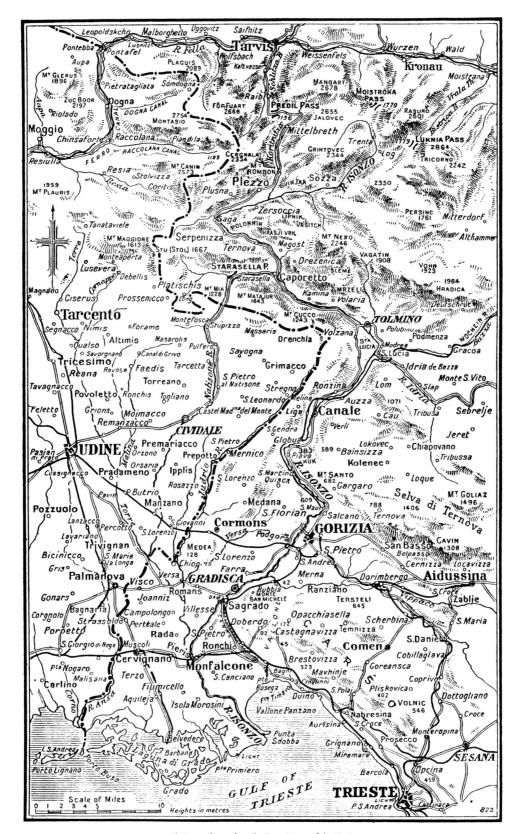

The Isonzo front. *(from* The Times History of the War*)*

admiration, for his part in the famous defence. Instead, he was warned to get his hair cut lest the general saw him. Monelli was met with a similar level of incomprehension when he admitted he had no rail pass. The officer could not fathom how the paperwork could be so terribly neglected just because a unit was up in the hills. The army observed by Julius Price and the army of which Paolo Monelli was an officer appear to have been in two different worlds.

General Cadorna had reacted decisively to the Austrian offensive in the north. A new army, the Fifth, was brought together in the southern Brenta basin, ready to block an Austrian break-out from the mountains to the north. He also appealed for guns, but the French at Verdun and the British on the Somme were unable to help. In spite of Price's reports, the attempt to trap the Austrians in a pincer around the Sette Comuni, the seven Germanic settlements around Asiago, failed as the enemy withdrew and the front stabilized on new lines. Between 15 May and 17 June the fighting in the Trentino had cost the Italians 52,000 men, of whom 40,000 were made prisoner, and the Austrians 44,000, of whom 2,000 were captured and 14,000 fell sick. Cadorna turned his attention to the Isonzo once more.

The Duke of Aosta's Third Army was able to put 16 divisions into the field, supported by 1,251 guns and 774 mortars, of which 138 were 10-in weapons to destroy barbed wire. Facing them were Boroevich's 9 divisions of the Austrian Fifth Army with 540 guns. On 6 August the heaviest artillery barrage the Italians had yet delivered fell on Austrian positions and it continued for 9 hours until, at 1600 hours, the Italian VIth Corps advanced. On the west bank of the Isonzo opposite Gorizia the 45th Division under Colonel Badoglio stormed Monte Sabatino and the Podgora, taking 8,000 prisoners in under an hour. The Cuneo Brigade seized Gafenburg on the Podgora while to the south XIth Corps attacked Monte San Michele and took it together with much of the north of the Carso. Price had been in Udine and rushed to the front. He found General Capello, commander of VIth Corps, at his headquarters in a large country house on the road east of Cormons at Vipulzano. Here Price looked out towards the front from the terrace.

> On our left was Monte Sabottina [Sabatino]. In front of us was Monte San Gabriele. The richly wooded undulating plain of Friuli, dotted with villages, stretched away from below the terrace. In the distance, a couple of miles or so away, was the Podgora Ridge, bristling with gaunt tree-stumps; beyond it you could distinguish the houses of Gorizia. To the right was the Carso and Monte San Michele, some five miles [8 km] away. . . .
>
> From Monte San Gabriele to Monte San Michele, a distance of, roughly, nine miles [14.5 km], was one continuous line of bursting shells of every calibre; it never ceased for a moment, and this we were told had been going on without a lull for forty-eight hours. . . . The whole country appeared to be in a state of irruption, and columns of smoke of various colours and fantastic shapes were to be seen rising everywhere like embryo volcanoes.

During the night of 7 August patrols of the Cuneo Brigade reached the banks of the Isonzo and, despite the blowing of the railway bridge by the Austrians, four battalions used the road bridge to cross the river the next day. Lieutenant Baruzzi of the 28th Regiment, 12th Division, raised the Italian flag at the station in Gorizia. Price, in the company of the Italian journalist Barzini, rushed towards Mossa, west of the Gorizia bridgehead. Price reported:

> During the early part of the night detachments of the Casale and Pavia brigades had crossed the Isonzo and consolidated themselves on the left bank, and the heights west of Gorizia were completely occupied by Italian infantry. The enemy was in full retreat, and had abandoned large quantities of arms, ammunition and *matériel*. Over 11,000 prisoners had been taken, and more were coming in. . . .
>
> Beyond Lucinico we were right in the very thick of it. The railway line to Gorizia ran through the village, but just outside the houses the rails had been pulled up and a solid barricade of stones had been erected across the permanent way. We got a splendid view of Gorizia from here – it looked a beautiful white city embowered in foliage, with no sign at all of destruction at this distance. On the high hills beyond, which one knew to be Monte Santo and Monte San Gabriele, little puffs of smoke were incessantly appearing – these were Italian shells bursting – the booming of the guns never ceasing. The Austrian trenches commenced a few hundred yards beyond Lucinico. . . . The ground all around was pitted with shell holes, and strewn with every imaginable kind of *débris*: the remains of barbed wire entanglements in such chaotic confusion that it was frequently a matter of positive difficulty to pass at all; broken rifles, unused cartridges by the thousand, fragments of shell-cases, boots, first-aid bandages, and odds and ends of uniforms covered with blood.

The two journalists went on towards the river, under the hot sun. The heat was already making the corpses of the defeated Austrians smell and they did their best to avoid the ghastly heaps of what, from a distance, looked like abandoned uniforms. Where the road went under the railway embankment just outside Podgora they found the tunnel turned into a commander's headquarters with two floors of rooms to give offices and bedrooms. General Marazzi was using the entrance as his field headquarters and gave them his time to bring them up to date on developments. On they went, past the slopes of the Podgora Ridge itself, stripped of vegetation by shell-fire, and into the village of Grafenberg, littered with the dead. Price continued:

> Meanwhile we were walking parallel with the Isonzo . . . and the Austrians, though in full rout, were keeping up a terrific flanking fire with their heavy artillery, placed on Monte Santo and Monte San Gabriele with the idea undoubtedly of destroying the bridges. Two were already wrecked beyond immediate repair, one of the arches of the magnificent railway viaduct had been blown up, and the long wooden

Italian troops launch an attack through enemy shell-fire. *(Guy Cavallaro)*

structure just above Grafenberg had been rendered useless for the moment. There were two others still intact: an iron bridge the artillery and cavalry were crossing by and a small foot-bridge we were making for.

Price and Barzini ran across the foot-bridge without coming to harm and sheltered under the high banks on the far side. There they found men of the 11th and 12th Regiments, the men who had forded the river and, indeed, been forced to swim part of the way, when the little bridge was being repaired a day earlier. Price recounted:

> Their eyes were bloodshot, they looked dog-tired, and they were, without exception, the dirtiest and most bedraggled lot of soldiers it would be possible to imagine. The uniforms of many of them were still wet, and they were covered with mud from head to foot.
>
> Yet in spite of the fact that they had probably all of them been on the move the whole night, and under fire most of the time without a moment's respite, they looked as game and cheerful as ever, and most of them seemed to be more anxious about cleaning the dirt from their rifles than resting.

Price and Barzini went on into the town where they found the café open, though with little to sell, in the main square and a number of civilians starting to emerge from shelter. An old man told them he was a teacher of Italian and that he had been in hiding since the start of the war; now he offered his services as a guide. With evening approaching they returned to Lucinico and their car and drove back to Udine to write and draw their impressions of the day.

On 10 August the Italians struck on the Carso once more and the Austrian defence between Monfalcone and Doberdo collapsed entirely. North-east of Doberdo the ruined village of Oppacchiasella was taken by the Regina Brigade and 1,565 Austrian troops were taken prisoner. Soon after Price and two other newspapermen made another journey from Udine to survey the situation. They spent a night in Gorizia, taking over comfortable rooms in an abandoned hotel and were disturbed somewhat by an unsuccessful Austrian counter-attack. The next day they went to find out what was going on on the Carso, following the left bank of the Isonzo through Savogna, Sdraussina and Sagrado. All along the way, under the shelter of the hills to the east, Italian troops were bivouacked and were making the best of the pause in the action to swim and wash in the river. They could get no further that day but returned a couple of days later and drove from Sagrado down to Fogliano and, turning left under the railway, to Redipuglia. From here the road climbed the slopes of the Carso, leaving Monte Cosich on their right. Price wrote:

> I shall never forget my first impression of this shell-swept waste; for what I had already seen of it was only from a distance, and though through powerful binoculars, one was not really able to form any conception of what it is like in reality. I had been prepared to see nature in its most savage mood, but the scene before me was so terrible in its utter desolation as to inspire a sense of awe.
>
> Imagine the Brighton downs [the hills on the south coast of England] covered from end to end with colourless stones and rock instead of turf; no sign of vegetation anywhere; ribbed in every direction with trenches protected by low, sand-bagged walls; bristling with wire entanglements, and everywhere pitted with huge shell-craters . . .
>
> . . . here nature appears to have connived at the efforts of man, and every hollow and every hummock form as it were potential bastions. The incessant thunder of the guns in the distance seemed, as it were, to be in keeping with the utter desolation of the scene.

The party of journalists went on to the ruins of Doberdo where they found a field dressing station and Red Cross men working under intermittent fire. Gazing out over the wasteland towards the east they could see how the defences were constructed. Price recorded what he saw:

> The peculiar rock formation of the whole area precludes any making of actual trenches except with enormous labour; to obviate this shallow furrows are formed and protected with stone parapets, finished with sand-bags (or rather bags of

The creation of a defensive position on the eastern Carso. The hostile, rocky terrain made entrenchment very difficult, but with the use of explosives natural hollows were enlarged by the Italians and shelters built of stone and sandbags.

small stones, as, of course, there is no sand here). The condition of these parapets and 'trenches' after continual pounding with high explosives may be left to the imagination. A gruesome detail must be mentioned: so difficult is it to excavate the ground here that the dead are not being 'buried' but simply covered over with stones.

As Austrian shelling increased the journalists departed, not without risk and with Price being dazed by a near miss. A few days later he was on the Carso again, this time heading for the village of San Martine del Carso, south of Monte San Michele. Once more he was daunted by the empty, cratered, rocky landscape. On they drove until, as Price wrote:

The chauffeur suddenly turned round and, pointing to what appeared to be a rugged slope just ahead, said quietly, 'Ecco San Martino del Carso.' I am hardened to the sight of ruins by now . . . but I must admit I had a bit of a shock when I realized that this long, low line of shapeless, dust-covered rubble actually bore a name. . . . The Austrian trenches commenced in amongst the ruins: they were typical of the Carso; only a couple of feet or so in depth, and actually hewn out of the solid rock, with a low wall of stones in front as a breastwork. So roughly were they made that it was positively tiring to walk along them even a short distance. To have passed any time in them under fire with splinters of rock flying about must have been a terrible ordeal, especially at night.

The Italian troops had exhausted themselves and on 17 August General Cadorna halted the battle. The gains had been the most impressive achievement by the Italian forces so far. Their losses had amounted to 51,232 men, of whom 12,128 were missing or made prisoner, while the Austrians suffered almost equal casualties, 49,035 men of whom some 20,000 were captured. Taken together with the success of the counter-attack in the Trentino, this was a result that was good for Italian morale and for the Allied cause, for Austrian reverses in Russia and British and French advances, even if at a high cost, on the Somme and at Verdun suggested that the Central Powers were not invincible after all.

After a two-week break to resupply, Cadorna renewed the assault on the Isonzo with the Seventh Battle. The Third Army, with 14 divisions, 966 guns and 584 mortars, attacked on the Carso on a line east of Doberdo/Monfalcone towards the hills, from north to south, of Nova Vas, Hill 208 and Hill 144. Julius Price was on the move again, and pointed out that this was terrain of a different kind. The district of the Carso north of Trieste had been planted by the Austrians with large tracts of fir trees.

Italian troops in a trench in the pine woods above Monfalcone.

On the Cristallo Ridge above Cortina. This photograph was taken in September 2002. *(Philippa Carling)*

Sheltered by the almost impenetrable cover which the dense growth of immature trees offers, the Austrians had constructed Torres-Vedras-like series of fortified positions among the trees along the ridges that intersect the district. . . . The trees are of too young growth to stop bullets; and hidden in their trenches the Austrians could sweep the approaches at ground level, lying low behind abbatis [timber defence works] and a mass of wire entanglements.

In spite of this hazard the Italians succeeded in taking the southern positions on the first day and Nova Vas was assaulted the next day. Price relates:

After a furious preparatory bombardment for hours by the Italian heavy guns, to which the Austrians replied vigorously, there was a sudden cessation of Italian fire. The crisis had come: the infantry were to attack. But while waiting word from elsewhere, there was a brief pause.

Next, suddenly, to the general amazement, within six minutes of the guns ceasing, one saw hundreds of men abandoning the Austrian front trenches. They held up their hands and waved handkerchiefs wildly in token of surrender. Out they poured, like driven rats stampeded by terriers from a barn. They came racing across the stretch of 'No Man's Land' between the opposing trenches, straight for the Italians, taking their chance amidst the Austrian shells, still falling briskly. . . . In all, 2,117 Austrian prisoners were made that day, including 71 officers.

On the same day the Italians launched an attack in the Cadore in an effort to drive through to Toblach. Monelli and the Alpini were there. He recalled: 'Whoever comes in time of peace to see the Prima Lunetta will think it is impossible that it could have been taken by assault and held, without even a single round of artillery-fire – this crest that rises up stark against the sky on one side and falls almost as precipitously down on the other.'

With the Cauriòl in their hands, the Alpini continued the attacks, taking Monte Gardinal the next day and then having to hold the heights. Monelli came under shell-fire, which he endured with detachment and fatalism, thinking more about the ordeal of his comrades on the Cauriòl which was now being battered by Austrian fire.

The weather turned foul and action on the Carso and in the mountains slackened off. Julius Price, concluding that the fighting season was over, went back to England. General Cadorna, who differed in his views, ordered the Eighth Battle of the Isonzo. It began on 9 October and was accompanied by an attack on Mounte Pasubio in the Trentino. The bombardment completed, the infantry attacked the next day at 1450 hours in pouring rain and took Monte Sober, east of Gorizia, Nova

Italian Alpini advance across a snow-covered mountainside.

The problem of supplying troops in the mountains was serious. In fair weather mules and dogs were used. In bad weather men carried food and ammunition aloft. *(Guy Cavallaro)*

Vas village and, again, Hill 144 in the Carso. The fog was so thick on 11 October that no fighting took place there and the battle was allowed to halt.

New efforts were made in the Venetian Alps a week later. On 19 October the guns were bombarding the Austrian positions. Monelli imagined his adversaries sitting stolidly in their dug-outs, smoking and playing cards, waiting for the shelling to cease and the attack to begin. The opposing summits were shrouded in mist. He felt they were fighting in complete isolation from the rest of the world, unremarked and unmourned. Any romantic notion of dying heroically for one's country was irrelevant in the murky gloom. Monelli reported: 'We couldn't take it, that damned hill. All the

Austrian trenches on Monte Piana, overlooking the route from Cortina
northwards to Dobbiacco. This site is now preserved as an open-air museum.
(*Philippa Carling*)

platoon of scouts – almost all the 265th –
were left lying among those boulders, in
the livid twilight, against the hostile
barrier of rock which suddenly became
alive with machine-guns lurking in their
nests, which our artillery had been
unable to touch.' Their losses were great,
and would have been greater if one man
had not had the courage to risk taking a
message forward to tell the Alpini to
withdraw. Then followed the inevitable
counter-shelling and counter-attack.

On 1 November, unbelievably, the Ninth
Battle of the Isonzo began. The Second and
Third Armies attempted to thrust out of
the low plains east of Gorizia. In mud up
to their waists, they struggled up the slopes
of San Marco, east of the town, and the
Toscna Brigade struck at the northern
ridge of the Carso from the River
Vippacco. With ferocious tenacity they
took the ridge and the village of
Volkovniak, but after three days progress
stopped and the battle ceased. Since 14
September, when the Seventh Battle had
begun, Italian losses here had amounted to
75,500 men. The Austrians had lost some 63,000 of whom 21,500 had been taken
prisoner. Both sides were nearing complete exhaustion. The Austrians, pushed back step
by small step, needed more men to defend the longer-line Italian advances created while
the Italians saw small gains for terrible cost.

Monelli and his comrades were relieved from the front line in the Alps but, after a
short rest, were sent back to the Trentino, at Tezze di Valsugana for the winter. Snow
fell. Supplies, when they got them at all, came up on the backs of the men, long lines
plodding through the deep banks of snow. The beauty of the scene mocked the
soldiers. The enemy and the elements threatened them. Everyday tasks, when the
weather was clear enough to perform them, were dogged by enemy snipers. Monelli
recalled: '. . . the soft peril of the avalanche gathers on high and rumbles down with a
tragic moaning; unexpected, unforeseen, illogical, not where broken pines foretold its
course, but by new ways, on to the huts and the dugouts where the necessity of war
has fixed them'. Huts and mule stables were engulfed. Men struggled beneath the pure
covering and suffocated there. Those that fought their way out became targets for the
snipers. This war held terrors and hardships other than the mud of Flanders.

SEVEN

BATTLES OF CAPORETTO AND PIAVE

A conference convened in Rome on 5 January 1917. It was attended by the new Prime Minister, David Lloyd George, and his senior military advisers as well as the commander of the British forces in Salonika, General Sir George Milne, on the part of the British. The French Prime Minister, Aristide Briand, was there with his Salonika commander, General Maurice Sarrail, and the Italian Prime Minister, Paolo Boselli, his Foreign Minister and General Cadorna completed the three-nation body. They were to consider the future of operations on Austria's southern flank in the coming year. Lloyd George arrived with ideas of his own, generated without consultation with his military. He foresaw two possibilities. The first was for a defensive policy which he subsequently claimed saved the situation that developed later in the year; that of making arrangements for the swift supply of heavy guns should Austria attack. The second was for an attack to be supported by the temporary loan of guns by France and Britain to back an offensive on the Isonzo. The problem was the temporary nature of the loan given that the weapons were required on the Western Front for the planned spring offensive. Cadorna could scarcely, in January, accept if the guns had to be given back early in April; he needed them for as long as the offensive might persist and weather conditions would prevent a start before late March at the earliest. In the end the conference produced few constructive decisions apart from improved supply and communication lines to Salonika.

Cadorna offered his own ideas to his Prime Minister some ten days later, making it clear that the limited support the French and British could give would confine his offensive to the Isonzo, but that this might still produce the decisive breakthrough all desired; possibly as far as Laibach (Ljubljana). Indications of the Austrians reinforcing their western flank, near the Swiss border, and the decaying political situation in Russia suggested that Italy was to become the objective of Austria's coming operations. Visits by the new French commander-in-chief, General Robert Nivelle, and the British Chief of the Imperial General Staff, General Sir William Robertson, in February and March led to a decision to help with guns, but in nothing like the strength mooted in January. The British sent ninety-six 6-in howitzers in early April of which forty went to the Carso. Robertson also had plans made for the transfer of six British divisions from France to Italy should the necessity arise. In April thirty-five French guns were also sent but details of where they were deployed seem to be missing.

In the Austrian camp thought was also being given to the future offensives in the Italian theatre. Conrad proposed an attack in the Caporetto sector, suggesting that the Italians were weakest there. However, his credibility had been undermined by the failure in the Trentino the previous year and he was replaced by the new Austrian Emperor, Karl I, on 1 March with General Artur, Baron Arz von Straussenberg.

The consultations of the great were accompanied by continual small-scale action at the front, alternating with boredom. On 9 February the Austrians attacked east of Gorizia, taking some 1,000 prisoners, but gaining no ground. However, two weeks later Italian guns destroyed the Austrian railhead at Tarvis in the Trentino. The next day an accident in the Carso sector killed four Italians and wounded others, among them Corporal Benito Mussolini.

Cadorna reorganized his forces on the Isonzo front on 4 March, creating the Gorizia Defence Command out of the left corps of the Third Army and the three right corps of the Second Army. The command of this formation was given to the victor of the capture of Gorizia, General Luigi Capello. General Piacentino's Second Army now consisted of a single corps with the Carnia Force attached. On the same day an Austrian attack east of Gorizia was thrown back and fighting took place in the Alps.

Corporal Monelli was transferred to a ski company in March, in spite of his protests of incompetence on skis and his wish to stay with his companions. Scarcely had he joined his new unit than they were ordered to turn in their skis because they were to become a climbing unit. After a short leave in Padua, Monelli was once more on his way to the Asiago and the distant sights of Cima Dodici. Here the company were put to road-making and kept at it well into May.

In France General Nivelle launched his much-advertised assault on the Chemin-des-Dames on 16 April. The next day the first of his men to mutiny left their positions. On 19 April Nivelle called on Cadorna to begin his attack on the Isonzo, but the plans

Italian mountain troops balancing skis on their shoulders. (Guy Cavallaro)

made could not be brought forward. By 20 April the French offensive had halted in failure and heavy loss. The date for the next Isonzo attack was altered from 7 May and on 12 May the Tenth Battle of the Isonzo started with a 2-day barrage by 1,058 heavy guns and 1,320 field guns on a 25-mile (40-km) front. Royal Navy monitors in the Adriatic were involved, as were French guns and British artillery.

At noon on 14 May Capello's forces attacked the hills defending the Bainsizza plateau east of Plava, taking Hill 383, Zagora and Monte Santo. The IInd Corps was in the forefront of the battle, commanded by Major-General Badoglio who had been promoted to the post only two days previously. He was further promoted to lieutenant-general that day. The Vodice saddle between Monte Santo and Monte Kuk was assaulted by IInd Corps and held against violent counter-attacks. The VIth Corps had taken Monte Santo and on 15 May IInd Corps took Monte Kuk. The British guns supported their grasp on these heights. Now the emphasis was moving elsewhere, for with too few guns to mount simultaneous attacks, General Cadorna had planned one assault on his left, drawing off, it was hoped, Austrian reinforcements, before launching the second on the far right against the Carso.

On 23 May the next blow was aimed at the Austrians when the Italian Third Army struck between the sea, east of Monfalcone, and Kostanjevica to the north-east, some 3 miles east of Oppacchiasella. Here the British monitors destroyed rail links with

Alpini bringing up supplies by mule.

Trieste, blew up an ammunition dump and denied the enemy the means to move up reinforcements. The land artillery shelled the roads at San Giovanni, north-west of Duino on the coast, and smashed trench lines on the Carso. At 1600 hours the infantry went into action, supported by 130 aircraft. Gabriele D'Annunzio, flying as an observer, won a third Silver Medal and was promoted to major. They took four hills that day and cleared the Austrians from their positions at Hudi Log, south of Oppacchiasella, the next day. The 4th Division reached Kostanjevica on 26 May but could not hold it against Austrian shelling. In the south they reached the River Timavo but could not take Hill 28 which dominates the little peninsula on the Adriatic shore. Monte Hermada, north-east of Duino, had been thoroughly fortified by the Austrians to protect the coast road to Trieste and the Italians made some progress on its

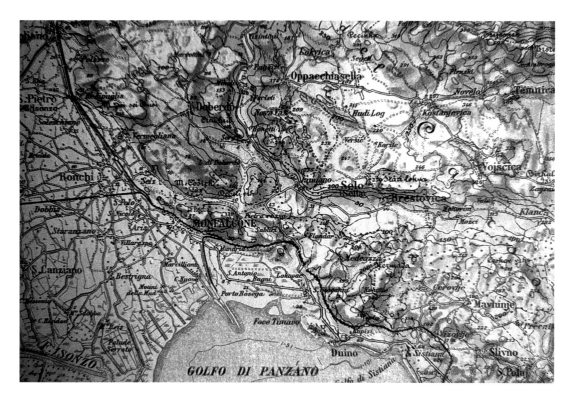

The Carso area from a contemporary map. Monfalcone is north of the
port complex on the gulf shore and Oppacchiasella is to the north-east.

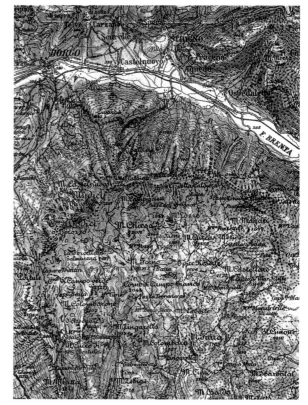

The terrain in which the Battle of Ortigara was fought, from a
contemporary map. From left to right along the valley at the top of
the map are Borgo, Castelnuovo and Agnedo. The mountain of Cima
della Caldresa is on the rose-tinted border south of Agnedo and the
Ortigara Pass is immediately to its south.

western side, but the impetus of the assault was now declining under the fire from the supporting Austrian strongholds at Duino and Brestovica, south and north. Austrian counter-attacks were typically fierce and on 4 June three fresh divisions brought from the Eastern Front were thrown in forcing the Italians back from Hermada. The battle came to an end with Italian losses since 14 May amounting to 157,000 men, 27,000 of whom had been made prisoner and about 26,000 were killed. The Austrian casualties came to some 75,700 including23,400 prisoners.

On 10 June the Italians attacked in the Trentino, north of Asiago and south of Castelnuovo and the Val Sugana. The fight became known as the Battle of Ortigara. A total of 12 divisions and 1,500 guns and mortars were employed over a front of 9 miles (14.5 km), with the bombardment starting at 0515 hours and going on until 1100 hours. The troops made a night march over the plateau and approached the camp fires of the assault force. They reached the slopes below the Cima della Caldiera as day dawned and made a bivouac among the rocks and scattered pines. On 10 June the Italian bombardment began and was answered by Austrian guns. Waiting in reserve, Monelli saw the prisoners start to come in, grey-faced and shocked, then the wounded. His unit set out to carry supplies forward in the gathering darkness, rocksides illuminated by the flash of explosives and slick with rain. The Alpini had taken the Agnello Pass and part of the Monte Ortigara complex of peaks, but the Austrians held on to the rest. Attacks on neighbouring mountains failed. The next day the Austrians poured more troops into the sector and prepared to counter-attack. On 12 June the rain began to fall in fresh torrents while the Italians endeavoured to build defences and shelters on the barren mountains. The attempt to regain the positions on Monte Ortigara was made three days later. The Italians cowered under the shelling as

An Italian communication trench on Monte Ortigara, not substantially changed from the time when Monelli and his comrades might have used it. *(John Chester)*

it targeted first the front line and then the rear. Monelli was among the reserves: 'All the enemy artillery, from the Corno di Campo Bianco to the Salubio, when they are tired of battering the foremost troops, have a go at the reserves, at us who are clinging as best we can to the rocks of the Caldiera. It happened this morning: a hail of big ones, great splitting bursts that raised a thick smoke which caught one's throat.'

The Italian assaults were renewed on 19 June. Monelli says nothing of this; apparently some events went unreported either because there was no opportunity to write or no inclination to dwell on recent experience. The attack on the summit of Monte Ortigara began at 0600 hours. There were 15 battalions of Alpini involved, supported by 145 aircraft which bombed Austrian artillery positions. Within an hour the summit was in their hands, but it remained overlooked by Austrian fortifications on Cima Undici and Cima Dodici. About a thousand Austrians, including their crack Kaiserjäger troops, were made prisoner. The reaction came six days later when Ortigara was attacked at 0230 hours by seven Austrian battalions supported by more than a hundred guns and mortars. All three heights of the mountain complex were retaken from the Italians. Counter-attacks were ordered, and included Monelli's unit. The men, their sensibilities dulled and their fear replaced by a fatalistic acceptance of what might or might not unfold in the next few minutes or hours, prepared to move. As they started one of their number was decapitated by a shell, and as they rushed down the slope preparatory to climbing the one opposite, machine-gun fire was concentrated on each defile through the rocks. Peering through their gas-masks, they gulped for air and, finally, Monelli took his off, risking the danger in exchange for a full breath of air. Down into the Agnelizza valley they went, among the skeletons and fresh corpses, the combined harvest of this battle and the one of a year before, then up only to see their comrades caught like flies on a window-pane, clinging to the mountainside, their wounds bright in the noon-day sun.

In spite of these hazards, Monelli met a fellow officer and they reported to General Porta. The orders were that the Cuneo and Marmolada battalions should recapture Hills 2003, 2101 and 2105. Having clambered out over the heap of dead in the cave mouth, the two men consulted over which route to take. Shell-fire fell on the one first selected. The Alpini struggled, climbed, jumped and clambered over the steep, sometimes sheer, face of the mountain. The situation became ever more confused. Shell-fire was repeatedly cutting the telephone lines and orders were received in fragments that made no sense. That night the 297th Battalion succeeded in rushing and taking Hill 2003. Monelli was told to reinforce the position and drove his reluctant men, gathered from a number of scattered units, forward with insults. One, a Bersagliere, volunteered eagerly and sprang to the advance. He was killed instantly.

The Alpini huddled under the intense barrage that night. They were offered reinforcements in the shape of the Tirano battalion. When it arrived it was made up of 3 dozen men, all that remained fit for action from the 600 who formed the unit only a few days before. Captain Ripamonte, defending Hill 2003, sent them back, saying they deserved six months' leave rather than another stint in the front line. They hung on

A pause in the conflict. Austrian soldiers deal with supply wagons, ignoring the Italian dead.

there for another three days, dealing with their fear as successive bombardments sent rock fragments skittering and slicing among them. Somehow men brought up food to them. A couple of officers mistakenly intercepted the pastries and Spumante intended for the General. They got a kind note in response to their letter of apology written when they found out whose food they had consumed. A messenger struggled up with a yellow envelope. It contained a memorandum forbidding the wastage of steel pen-nibs. A good deal of alcohol was needed to comfort the messenger. As dawn broke on the fifth day the alarm sounded the news that Hill 2003 had fallen to the Austrians. Private Pretto arrived to tell of his night of peace before a Hungarian battalion struck in a shower of grenades. Captain Ripamonti was reported wounded; Pretto had seen an Alpino trying to carry him away. A message came to say the Captain's rescuer had himself been killed and Private Sommacal got up to seek the wounded man, followed by a stretcher-bearer. The Austrians held their fire.

At noon the shelling paused. Monelli took the opportunity to stack up some sandbags before the firing began again. They were pinned down, unable to move forward or back. When night fell they got orders to retire and away the few survivors crept, down the Agnelizza valley to a cup of soup and a dry, warm hut. The next day they could not credit the reality of the sunshine, the fact that they were alive. Then the paperwork began; the lists of dead, wounded and missing.

The line in the Trentino had changed not at all. The Austrians had lost some 8,830 men. The Italians had a total of 23,736 casualties. Of these the Alpini losses came to 12,735. About 950 officers had been killed or wounded. The waste was much resented in the Italian Army where the point of the campaign, distracting the Austrians from the Russian operations in Galicia, was not understood. On 9 July a mutiny in the Catanzero Brigade had to be put down by force. Murmerings stimulated by revolutionary developments in Russia added to the unease. General Cadorna was apparently unaware of this, although sensitive to socialist growth in domestic politics, and fixed on delivering the action he had promised to the Allies during the previous year. While the British were making ready for the Third Battle of Ypres, he was planning the Eleventh Battle of the Isonzo – also known as the Battle of the Bainsizza. Cadorna had travelled to Paris and met General Foch and General Robertson on 24 July to ask for 10 divisions and another 400 guns, but in spite of Foch's sympathy, he got nothing as the British were determined to give everything they could to the Ypres undertaking. In a letter to Cadorna of 17 August Robertson confirmed this determination.

Yet another reorganization was undertaken on the Isonzo front. The Gorizia force under General Capello was merged with the Second Army and Capello was put in command. He faced a front from Plezzo, north of Tolmino, to the Vipacco River, south of Gorizia. The Second Army had twenty-six divisions, including VIIIth Corps' four, a special force for the security of the Gorizia bridgehead, and approximately a thousand each of heavy guns and of mortars. From the Vipacco to the sea the Third Army was on the Carso with its 18 divisions, 700 heavy guns and 800 mortars. A new kind of soldier, the *arditi*, the daring men, had been formed into storm troop units to undertake special tasks. The details of the coming action were left to army commanders to decide; Cadorna issued them with

Map of the Isonzo front between Tolmino and Gorizia, with an inset showing the Carso area further south. *(from* The Times History of the War*)*

The terrain of the Bainsizza, showing the extent to which the description of the area as a plateau is misleading. *(Imperial War Museum Q55981)*

their objectives. The Third Army was to strike for the rest of the Carso and for Trieste while the Second Army was charged first with the taking of the Bainsizza plateau and, second, with the capture of the Selva di Ternova to the south of the plateau. The Isonzo River runs through a steep-sided valley, becoming almost a gorge, from its confluence with the River Idria at St Lucia, south of Tolmino, to Salcano, north of Gorizia. It flows south-west to Plava and then runs south-east to Salcano, and it was on the former stretch that Capello decided to make his assault across the river and from the small Plava bridgehead, against the heights bordering the Biansizza plateau.

The preparatory artillery barrage began at 0600 hours on 18 August. The Second Army established six pontoon bridges over the river, eight fewer than planned, but from those and from Plava they advanced briskly. The force from Plava went almost due east to take the village of Britof on the little Rohot River while the Austrians shelled what they wrongly guessed was the line of approach to the village across the river from Anhovo. The building of more bridges between Anhovo and St Lucia occupied the night of 19 to 20 August and by dawn twelve Italian battalions were on the left bank. Mist lay heavy in the valley and concealed the Italian movements during the morning, but as the day went on it dispersed, revealing them to the Austrian machine-gun posts in the rock dug-outs and caves up the hillside. The 1st and 5th Bersaglieri Brigades pushed up the slope between Canale and Auzza and gained the edge of the plateau north of the village of Vrh and spread east and south. More troops followed and the Tortona Brigade seized Monte Kuk 711 (one of several heights of the same name, distinguished from each other by the number of metres they stand above sea level).

Italian troops crossing the Isonzo on a pontoon bridge. *(Guy Cavallaro)*

A considerable hole had been smashed in the Austrian line.

In the Carso the Italian XXIIIrd Corps broke through the Austrian 12th Division at Selo and in the Hermada area they regained the positions from which the Austrian counter-attack had driven them in June. On the ridge north of Kostanjevica, at Faiti Hrib, Austrian resistance was near fanatical, but the Pallenza Brigade managed to occupy a position to the south-east and held on grimly. The losses, however, for these small advances were great and Cadorna decided to reinforce the success on the Bainsizza and suspend operations in the south.

On 22 August the Emperor and the Austrian chief-of-staff, General von Arz, visited the Fifth Army commander, General Svetozar Boroevich von Bojna. They revealed to him the plan for a crippling blow to be struck on the northern Isonzo shortly, one that would involve additional troops from the German Army and for which eight divisions had already been ordered to move from the Russian front. Boroevich responded by suggesting an immediate withdrawal from the Bainsizza to a line running roughly south from Tolmino. This was agreed and orders were given at 0900 hours on 23 August. That same morning the Florence Brigade attacked eastwards from the Rohot valley, reaching the edge of the plateau at Rutarsce, and began to roll up the Austrian positions to the south-east. The IInd Corps was thrown in south of Jelenik and by the next day the Italians had taken Monte Santo, one of the two peaks that had been so significant in the assault on Gorizia. Soon progress began to slow. The arid plateau is traversed with hills and gullies, making movement difficult and drinking water scarce. By 27 August the advance had reached Volnik in the east and the slopes leading up to Ternova in the south, but it had outrun the artillery. Cordona ordered a pause, while pressure on Monte San Gabriele was maintained. Here the Italians had taken Santa Caterina, a hill half the height of their final objective standing to the south-west, and Hill 343 immediately to Santa Caterina's north. On the northern slope of Monte San Gabriele a foothold had been established under Veliki Hrib, or Hill 526, leaving the road up to it from Stella di Dol the only access to the Austrian positions on the summit ridge, an area some 2,000 yd (1,830 m) long by 800 yd (730 m) wide. This eminence dominated the route along the left bank of the Isonzo and the Gorizia sector to the south and west.

On 30 August the Italians took Veliki Hrib and during the next two days clawed their way to a position just below the summit. On the morning of 3 September three Italian columns attacked from the west and north, the centre column getting into the Austrian defences and driving a wedge into their line. About 1,500 prisoners were taken. The correspondent of *The Times* reported:

They had done the impossible, and now reserves came up to sit down and hold the salient, closely pressed by a desperate enemy and smitten by all the massed guns from east and south. For the Austrians to prevent the complete occupation of San Gabriele was a matter of life and death. If once it was altogether gone the way lay open to an Italian advance east of Gorizia and the consequent enfilading of the all-important positions on the northern rim of the Carso. The enemy had to sacrifice anything in order to gain time to improvise a new defence on the Ternova plateau and the low ground that leads down behind Gorizia to the Vippacco.

Over the next ten days the fighting on San Gabriele was hard, hand-to-hand combat. Tiny gains and losses of ground cost many lives. A massive Austrian attack on

Some of the few Italians made prisoner in the Eleventh Battle of the Isonzo. *(Guy Cavallaro)*

12 September regained only a little ground and although the fighting staggered on in fits and starts, the Eleventh Battle of the Isonzo was over. On 18 September Cadorna ordered a defensive policy to be adopted. He informed the Allies and they responded by suspending any further supply of heavy guns and started to withdraw those they had already sent. The French took back those that had not yet got to the front and the British pulled out eleven of the sixteen batteries on this front. Since 18 August the Italians had suffered the astounding number of 166,000 casualties, of whom only 18,000 had become prisoners of war. Some 40,000 had been killed. Austrian losses were in the region of 85,000 men, nearly 29,000 of them captured.

The importance attached to San Gabriele by the Austrians in the eyes of the correspondent of *The Times* may have been somewhat exaggerated, for preparations were in hand for their new offensive from the Tolmino front as an answer to Italian success, expensive success though it had been. With the fall of Riga on 5 September the Germans were able to release troops from the Russian front and also send some from Alsace-Lorraine and Roumania, together with some specialist mountain and storm troops. They constituted part of the Fourteenth Army under General Otto von Below, who was appointed on 9 September, with four corps, two German, under von Stein and von Berrer, and two Austrian, under von Krauss and von Scotti. They were assembled in secrecy north and east of the Julian Alps in September, ready to advance

The Austrian Kaiser Karl inspecting the elite storm-troopers. *(Guy Cavallaro)*

The village of Caporetto (Kobarid). *(Guy Cavallaro)*

over narrow roads and high passes to occupy the northern front with the Second
Isonzo Army to their left and the First beyond them on the Carso. At the same time
fresh troops were sent openly to the Tyrol and the Austrian–Swiss frontier was closed
to suggest an impending attack in the west. General Cadorna could not neglect the
possibility and had further cause to adopt a defensive posture on the Isonzo.

The terrain west of the Isonzo in the Tolmino sector consists of deep valleys separating
the mountains. Immediately opposite is the Colovrat range, a v-shaped massif pointing at
Tolmino with the mountain of Na Gradu at the point and from there a ridge running just
north of west through the summits of Kuk and Mrzli vrh to end at Monte Matajur. On
the same line, beyond the River Natisone, looms Monte Mia. From Na Gradu south-
westwards are Monte Jeza, Monte Globochek and, close to Plava, Monte Corada. North
of the Colovrat on the River Isonzo is the town of Caporetto from where a valley runs
west to the northern end of the Friuli plain, leaving a ridge on its north through Monte
Stol to Monte Maggiore. A valley route to the west exists north of this range, originating
at Plezzo on the Isonzo. There are thus two westerly roads available, both commanded
from mountain ranges, the possession of which guarantees safe passage for those below,
provided they are friends. Further south the V of the Colovrat, once taken, oversees the
river routes to the south-west, Cormans and Udine. East of the Isonzo and north of
Tolmino the mountain range runs though Monte Versic, Monte Nero, Monte Rosso to
Sieme and Mrzli and Monte Vodel (see map on p. 138).

The Italian perception of what was clearly an offensive build-up east of the Isonzo was that an attack would be mounted to regain ground lost recently, mainly striking south and west of the Tolmino position. Cadorna stated that, as the country north of Tolmino was so difficult, he was holding it lightly. His control of his armies was affected by General Capello's being ill and advised by his doctors to leave the front. Cadorna's orders made clear that the front line was to be held lightly and supported with artillery. The XXVIIth Corps was to pull back from the Bainsizza south of St Lucia and protect the right bank of the Isonzo. In fact only part of the corps completed the move before the battle and that was deployed in strength in the front line, vulnerable to a breakthrough. The IVth Corps, north of Tolmino, held the northern end of the Monte Nero ridge lightly but the southern end, which was a poor line of positions, strongly. The plan developed by Lieutenant-General Konrad Krafft von Dellmensingen, General von Below's chief-of-staff, called for the corps of Krauss and Stein to break through in the north while Berrer and Scotti tackled the Colovrat. The advance would be covered on the southern flank by the First Isonzo Army. General von Below made his tactics clear in his final orders:

> The governing principle for any offensive in the mountains is the conquest and holding of the crests, in order to reach the next objective by way of these land-bridges. Even going by round-about ways on the crests is preferable to crossing valleys and deep gorges, since these take longer and entail greater exertions. The valleys are to be used for the rapid bringing up of closed reserves, the field artillery and supply units. Every column on the heights must move forward without hesitation; by doing so opportunities will be created for helping neighbours who cannot make progress, by swinging round in the rear of the enemy opposing him.

At 0200 hours on 24 October Lieutenant-General Richard von Berendt's artillery barrage began. Gas shells poured down on Italian positions for two-and-a-half hours. Then there was a pause. The rain started to fall, light at first, then with increasing force on lower ground while snow fell on the heights. At 0630 the bombardment was renewed with high explosive and then with trench mortars; an unprecedented weight of gunnery that smashed Italian defences and cut communications. The Italian artillery did not, in gas and confusion, reply. At 0800 two huge mines, on the Monte Rosso and the Monte Mrzli, blew up and the Fourteenth Army swept forward. By 0930 Krauss's men had broken the Italian IVth Corps' front. Just north of Tolmino, at the junction of IVth Corps and XXVIIth Corps, Stein's troops hit the Italian line when the relief of the Alessandra Brigade, IVth Corps, by the Napoli Brigade of XXVIIth Corps was in progress. The Napoli Brigade was destroyed and the Germans thronged over the river. Part of Stein's force attacked north of the Colovrat Ridge, aiming for Monte Matajur. The rest of Stein's men headed north-west and had taken the village of Caporetto by 1600 hours. The IVth Corps collapsed and a wide opening appeared between Plezzo, Saga and Caporetto.

...

South of Stein, Berrer and Scotti were facing the front on which Cadorna had anticipated an attack but, none the less, Berrer's men were on the eastern end of the Colovrat by nightfall and Scotti had penetrated to Globocek. Cadorna ordered reinforcements forward to Bergogna and Nimis that evening, but in the south he was obliged to order a withdrawal from the Bainsizza front. He then set about organizing a retreat to the River Tagliamento while pinning a series of defence lines to Monte Maggiore, to the north of Udine. The first of these, depending on Monte Stol, fell the next morning when, entirely surrounded, the Alpini could hold no longer against the Austrian 22nd Division. Cadorna framed orders for a retreat but, having consulted General Montuori who, standing in for Capello,

Austrian troops load a heavy mortar. *(Guy Cavallaro)*

An Italian communication trench in the mountains. *(Guy Cavallaro)*

considered the line could be held, did not issue them.

The general behaviour and attitude of the Italian troops, with some notable exceptions, was feeble – the outcome of insensitive leadership and excessive and expensive combat. It can be appreciated by following the progress of Lieutenant Erwin Rommel of the Württemberg Mountain Battalion. At about 0500 hours on 24 October, as the bombardment slackened, Rommel was ready to take part in the attack on Na Gradu on the Colovrat. The shelling grew in volume once more before ceasing at 0800 hours when Rommel led his men forward towards the lesser peak of Monte Hlevnik across wooded country. Through the mist

and strengthening rain they made their way as quietly as possible until the leading section came under fire near the Italian barbed wire. In heavy rain Rommel led a flanking group up a steep, rocky gully to emerge on the hill below the line of wire across the ridge leading to the summit. The wire disappeared into a wood and along the edge of the wood was a path along which Rommel sent a small detachment to pass through the wire as the Italians were clearly wont to do. Lance Corporal Kiefner led off and soon sent a message to say he had taken a dug-out and its defenders without firing a shot. Through went the rest of Rommel's force to take a series of dug-outs in which the Italians were trying to keep dry. As they went for the summit they met the

On 24 October the Isonzo valley was shrouded in rain and mist, with snow on the high ground, as seen in this modern photograph. *(Guy Cavallaro)*

3rd Battalion Bavarian Life Guards. They were all forced to pause as their artillery was still shelling the summit, but Rommel took his men into dead ground and outflanked the position which then fell to him. The taking of Na Gradu was not, for Rommel, a happy business as he was outranked by the Life Guards commander and made to serve a support role.

The next morning the Württembergers made their way along the side of the ridge, outflanking Italian positions and looking for the right place to assault the top of it. A chance encounter with a hillside strongpoint, which they again captured in silence, settled the matter and up they went. They were facing a position with wire running across the ridge from side to side and Rommel, leaving a machine-gun unit to guard his rear, ordered a double flanking attack on the Italian lines. His side was stopped as the other went into action, so Rommel swiftly retraced his steps and led his men against the rear of the Italian battalion that had pinned down his other company. The surprise alone seemed enough to obtain the surrender. By 0915 hours of the second day Rommel had taken half a mile (800 m) of the ridge and 1,500 prisoners of the Arno Brigade.

The next peak on the ridge was Kuk. Rommel moved against the southern flank, but becoming aware that the Life Guards were about to engage the position from the east, he moved on to block the north–south road from Caporetto to Polava, which passed between Kuk and Mrzli vrh, on the southern side of the ridge. This had been done by 1230 hours, but by now he had only his 4th and his 3rd Machine-gun Companies with him. Here he collected Italian prisoners as troops came down the road, culminating, after a brief fire-fight, with the capture of more than 2,000 men of the 4th Bersaglieri Brigade.

That night Rommel took an augmented force to occupy the village of Jevscek and on the morning of 26 October was forced to take Hill 1096 by frontal assault, his men well spread out but, given the nature of the position, obliged to hit it head on. The next height, Hill 1192, was taken by the usual flanking and encircling tactics by 0830 hours. Mrzli was next, and as he approached Rommel became aware of a large crowd of Italian troops milling about in uncertainty. With only a few companions he walked into the mob, waving a white handkerchief and calling on them to give themselves up. Suddenly they threw down their arms and swarmed towards him, thrusting their officers aside. More than 1,500 men of the 89th Regiment, Salerno Brigade, had surrendered. The final objective was Matajur and here, fearing serious opposition, Rommel made a cautious advance, again on the flank by dropping down the side of the ridge, supported by well-sited machine-guns. Hard fighting was not required. Surprised and outflanked, the troops of the 90th Regiment, Salerno Brigade, laid down their arms. Rommel's tactics had been brilliant, but vulnerable to any determined and courageous resistance. The spirit had been lacking and some 9,000 Italians had been taken prisoner at a cost to Rommel's detachment of 6 dead and 30 wounded.

Cadorna was now becoming aware of the extent of the collapse of his line on his left where the Second Army was folding up. He had already ordered the Duke of Aosta to start to move his heavy artillery to the west and his Third Army was to be noted for its steadiness in making an orderly retreat. At noon on 26 October Cadorna ordered a general withdrawal to the Tagliamento River, about 30 miles (50 km) west of Udine. Both the French and the British were asked for troops, the former reacting supportively and the latter reluctantly, but neither could act quickly enough to stem the military tide sweeping across the Friulian plain. The Tagliamento is a lowland river, dividing into numerous smaller streams many of which, in the dry weather, are waterless, but in the wet it can become a rushing mass of water over a mile wide. In order to smooth the withdrawal, Cadorna allocated specific bridges to his armies: to the Third a stone bridge and a railway bridge at Latisana and a pontoon bridge at Madrisio and the foot, railway and stone bridges at Codriopo; to the Second the trestle bridge at Bonzicco, the foot and stone bridges at Pinzano and the railway bridge at Cornino. The Bonzicco bridge washed away almost immediately in the swollen waters of the flooding Tagliamento, for the rains that had soaked Rommel's men had put the river in spate. Further, the Pinzano and Cornino bridges could only be reached by rushing across the enemy front, so pontoon bridges were proposed to solve the problem. The floods prevented their construction.

The journalist G. Ward Price was working for the British Newspaper Proprietors' Association as a war correspondent and had been sent to the Carso, where British batteries were serving with the Third Army, earlier in October. He had scarcely arrived when the crisis occurred: '. . . it became clear that the rout of the Italian army had already begun. It figures in the history of that war as the Retreat from Caporetto. The main road from the front was filled with disorganized Italians who had deserted their posts and were streaming to the rear with cries of 'A casa! [Homeward bound!]' and

'Finita la guerra! [The war is over!]' Price was advised by the commander of the British artillery to leave with the liaison officer going to headquarters in Udine:

> It proved to be a nightmare drive back to Headquarters among the Italian fugitives. We could do no more than creep through the confusion of retreat. Every now and then the darkness of the night was shattered by the flash and detonation of ammunition-dumps being blown up. On the way we picked up a wounded Italian who had been abandoned by his comrades. It was with great difficulty that we got rid of this casualty to a military hospital, which was itself being evacuated.

The speed with which a partial withdrawal had been turned into a complete retreat took the Third Army by surprise, and confusion was the inevitable result. Luckily the Austrians under General Boroevich were equally unprepared and did not give chase.

The first line of retreat was to the River Torre but VIIth Corps of the Second Army failed to prevent von Berrer's 200th Division reaching and crossing the river at about 0400 hours on 29 October and moving towards Udine. The commander was close behind his forward troops and entered Udine himself early that afternoon where an alert member of the Italian carabiniere saw him, appreciated that he was a senior officer, and shot him dead. Not all the invaders moved so fast. The Austrian troops, in particular, had suffered deprivation in the mountains and now found themselves amid the plenty of the villages of the Friuli. They paused to refresh themselves, often to stuff themselves to bursting. Their advance slackened. Moreover, the speed of the advance had surprised the Austrian and German senior commanders. Berrer's successor, General von Hofacker, conceived the plan of cutting off the Italian retreat and turned his troops towards Latisana, on the Tagliamento and the main east–west coastal road. Scotti turned with him. That night the Fourteenth Army commander, von Below, gave orders for a general pursuit.

At Pinzano, close to the foothills in the north, the Italians prevented a crossing, but at Codroipo, on the road westwards from Udine to Pordenone, there was a massive traffic jam. The delay gave the Italians the chance to blow the bridges, leaving some 12,000 of their own men on the eastern side of the Tagliamento together with all their equipment and artillery. South of Udine at Pozzuolo the Italian XXIVth Corps fought a vigorous rearguard action until night and then withdrew across the Tagliamento at Latisana and Madrisio. The Austrians and Germans had failed to secure the river crossing they so urgently required and a substantial part of the Italian Army had escaped. The Fourteenth Army had been allowed to become mixed with the Second Isonzo Army. The chance to regroup for an orderly retreat to the Piave River had been permitted to Cadorna. It was not until the evening of 31 October that the Austro-German forces had sorted themselves out.

G. Ward Price had been advised by the British Liaison Officer, General Delmé-Radcliffe, to leave Udine and hurry to the rear: 'It was pouring with rain, which had the effect of delaying enemy pursuit. After forty-eight hours' slow travelling by

Storm-troopers prepare to attack, wire-cutters and grenades in hand. *(Guy Cavallaro)*

The Austro-Hungarian success was not without cost. Their dead lie in the cemetery at Caporetto. *(Guy Cavallaro)*

Shattered wagons lie in a
riverbed while an otherwise
orderly retreat continues.

cattle-truck our train crossed the Tagliamento just in time before the railway bridge
was blown up by Italian engineers. This checked the enemy advance, and meanwhile
fresh Allied troops were manning the line of the River Piave to the north of Venice.'
The Allied troops he refers to were, presumably, the French whose 64th and
65th Divisions began to arrive near Lake Garda on 3 November, but as his memoir
was written a good deal later it may be faulty on precise troop movements and their
dates.

  For the Alpini in the Trentino and the Dolomites, it was a time of uncertainty and
worry. On 30 October Monelli wrote of the disaster and complained of the inaction
on his front and of the irrelevant fussing of officers giving futile orders. There was
little news to rely on and an increasing sensation of isolation.

  On 31 October both General Foch and General Robertson were in Treviso
conferring with General Cadorna and with each other. They agreed that the
four French and two British divisions already on their way to Italy would suffice to
reinforce the Italians when, and when was seen as more probable than if, they made
their stand on the Piave. The French troops were directed to Verona while the
advance parties of the British reached Treviso on 1 November. They, the 23rd and
41st Divisions, were to come under the command of Lieutenant-General the Earl of
Cavan. His general staff officer, Brigadier-General the Hon. J.F. Gaythorne-Hardy,
and his ADC, the Prince of Wales, accompanied him to Padua on 5 November. The
troops were scheduled to arrive on 20 November. On 4 November a meeting took

place at Rapallo and G. Ward Price, hearing that General Sir Henry Wilson was among those coming to it, met him in Milan:

> A party of Italian officers was waiting on the platform to salute this distinguished visitor – all of them, doubtless, chosen for their knowledge of English. They must have been edified by the general's remarks to me as he walked up and down within earshot of this reception committee.
>
> 'Well, what do you think of the Italian army now?' he asked in resonant tones. 'Licked for good, eh? I don't think so. They've got feet enough; they've got hands enough, if only they'll use them. What we don't know is whether they've got hearts enough.' (In actual fact General Wilson used much stronger terms in his reference to the physical equipment of the Italian forces – but they are unprintable.)

Once behind the Tagliamento and with time to reorganize, the Italians found heart and attempts to cross the river were thrown back almost everywhere. In one place, in the north at Cornino, north-west of Udine, the heart was lacking. Here the Italians had blown the bridge on 30 October, but destroyed only the eastern-most span. The Germans were allowed to repair it and, on 2 November, rush over. No attempt was made to halt them. The line was compromised and, on 4 November, Cadorna began the retreat to the Piave line. This ran from the marshes north-east of Venice along the river past Papadopoli Island, passed east of Montello and Monte Grappa northwards to Feltre before turning west on the Trentino front. By 9 November the withdrawal, covered by some fierce rearguard fighting by XVIIIth and IXth Corps, was complete. The Fourth Army, pulled back from the Dolomites, was in the north and the Third was in the south. No sooner had this been completed than Cadorna was replaced by General Armando Diaz. Italian losses in the Battle of Caporetto amounted to 320,000 men of whom 265,000 became prisoners of war. The Central Powers had taken 3,152 guns, 1,732 mortars, 3,000 machine-guns, 2,000 sub-machine-guns and more than 300,000 rifles for the loss of about 20,000 men.

The repositioning took place in the mountains as well. Lieutenant Monelli had been driving his men to build shelters, create breastworks and prepare for a long winter defence of their positions. On 9 November they were ordered to abandon these works and fall back through the snow. The next day they were on the flank of Monte Tondarecar.

The First Battle of the Piave started on 11 November and it would continue in fits and starts to the end of the year. The Austrians had reached Belluno and Feltre the previous day and now, at the southern end of the line, they got over the river at Zenson, 20 miles (32 km) north-east of Venice and managed to hold on to a couple of islands. Help from the Allies was becoming more tangible. General Sir Herbert Plumer arrived on 13 November to take over from Cavan and made the British 23rd and 41st Divisions available as soon as the Italian commander-in-chief could provide transport and billeting. He also agreed to ask for another two divisions and a cavalry brigade. The French 46th and 47th Chasseurs Alpins had arrived on 12 November.

The Austrian 1st Mountain Brigade entered the Val Sugana and took the height of Primolano, above St Vito, north-east of Monte Tondarecar which itself is north-east of Asiago and Gallio. Monelli was aware of their approach. On 13 November he took his company into the line behind the barbed wire the Italian engineers had managed to string across the very summit of the mountain. Two days later he was able to report that the enemy had not got through. He wrote the same of 22 November. The Austrian dead lay in the woods, on the open slopes and among the wire.

Fighting continued in the Asiago region and also on Monte Grappa where the Austrians and Germans attacked on 18 November. The crisis came four days later when Monte Tomba fell but IXth Corps managed to throw them off. Monte Pertica, immediately to the north-west, was hotly disputed; indeed, the whole of the Monte Grappa complex between the Upper Piave and the Brenta valley was the scene of intense action for a week.

On 2 December the British forces took over the Montello sector and the French entered the line at Monte Tomba. But the Central Powers were having to come to terms with the fact that their offensive was running out of power and starting to cost too much, and on this day von Below received orders to suspend it. The exception was that the position in the mountains was to be improved.

British trenches in the Montello sector overlooking the River Piave. *(Imperial War Museum Q26115)*

The Venetian plain from the edge of the lower Dolomites. The escarpment in the distance on the left was the point of the furthest advance of the Austrians in 1916. *(John Chester)*

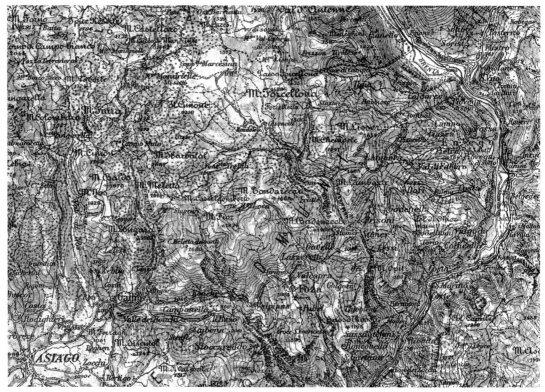

The mountains north-east of Asiago and west of the River Brenta in the Setti Communi, the terrain defended by Paolo Monelli and his comrades, from a contemporary map. Monte Tondarecar is right of centre at the top of the map with Castelgomberto just below to the left. The village of Gallio is bottom left and Asiago lies to its south-west. St Vito is top right, east of the River Brenta.

In the mountains Monelli saw drafts of new men come into the line, boys born in 1899. His unit was relieved by the Bersaglieri and the Alpini moved to positions below Castelgomberto. They huddled in damp, dripping caves. The flash of shell-fire on Monte Grappa could be seen. There were mumblings about the ability of the troops that had replaced them to hold on to Tondarecar. On 4 December the defenders of Castelgomberto knew they had held their positions but that the enemy was penetrating the line to left and right of them. Suddenly the gunners were being ordered to fire over open sights, and the next instant the Austrians were in among them. Desperate hand-to-hand fighting left Monelli with a kaleidoscope of impressions before he found himself with the survivors forming new positions around Castelgomberto. He could hear cries and shots as the 300th Regiment attempted to hold their ground, led by his own commanding officer, Captain Enrico Busa, who had gone across to help. Suddenly one of the men ran back, Tarchetti, with the news that Busa was dead – shot through the forehead. They huddled down in the cold wind, hoping for a counter-attack to relieve them. They had no food or blankets. They waited. The next day, 5 December, dawned after a night of enemy attacks. They were terribly cold and hungry. They had ten cases of trench-mortar bombs, so they shot them off steadily to prevent the enemy resting. With the dawn machine-gun fire came down on them. Their ammunition was at last exhausted. The few remaining were forced to surrender. Monelli recorded his feelings:

> Bitter tears, and a pang of agony so sharp that one feels that death itself will not blot it out. . . . And I see the oldest of my Alpini, who survived with me the battles

The summit of Monte Grappa still bears the scars of the trenches from which the Italians halted the advance of the Austrians, who were coming from the right of the picture. (John Chester)

of Valsugana and Cauriòl, three winters of war, the butchery of Ortigara, all that were left from a long series of deaths in all these valleys and on those lost heights, weeping at the shame of capture. I don't know the name of the man beside me who says: 'What will my mother say?' But I see his face, burnt by the hot breath of battle, glistening with tears.

Monelli went into captivity, which he survived, and as he did so the Italian line was re-formed on the south side of the Asiago plateau running from the River Assa in the west towards Valstagna on the Brenta in the east. From there it went north of Monte Grappa to the Piave and along the river to the sea. The cost of establishing this line had been the loss of about 140,000 Italian men of whom half had been made prisoner.

In 1918 the Austrians planned to take advantage of the withdrawal of Russia from the conflict to launch a major attack on the Piave line. This was made more attractive when, in late March, the Germans began their series of offensives in France, thus ensuring that no reinforcements would be sent to Italy. A feint was made at the Tonale Pass north of the Adamello massif on the western flank of their front on 13 June but it was so vigorously resisted that it was soon abandoned. The Second Battle of the Piave as such began on 15 June, three days before a planned offensive by the Allies. The Austrian strength had been shared between the Army Groups of Conrad in the mountain sector from the Asiago to Monte Grappa and that of Boroevich on the Piave frontage.

In the Asiago sector the line from the River Astico to the Brenta was held by the Italian Xth Corps, the British XIVth Corps (48th and 23rd Divisions), the

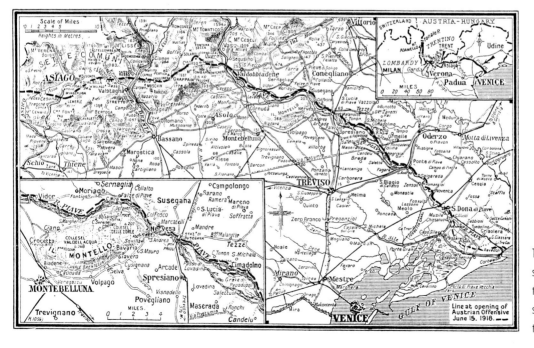

The Piave front from Asiago to the sea with, inset, a detailed map of the Montello to Papadopoli Island sector. (from The Times History of the War)

British troops in the mountains, washing and resting. *(Imperial War Museum Q26673)*

French XIIth Corps and the Italian XIIIth and XXth Corps. They had some intelligence reports prior to the attack, but the British were told that the main thrust would be to their right, although they might be shelled. They were. It started at 0300 hours and consisted of gas, shrapnel and high explosive. The British response was languid where there was any response at all. Communications were destroyed almost at once by the enemy because, given the rocky ground, telephone wires had been slung through the trees. When the trees fell under shell-fire the lines were broken. The defensive barrage the infantry expected was absent; they had to deal with the Austrian infantry's attack at 0700 hours unsupported.

On the left of the British XIVth Corps, alongside the Italian 12th Division, Xth Corps, was the 48th Division facing the valley of the River Ghelpac, a tributary of the River Assa, between the confluence of those streams and the edge of the woods facing the hill of Canove. To their right was the 23rd Division and beyond them the French XIIth Corps, on a front south-east of Asiago, the centre of which faced Pennar. The Austrian line was at some distance, up to a mile (1.6 km) away in places, and the existence of forward posts inhibited the British artillery from creating a defensive barrage lest their own men were caught in it. The Allied front line did not follow the edge of the woods, but passed in and out of them. Nor was it well designed for defence, for the intention was to attack from it at much the same time as the Austrians, who, in the event, moved first.

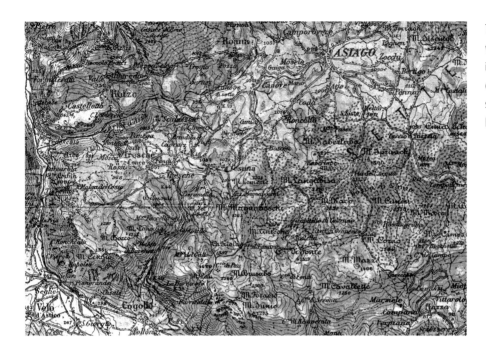

The ground held by the British south of the Asiago valley, from a contemporary map. The Astico valley is on the left and Asiago is at the top, right of centre. The wooded hills held by the British are south of Asiago. To the west and a little south the River Assa flows towards the Astico.

The Northumberland Fusiliers, Durham Light Infantry, York and Lancaster Regiment and Sherwood Foresters were in the front line of the 23rd Division. Their greatest problems were caused by an assault on the San Sisto Ridge, a wooded spur reaching northwards towards Asiago and broadening within the 23rd's lines which, if taken, would give the enemy a raised position from which to fire east and west, enfilading the trenches. The Austrians managed to oust the 11th Sherwood Foresters from a length of their trench and clamber up the ridge beyond. Lieutenant-Colonel C.E. Hudson led a counter-attack and was wounded, but the eventual re-taking of the position at about 1400 hours restored him to his own side. His bravery was rewarded with the VC.

It was on the 48th's front that the greatest danger arose. The road running south-west from Asiago to Cesuna passed through the front and the Austrians broke through to the east of it, in front of Mount Lemerle, on the front of the 4th Ox & Bucks. The situation was made more complicated because the main ammunition dump, at a location dubbed Handley Cross, between Lemerle and Magnaboschi to the south, had been hit. Explosions went on all day, endangering the men and denying supplies of ammunition. A breakthrough on the Cesuna Road was a possibility as was one on the right, at the junction with the Northumberland Fusiliers' line. The defence was an improvised affair, with infantry helping the gunners reposition their weapons to fire over open sights and non-combatant men joining the action to make up the numbers. The Austrians, however, lacked the zest and skill of Rommel's troops and an officer of the 11th Northumberland Fusiliers showed outstanding courage and initiative in carrying out a number of counter-attacks personally as well as organizing any men from a number of scattered units to form defensive positions. Another VC of the day

The western end of the Asiago plateau, looking from Cesuna, in the British lines, towards the village of Rotzo behind the Austrian lines. *(John Chester)*

The memorial to Lieutenant-Colonel Knox, 1/7th The Royal Worcestershire Regiment, one of only two such monuments in Italy. *(John Chester)*

Barenthal British Cemetery, close behind the British front line of 1918 and alongside one of the narrow, vulnerable tracks coming up from the south. There are 125 men buried here, of whom 9 are unknown. *(John Chester)* was 2nd Lieutenant J.S. Youll. For the commander of the 48th Division, Major-General Sir Robert Fanshawe, the difficulty was finding out what was happening when telephone contact had been lost. Once he had news he sent Lieutenant-Colonel F.M. Tomkinson, commanding 144th Brigade, to counter-attack from the left. By 2130 hours most of the ground lost had been recovered and a further attack at 0430 the next day regained the old front line and all the guns that had been taken the day before. The chief sentiment afterwards was embarrassment, for the British had been attempting to train Italian troops and had been obliged to rely on their support in this fight. The line, however, was held without any major withdrawal taking place as a result of the determination and courage of the infantry.

The Austrians also attacked in the Monte Grappa area, capturing five Italian positions, but three were taken back on 16 June. It was on the lower Piave that the most serious penetration took place. The Austrian Isonzo Army got over the river at three places on a 20-mile (32-km) front, while the river was also crossed by the Sixth Army at Montello where a bridgehead was secured and about 4,000 prisoners taken. Allied airpower was dominant and the Royal Air Force bombed the bridges thrown across the Piave, compounding the challenge presented by heavy rain which had put the river in spate. Downriver frantic bridge-building still left the Austrian XXIIIrd Corps short of supplies. The Italians mounted a ten-division counter-attack on Montello on 19 June and renewed their assaults on the southern bridgehead on 21 June. The Austrians had no reinforcements to offer their generals. Boroevich was forced to withdraw and by 24 June none of his men, other than casualties, remained west of the Piave. It was Austria's last offensive.

The campaign had been a disaster for the Austro-Hungarian Army. Their casualties amounted to something between 135,000 and 150,000 men, of whom 24,475 were prisoners of war. Of these prisoners perhaps half had simply given themselves up, so poor was morale. They had also lost 70 guns, 75 mortars, 1,234 machine-guns and over 37,000 rifles. In the air more than 100 of their machines had been destroyed as well as 9 balloons.

The Allied losses were by no means trivial. The Italians had suffered 84,830 casualties, of whom about 30,000 were taken prisoner, the British 1,959, including 319 prisoners and missing, and the French 564 men.

On 27 June the Italians were reinforced by the arrival of the American 332nd Infantry Regiment which was to enter the line in September. As July progressed, the Italians consolidated their victory and another 3,000 Austrians passed into captivity on 2 July with renewed fighting in the Monte Grappa sector. On 8 July an eighteen-year-old American Red Cross canteen driver, Ernest Hemingway, was wounded when with Italian Arditi troops at Fossalta di Piave. He was handing out chocolate to his allies when an Austrian mortar round hit their dug-out. Hemingway was decorated for his courage in remaining to assist those more seriously injured than himself.

Whereas the Italian morale had been decidedly low prior to Caporetto, it was now fully restored and the Austro-Hungarian armies were crumbling. Their men came from many countries and communities, often unwillingly, and a large number of them were eager to desert. It was, one of them is reported as saying, the river itself that prevented them – it was very difficult to get to the other side. Crossing the river in sufficient numbers and with effective lines of supply was the next problem for the Allies.

General Diaz declined to be hurried in his preparations for taking the battle to his enemies. He planned to cut the Austrian forces in two, attacking in the Monte Grappa area to separate the Trentino from the Piave front, before advancing on a broad front across the river and pushing the Austrians back to the east. On 1 October he invited Lord Cavan to form a new Tenth Army made up of the Italian XIth Corps (23rd and 37th Divisions) and the British XIVth Corps (7th and 23rd Divisions). The force at Diaz's disposal by 24 October numbered about 2,000,000 Italians, 78,600 British, 44,000 French and 5,000 Americans – 57 infantry and 4 cavalry divisions. He had 7,720 guns, 1,745 mortars and 600 aircraft. The Austrians had some 1,810,000 men in 54 infantry and 6 dismounted cavalry divisions, 6,145 guns and 564 aircraft.

The single American regiment, 332nd Infantry, was all Diaz got from General Pershing. He had asked for an entirely impossible twenty-five divisions! The 332nd moved to Treviso early in October and then occupied itself in a series of ostentatious demonstrations. Its battalions, always dressed and equipped slightly differently, marched out in separate directions each day and crept back after nightfall. The impression of a large number of American troops was conveyed, it was hoped, to the watching Austrians. As the next battle grew near the Americans were attached to the Italian 31st Division, but on 29 October became part of the British XIVth Corps, Tenth Army, and fought under that command until the Armistice.

The main objective of the Battle of Vittorio Veneto was the town of that name north of Treviso and close to the hills as it was a vital supply centre for the invaders. The Italian Eighth Army was to be the centre of the effort with the Twelfth on its left and the Tenth on its right. They were to attack in the dark, in order to be able to cross the broad waters of the Piave without being decimated by Austrian shell-fire, over pontoon bridges. The Eighth Army had to set up eight bridges, the Twelfth two and the Tenth another two at Papadopoli Island. Major-General Sir J.M. Babington, commander of 23rd Division, suggested the Papadopoli operation should begin the night before the main attack in order to establish positions on the island itself, beyond the main branch of the river, and make the final crossing that much easier. This was agreed. Preparations were made in as much secrecy as possible with the British troops kept from their front until 18 October and their officers dressed in Italian uniforms to reconnoitre. The only matter in question was when the battle would begin, for once again the river was in flood. On 21 October the final orders were issued.

Papadopoli Island was occupied by the Austrians who had dug trenches as deep as possible without river water seeping in – about 3 ft (1 m) – and strung barbed wire which was now largely overgrown with grass and weeds. The plan was for the British to take the northern end of the island and the Italians the southern. At 1900 hours on the night of 23 October Lieutenant-Colonel Richard O'Connor of 1st Battalion Honourable

The memorial to the British 7th Division on the banks of the Piave. The modern bridge to the island of Papadopoli, right, is visible to the left of the monument.
(John Chester)

Artillery Company led the advance party of his battalion and of 1st Royal Welch
Fusiliers across the river using flat-bottomed boats handled by local men. They found the
river consisted of a stream of moderate width, then a sandbank, then another, narrower
stream, both these unfordable, before another sandbank and the final, wider but
shallower stretch of stream. The noise of the river itself covered the sounds they made. At
2015 the first two platoons set off, seven men and a boatman to each little vessel and ten
of the twelve boats made it. The first seventy men then found and took the first defence
line at bayonet point, capturing the twelve men in it. Downstream the Italians had less
luck and were fired upon before they could make the final part of the crossing.
Meanwhile, Pontieri Company and 101st Field Company, Royal Engineers, built
two pontoon bridges to get men over the unfordable part of the river and these were
used before daylight to get the rest of the troops over. They were then dismantled and
hidden to avoid their destruction by enemy fire. The Honourable Artillery Company
advanced south-east and, now with the Welch Fusiliers, cleared the defenders out of the
northern half of the island to gain all their objectives by 0500 hours on 24 October.

The rain continued to fall and the Piave continued to rise, preventing operations
upstream from starting. It would be 26 October before Diaz could give the word to
advance there. So the British, soaking wet and cut off during daylight, had to endure
the Austrian shell-fire as best they could. They avoided the old trenches which, as they
expected, were heavily shelled, and kept their heads down. Work on getting a full-size

pontoon bridge went on during the night and the next day turned out fine and sunny. The rest of the island was captured that night and held against counter-attacks from the far bank, so that by 0900 hours on 26 October Papadopoli was in Allied hands.

The strength of the waters of the Piave continued to be troublesome on 27 October, but by the end of the day the Eighth Army had two bridges in commission much of the time and had established a bridgehead on the far side with about two divisions safely across. By 0230 on the same day three French battalions got over in the Twentieth Army's sector and in spite of shell-fire breaking the bridges from time to time five battalions were across by the end of the day. The Tenth Army now had to cross from Papadopoli to the eastern side where a flood defence consisting of a high riverside bank, the 'Bund', made an excellent defensive breastwork, augmented with barbed wire between it and the river. By 0300 on 27 October the British had brought more of their men over to the island and were ready for the next stage. At 0645 the artillery barrage reached the Austrian front line. The British moved forward to wade the turbulent stream, linking arms for safety. Those who lost their footing could not, under the burden of their equipment, regain their balance and so drowned. By 0700 the first men were on the Bund and had cleared the trenches. Some units, notably the 11th Northumberland Fusiliers and 12th Durham Light Infantry, ran into difficulties with wire and more determined defenders, but by 0710 they were ready to follow the

The grave of Elisa Franceschini, an Austrian nurse, who is buried in the Austrian Military Cemetery at Slagenhofi, in the mountains north of Asiago. (John Chester)

A post-war monument on the Pasubio declaring 'Here no one passes.' (Guy Cavallaro)

After the battle, November 1918, further pontoon bridges were needed over the Piave. Here Italian engineers construct a bridge to Papadopoli Island past partially cleared barbed wire entanglements. *(Imperial War Museum Q26694)*

lifting barrage towards the next line of trenches and, with one or two hold-ups, had taken their objectives by 0810 hours. The only problem was that the flanks were unsupported, notably on the left where the Eighth Army had not crossed yet. Meanwhile, in the north at Monte Grappa, the Italians were making some progress and ample aggravation to ensure that the Austrians were fully occupied there.

Diaz solved the Eighth Army's problem by allocating its XVIIIth Corps to the Tenth Army and Cavan sent it across his bridges to advance in concert with his troops. This broke the resistance to the Eighth Army and XVIIIth Corps was able to rejoin it on 29 October. By this time the Austrian Sixth Army had already been ordered to fall back and at 0830 hours on 29 October the first request for an armistice was made to the Italians at Serravak in the Adige valley. The next day the Italians were in Vittorio Veneto.

The armistice was signed at 1800 hours on 3 November and it came into force at 1500 hours the next day. Austrian losses amounted to about 30,000 killed and wounded and 427,000 made prisoner. Italian casualties totalled 37,819, British 2,135, French 778 and American 7, incurred when the 332nd Infantry crossed the Tagliamento River and took Codiropo.

The defeat at Caporetto was avenged, but that reverse, though dramatic and substantial, must be seen as part of a war in which the Italians had, for much of the time, taken the conflict to Austrian territory and, in the dauntingly adverse terrain of high, snow-covered mountains and of harsh, barren hills, inflicted great damage on their adversaries. The Italians had lost some 680,000 killed in the war and demonstrated, incontestably, outstanding courage.

THE
SALONIKA FRONT

'. . . undoubtedly this factor [the malarial mosquito] contributed considerably to the wave of sickness that passed over the Army. Under the severe conditions imposed on them by month after month of blazing heat, the men were used up and of low vitality. In every battalion men went down by the hundred . . .'

H. Collinson Owen's comments on the conditions faced
during the summer of 1916

Overleaf: Graves of British soldiers killed in August 1916.

EIGHT

BRIDGEHEADS IN THE BALKANS

At the start of the war Austria-Hungary had invaded Serbia with a view to defeating the tiny nation in the north-west of its territory without being drawn into the mountains to the south. The Serbs were guarding against the obvious ambition of the Bulgarians to add to their domains by acquiring Macedonia from their erstwhile allies against the Turks, the Greeks and the Serbs. The Bulgarians were not at first involved in the new war, but were waiting until it became clear which side would grant them the opportunity for the expansion they desired. The Greeks, under the government of Eleutherios Venizelos, also had expansionist ideas but the King, Constantine, was both a successful military general and the husband of the German Kaiser's sister. Thus, while the monarch was inclined towards the Central Powers and domination of the Balkans with Bulgarian help, his Prime Minister was opposed to 'Slav domination' and wanted to side with the Allies to gain what might be had at Turkey's expense. Military operations in this theatre were, in consequence, inevitably complicated by the mysteries of Balkan politics.

The Austrian campaign in north-western Serbia did not succeed, but just as the Gallipoli campaign stalled and was diagnosed as a failure by the Allies in 1915, the Central Powers determined to eliminate Serbia with Bulgarian help. A link between the Germans and Turkey would thus be created to surround the Russians. The renewal of the Balkan campaign became known when, on 22 September, the Bulgarian Army was ordered to mobilize. The Serbs called for assistance from the Allies. The French general, Maurice Sarrail, ousted from his command on the Western Front, was being granted the command of forces at Gallipoli and the responsibility for the Balkans as a whole was an obvious development. Reinforcements intended for Gallipoli were diverted to Salonika (Thessaloniki), but as they approached the Greek government fell and the King installed politicians supportive of his pro-German stance.

Salonika's location was important. The city lies at the head of the gulf of the same name on the north-eastern side of the peninsula that is the greater part of Greek territory. A ring of mountains overlooks the coastal plain here, with Mount Olympus to the south-west and a chain of peaks going roughly north from it to the border with, at the time, Serbia where Mount Kaymakchalan (Kaymakčalan) overlooks the towns of Florina and Monastir (Birola). The Moglena Mountains run eastwards, with the River Crna (Tcherna) flowing to the north to the valley of the Vardar which drains into

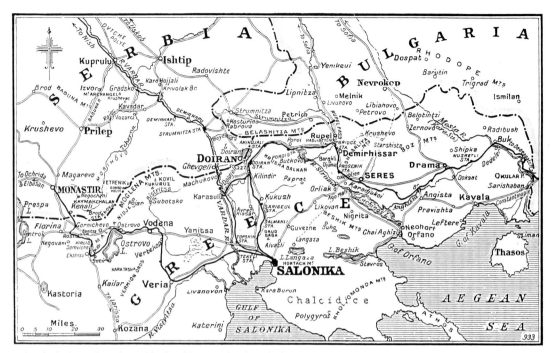

The Salonika theatre of war. The Greek borders of the time with Serbia and Bulgaria were largely mountainous while the valley of the River Struma, which reaches the sea at the Gulf of Orfano, was then a breeding ground for the malaria-carrying mosquito. *(from* The Times History of the War*)*

The Belashitza Mountains seen from the Greek side. The Bulgarian border ran along the crest of the range. *(Turrall)*

the Gulf of Salonika. East again the mountains rise to embrace Lake Doiran and, passing north of it, the Belashitza Mountains forming the Bulgarian border are broken by the Rupel Pass and valley of the River Struma flowing towards the Gulf of Orfano. The Vardar valley is the main line of communication northwards through Uskub (Skopje) and Pristina, bringing the railway down from Belgrade. West of Lake Doiran the railway divides at Karasuli, one line continuing to Salonika and the other heading east through Seres and Drama on its way to Constantinople (Istanbul). Communications to the west and Albania on the Adriatic Sea are difficult, passing through Monastir in the mountains, past the lakes of Prespa and Ohrid before making the descent to the coast. From Salonika eastwards there are more high hills, the Beshik Mountains, separating it from the Struma valley.

On Tuesday 5 September 1915 the Austrian and German guns opened their bombardment of Serbian territory preparatory to invading near Belgrade. On the same day the first French and British troops arrived in Salonika. H. Collinson Owen edited the British trench newspaper the *Balkan News* during the campaign, and later wrote of the impressions of a British supply officer on reaching Greece:

It is difficult to treat seriously the situation in Salonica in the beginning of October, 1915. The setting of the Place de la Liberté, with its cafés spread along each side of the brilliantly lighted square, where the Greek officers during the first mobilisation disported themselves in brilliant uniforms with their smartly dressed women-folk, was suggestive of the opening scene of a Balkan comic opera, and this atmosphere was intensified by the general topsi-turviness of the situation.

Imagine a British Army landing in a neutral country, supposedly friendly, but actually engaged in active and organised opposition, of the passive resistance variety. Imagine the German and Austrian Consuls in a town containing more than a sprinkling of their own nationalities, of Turks, Bulgarians, and other enemies, counting each British soldier and gun as they passed the dock gates, and concocting in the evening their daily telegram sent by Greek wireless to Berlin. Imagine the mail train passing through the British Base up the British Lines of Communication, to the British Railhead at Doiran, with its daily freight of spies and alien enemies, bound for the hostile capital of Constantinople, and returning thence without let or hindrance. Imagine all these things, and you have a fairly accurate picture of early days in Salonica. A situation which would doubtless have appealed to the librettist, but which did not argue well for serious military operations.

This officer had been, in fact, in the town for some days when the troops arrived as he was part of the advance party that landed on 1 October and was responsible for making ready for the main force. The seven British and two French officers had been put on a destroyer at Mudros on the night of 29 September and pushed ashore near the White Tower, having opened sealed orders that directed them to the British Consulate for more detailed instructions. The Consul was away and his Vice-Consul,

The peak of the Grand Couronné, the highest mountain west of Lake Doiran, seen from the Petit Couronné, a Bulgarian strongpoint. Today the trees and scrub have covered what was a more open scene in 1916. *(Alan Wakefield, Simon Moody and Andrew Whitmarsh)*

although he had been warned an hour earlier of their arrival, had no other information for them. The French, wisely, donned civilian clothes while the British remained in uniform and thus risked arrest. The un-named supply officer recalled:

> The next few days were spent in reconnaissance of the harbour, railway and local topography, and in entering into various agreements and purchases, most of which were subsequently annulled by the action of the Greek Government, which stepped in and requisitioned nearly the whole of the articles purchased and the buildings hired. We managed to borrow a set of maps from the Standard Oil Company, which proved to be invaluable, as none were obtainable elsewhere. Two of us were arrested for making a reconnaissance of the Croisement Militaire, but fortunately the subaltern commanding the guard had been an engineer in Belgium before the war and had pro-entente sympathies. He was easily persuaded to let us go again.

On October 2nd a wire was received from the British Minister in Athens saying that our arrival was unexpected, that it was causing political embarrassment, and that we ought to return whence we came. This was rather a blow, but we replied

ANZACS at Mudros after being withdrawn from Gallipoli. Guy Turrall served with them in that campaign before being sent to Salonika. *(Turrall)*

that we were sent out under War Office instructions, and could not leave without orders from the same source, and asked the Minister to repeat both cables home. The political situation certainly *was* delicate, and to judge by the local papers our arrival had occasioned considerable consternation. There were stormy scenes in the Greek Parliament, and in the end the Greek Government protested against the landing, but did not take any active military steps to prevent it.

At 9 p.m. on the night of the 2nd we heard through French sources that our position was being officially recognised, and this was confirmed at 11 p.m. by the Greek authorities. This removed the danger of internment for the time being, but did not have much practical effect in reducing our difficulties. We found ourselves blocked at every turn by a solid phalanx of Greek obstructionists. We found that everything that we wanted could only be obtained by referring to half a dozen different officials, each of whom did his best to delay matters, but the whole business was so insidious and so cleverly manoeuvred that I do not think any of us suspected hostile intent until months afterwards.

The orders governing the troops appear to have been equally confused. The British 10th (Irish) Division under Lieutenant-General Sir Bryan Mahon was ordered to remain close to Salonika itself for the time being. The French 156th Division, under General Bailloud, was charged with establishing a link with the Serbs who were based at Nish (Niš), far up the railway beyond Uskub. He set off at once, but was immediately recalled to await the arrival of the 57th Division. On 9 October the Austrians entered Belgrade and also invaded Montenegro and the Bulgars attacked the Serbs two days later. Sarrail reached Salonika on 12 October, the same day as his 57th Division, and immediately sent troops up to the frontier with Serbia. The next day, as the main Bulgar thrust began along the River Nisava towards Nish, the French 176th Regiment was over the border into southern Serbia. As they pushed on the French ran into increasing difficulty. The roads, where they existed at all, were scarcely more than cart-tracks and the bridges over the Vardar were built to carry the railway and had no provision for men on foot or road vehicles.

Further north the Serbs were fighting stubbornly, but the French could do little of significance to help. On 21 October, as the Bulgars entered Uskub, the French were in action against the 14th Regiment, Second Army, at Strumica (Strumnitza) station and the next day the British received authorization to assist their allies, but by 26 October the Bulgars had cut the lines of communication with the Serb armies. Mahon sent some Royal Engineers to assist the French and they were able to construct a bridge at Krivolak by 9 November. In that interval the French had thrown back the Bulgar 11th Division with heavy casualties, and their 156th Regiment had attacked north-west of Lake Doiran, but these efforts did nothing to distract the Central Powers from their objective – the destruction of the Serbs. On 5 November, as the British 22nd Division began to disembark at Salonika, the Bulgars took Nish and thus gave their national railway system, which linked with Turkey, access to the railway north to Austria.

The weather was also playing a part in the action. Rain turned to snow and the troops in the mountains suffered accordingly. The British were to sustain about 1,500 casualties as a result of the cold alone before this initial foray. The Serbs retreated to Kosovo which they had just regained from the Turks, 500 years after losing it in

Lieutenant Turrall mounted. He had the sadly destructive habit of trimming his photos to create irregular shapes or to crop off part of the image. *(Turrall)*

a battle that had become a national legend. The Austrians closed from the north and the Bulgars from the east. On 19 November the final, desperate fight began while the French made a last attempt to get through from the south. On 21 November the Serbian commander-in-chief, Field Marshal Radomir Putnik, gave the order to retreat to Albania. On 23 November the chief city of Kosovo, Pristina, fell and the great trek began. In four columns, with most of their now useless wheeled transport left burning behind them, the remaining Serbs, some 200,000 of them, still under arms, turned to the mountains. After terrible suffering, and laggardly assistance once they had reached the Adriatic, they were evacuated to the French-held island of Corfu, about 5,400 of them having died on the way.

In the first two weeks of December the French and British pulled back into Greece. The Bulgars halted on the frontier. The political leaders of Britain and France convened at Calais on 4 December and the British declared that they were pulling out of both Gallipoli and Salonika in order to defend Egypt and Mesopotamia. Two days later at Chantilly the decision in respect of Salonika was reversed. The Allies in Salonika went to work to secure their positions.

Two young English officers were on their way to Greece in December. R. Guy Turrall was starting his degree course at Cambridge when the war began and he immediately enlisted in the Royal Engineers. He served with the New Zealanders at ANZAC Cove in the Gallipoli campaign and was upset at being withdrawn. Now, twenty-two years old, he was with 127th Field Company, 22nd Division, and arrived in Salonika almost a month after the main body. Four-and-a-half years older than Turrall, Henry N. Lyster had been working for the Imperial Ottoman Bank in London, the organization for which his father worked in Constantinople, when war broke out. In the first weeks of the war he was responsible for the retrieval of the bank's gold reserves from its Paris branch, a task completed by using trains, ships and a covey of taxi-cabs with not a hint of a security man involved. Lyster joined the 4th/3rd City of London Royal Fusiliers, Territorial Battalion and eventually found himself with the Lancashire Fusiliers at Sulva Bay. On 24 December they were shipped back to Mudros. The two men did not meet during the Salonika campaign, although they did do so later, Turrall becoming godfather to one of Lyster's sons. Both of them have left records of their experience.

Turrall was a little inclined to wax lyrical if given a chance, but was modest enough to leave among his papers letters from friends who took him to task for overdoing it. He wrote of his first impressions of Salonika after arriving for the second time, in April 1916, from leave in Egypt, and being ferried from the transport ship

. . . across the green water to the Quay on the left of a long line of masts & native ships that jostle one another all along the sea front of the White Tower . . . we have to wait for lorries – late as usual. When we do move off, the streets are found to be cobbled & disappointingly dirty, filled with mud & puddles from a recent rain. Piled high behind with us & luggage, breathing forth petrol smoke & fumes of lubricating oil the jolting lorries rumble thro the noise & bustle of uninviting streets, where scenes are too new & varied to convey impressions, except they be of bustle & confusion in which Greek baggy trousers and French transport drays vie for recognition. And so we curve along splashing out the mud to either side upon an indifferent & motley community, & pass through a busy but dilapidated square (that afterwards we all shall know & speak of as Piccadilly Circus). . . .

Later on Turrall and some companions made a visit to the town.

As for the town; well, first impressions are strengthened. After the bright streets & wholesome hotel interiors of Alex[andria] there is a decided nth rate atmosphere in Salonika. If it were as eastern as, from the bay, the minarets & blue washed houses by the old wall seemed to indicate it might be one would not so much object to the mud & mire that swamps cobbled roads & pavements alike in one dark slime; but to find such a state prevalent among houses that ape the style of Western Europe – well, no wonder my thoughts are returning again & again to the good ship & to the light & colour of the distant shore of Egypt. . . .

Turrall goes on to complain of the shabby, colourless and mixed style of dress of the people he sees in the streets, so much less attractive than in Alexandria.

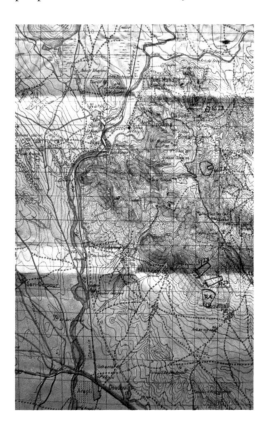

One sight, however, appeals to me, that is the native quay along which all manner of strange native craft are jostling sides & rocking & nodding on the dirty green water of the harbour. Compared to this old world sight the packed electric trams that run east & west along the front are hideous, jarring anachronisms so that on summing up about the most one feels inclined to say is that the town does not smell as bad as some pretend. It is not long before we have recourse to dinner hoping that might liven things up a little;

Detail from the Samli 1:50,000 sheet, marked with the positions of the 65th (east of the Matterhorn), 66th and 67th Infantry Brigades and the Royal Artillery, 22nd Division during the construction of the Birdcage. The railway running north alongside the Galiko River goes to Salmanli and beyond from Salonika. *(Turrall)*

& at the Olympus Palace Hotel facing the quay we obtain amid most indifferent surroundings, an indifferent meal for which twice as much is demanded & paid as one might expect to pay at the Carlton or Savoy. By the time of our return in darkness to Karaissi disillusionment is complete, & one is devoutly hoping that tomorrow will bring orders to proceed at once up country to our respective units.

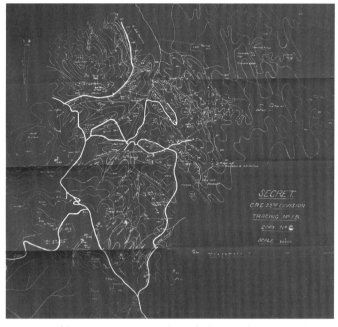

Copy No. 128 of the 1:20,000 tracing No. 1B showing the disposition of the 65th Brigade's trenches (in red) of the Birdcage on which Turrall worked. The road (in yellow) top left wraps round the east and south of the Matterhorn. *(Turrall)*

Generals Sarrail and Mahon were apprehensive about Bulgar intentions and the area around Salonika was fortified. To the west the flat land was marshy and defended by the River Vardar, then, east of the railway, a ridge ran north of Lake Langaza towards another lake, Beshik, from which a stream ran down a gorge to the little town of Stavros on the Gulf of Orfano. This line, some 70 miles (112 km) long, was to become the perimeter of the Camp Retranché de Salonique, the entrenched camp of Salonika – known as the Birdcage. British gunboats were hauled overland to the lakes, engineers poured concrete and lorries bogged down in the mud. Collinson Owen described the activity in and around the city.

The hard winter of 1915, then, and the opening months of 1916 was a period of feverish activity on the part of the Allies. The great transports that came into the splendid bay discharged troops or munitions daily. There were docks, camps, offices, transport, telephones, dumps, hospitals – a thousand and one things to be organized. . . . The Allied cavalry patrols, far up-country, beyond the line of the 'Birdcage', kept a watchful eye on the Bulgar, who, as a matter of fact, was digging himself into the positions which he was to hold for three years.

Christmas found Henry Lyster at Mudros.

We arrived at Mudros on Christmas Day and had bully beef and biscuits as our special fare. In the afternoon a nearby hospital asked the Officers to go for tea. Our poor C.O. could not make it as he had swollen feet and would not go sick. We had to help him all the way from the pier to our camp on arrival. To again have a nice cup of tea, nicely served, was very pleasant, and we were very greatly thankful to the sisters for their hospitality. It was raining hard but I could see not far from our camp a small village. On returning to camp I suggested to the C.O. to allow me to go there to try and buy some vegetables. This he readily accepted. I took with me two men and off we went. I found the village well stocked and we purchased meat, vegetables and eggs. On the way out of the shop someone on horseback well covered in oilskins asked me who I was. I replied 2nd Lt. Lyster, Royal Fusiliers and then told him we were from Number 1 Rest Camp. He then asked, 'What language were you speaking to these men?' to which I replied Greek. That was that. We were received with loud cheers when we got back to our camp loaded with our provisions, which would have allowed us to have real good grub at least on Boxing Day. At about midnight I was woken up by an orderly who said he had a telegram for me. This came as a surprise and a shock thinking it might be bad news from my family. The telegram, simply stated 'G.O.C. Islands request the pleasure of Lt. Lyster to lunch tomorrow 26th December'. No signature, no indication as to who sent it or who was to be my host. In the morning I showed the wire to the C.O. but when I asked him who was the G.O.C. Islands he could not tell me. I replied that this must be a mistake but he said that I had to go even if it was a mistake. My remarks that I would much rather stay in camp and eat our lovely stew made no difference and after asking some unit to supply us with transport and poshing myself up as well as I could I left to meet the Big Man.

Lyster was surprised to be offered a sherry by a general and taken to the mess for lunch. Still wondering what he was doing there he was taken into the general's office and things were made clear. The man on the horse on Christmas Day had been this same general, the GOC Islands in command of this rear zone. The hunt was on for men who could speak Greek and French, the two languages most commonly used by the inhabitants other than their own. Lyster was to go to Salonika as an interpreter. The young man objected and pointed out that, as an officer of a combatant unit, he could not be required to join a non-combatant one as acting as an interpreter would involve. The general was not pleased. He tried persuasion, then, annoyed, sent a satisfied Lyster back to his unit.

That night another telegram arrived. It told Lyster to report to SS *Argonaut* with all his kit. He did so and, on being told he was going on a special mission, again refused. The officer to whom he was speaking became very angry, but the lieutenant stuck to his argument – his was a combatant unit. He could not be ordered to leave. The officer left him for a moment and returned with the general who was all smiles. Yes, indeed, Lyster was quite right about the rules, which was why he had been transferred to the Intelligence Branch, General Staff, which was a combatant unit. He was immediately put on board a small fishing boat with just the pack he was carrying and he never saw his Fusiliers again.

An envelope was given to him containing orders to the effect that he was under the command of the army captain present on the vessel, so he asked what he was to do. Just come along and look around, was the gist of the reply. The next morning they moored in the harbour of a small island.

On arrival we were met by a junior officer who had a talk with the Captain and then informed me that he had a suspicious character which he wanted me to watch very carefully. I was introduced to my quarry. He had a semi-military uniform with the rank I was told of a Greek captain but he introduced himself as Colonel Yoannou. He spoke a strange sort of Greek and had a beard of about a fortnight on him and his boots had not seen any blacking for months and were full of mud. The first thing he asked was for the loan of a car. I translated this to the Captain who of course refused blankly. I pointed out however that it might be a good idea if a car was given him and that I went with him thus being able to see what this man was after. The Captain agreed that this would be a good idea so the car was produced after all. The Greek did not object to my going with him, on the contrary he seemed pleased at the idea. The Captain told me that if I did not return within 24 hours I would be posted missing and troops sent to arrest the Greek. What a journey we had. Roads did not exist and every now and then we left the track and cut across country, to save time said my mentor. This did not always prove the case as we had to return twice as we found ourselves facing cliffs overlooking the sea. Eventually we did manage to make for the village we were supposed to see. At first we saw no one. The Greek however blew a whistle and out of a house emerged rather sheepishly two or three men. When they saw however who had beckoned them they rushed forward and kissed his hands. He spoke like a leader and asked why the men were not on duty. One of the men whispered something to him and he said, Have no fear I am with an ally. This reassured me somewhat for the looks of these men were even worse than of my 'friend'. They then told him that on spotting the car a long way off the men who were on parade to await his arrival had dispersed as they never expected him to come in a car, and 'you know, we do not want people to know what we are up to'. This was getting really interesting. One of the men returned to the house, came out with a bugle which he sounded and from different angles men started running to the 'piazza'. There must have been about 300 men, all fully armed. They fell into rank but their eyes were more on me than on the Colonel. This did not please me. Some officer having called the men to attention the Colonel gave them an address. In a few words he said that soon these men would no longer hide but would be incorporated in the army under the guidance of 'our Great Allies the British'. This was received with loud cheers to which I felt like joining. After a few more words of encouragement the Colonel suggested we all had something to eat. This was also well received. Obviously the organisers of this 'plot' had expected the Colonel for they produced a marvellous meal which could not be described as impromptu for we had the largest fish I had ever seen and a whole lamb cooked on a spit on wood fire. During the meal I paid great attention to what was being said round me which helped in compiling my report to G.H.Q. when I got there. I knew already however that far from being a suspicious character Yoannou had been building, it is true secretly, but mostly from the Royalists, an army which eventually became the Archipelagos Division of the Greek Army and later the Army Corps, which he commanded.

On getting back to the fishing boat Lyster reported to his CO who was so pleased that he declared they must sail for Salonika at once. Colonel Yoannou asked for passage with them and was, in due course, delivered to GHQ by Lyster who reported once more before being ordered to proceed to join 31st Brigade. His journey was fraught with difficulty. The driver of the staff car did not know where to go so at Piccadilly Circus they asked the way. When they found their destination it emerged that what they were given as the name of the place was wrong. Back to Piccadilly Circus, but by now it was dark and as the true destination was 30 miles away and no lights were permitted, it was best to stay where he was. Lyster did so, with a Scots unit. It was New Year's Eve. They were having a 'bit of a do' and Lyster was welcome. Next morning he awoke after the limbers going up country had left, so he walked the 30 miles (50 km) to be roundly rebuked by his new CO as a liar (he could not have walked) and a laggard (he was a day late). When the Brigadier had gone to bed Lyster's new fellow officers made him comfortable, but it was not a good start.

Lyster never did get on comfortable terms with his Brigadier, but neither did other officers. He carried out a five-day reconnaissance in the week after his arrival, forward of the lines, to see if a particular village was occupied by Bulgars (fortunately it was not) and brought back a good report with details of the village and the surrounding country. The work on the Birdcage was in full swing.

The men were now all hard at it in the Brigade, digging like hell, and putting barbed wire in front of the lines. Maps had to be made of the new work and my job was to compile a daily work map showing day to day the work done. It had started snowing again and the men were complaining about having to work under these circumstances. One particular day the Brigadier went to inspect the work of a certain unit and found all the officers in the mess drinking before lunch time. He placed the whole lot of them under arrest. As a reprisal all the men refused to work. The Brigadier had to give in. Life in this headquarters was anything but pleasant.

Relations with the Greeks remained difficult. Sarrail had, as soon as the first bomb fell on Salonika on 30 December 1915, thrown out all enemy nationals including the diplomats who had, of course, been sending full details of Allied arrangements to their governments. The Greeks were not pleased. On 12 January he had the bridge over the

Floca's, the fashionable place to entertain a lady, although these gentlemen appear to be content with their own company. (Turrall)

Struma at Demirhissar blown up, clearly a defensive necessity. The Greeks were furious. On 28 January, in a substantial operation, he took the Greek fort of Karaburum which overlooked the approaches to the Gulf of Salonika. The garrison withdrew without argument. The position of the Allies in their enclave at Salonika was becoming thoroughly established.

Lieutenant Lyster's luck changed when the 31st Brigade was relieved by the 81st. He had been left in charge at Brigade HQ when a party including another Brigadier turned up and had to be shown round. When the young man had to explain he could not offer them a drink in the mess as only tea was permitted at that particular time, the visitors were clearly put out, so he invited them to his own quarters in a well-situated dug-out where they were better entertained.

> The new Brigadier for the first time said that he was the Officer commanding the 81st Infantry Division [in fact 81st Brigade], that his name was Crocker and that they were due to come and relieve the 31st I.B. He then said bluntly: 'Are you happy here?' to which I replied, just as bluntly, 'Not at all Sir'. 'Would you like therefore to be transferred to my Brigade?' to which I replied readily 'I would love it Sir'. They left asking me to pass their compliments to Brigadier Nichols and added with a twinkle in their eyes that they regretted missing him. Life seemed easier after that visit. Eventually the transfer took place. The Royal Engineers appeared first and started building a proper Brigade Headquarters on the spot I had suggested and although my transfer had not been promulgated, O.C.R.E. told me that he had received orders to contact me for ideas as to where to place the different offices and billets and mess. They did a good job and when the

Brigade marched in the place was nearly finished, for a day or two we lived in tents again but soon all was ready and a housewarming party given when two officers from each unit were invited to dinner. What a change of atmosphere in this mess. One was met by smiles from everyone, we were a happy family in the 81st Brigade headquarters. Work was properly divided and an air of efficiency prevailed right the way through the Brigade. But what a fine lot of units we had too. Royal Scots Fusiliers, Argyll and Sutherland Highlanders, the Gloucesters.

The work of building the Birdcage proceeded but liaison with the French formation alongside left something to be desired. Lyster was arrested by some French officers when in a village he names as Zaglivery, to the rear of the British lines. The French declared they were carrying out a reconnaissance forward of the entrenched zone and that he must therefore be a spy. It was not until he could persuade them to speak to the residents that they recognized their error. As he was fluent in French Lyster was sent for a couple of weeks as a liaison officer to the neighbouring French HQ. He found it an interesting experience.

I was billeted in a very fine hut and was given a batman. Office hours were 8 to 12.30 then lunch after which none of the Officers were on duty except the duty officer of the day. After what was every day a sumptuous lunch lasting over an hour everyone left. The first day the General asked me what I intended doing. I said I was hoping to have a look round. 'Oh no', he replied 'that will be done later. You better come with me to Salonica' and he took me to town in his car. On the way there he said 'Of course you will go now to see your girl friend', but having told him that I had only been in Salonica once on my way to the front he was sorry for me and told his driver to go to a certain house. There he said I was to tell the lady of the house that he had sent me and he added 'You will be made at home and a nice selection of girls will be brought for your delectation.' He told me not to pay more than 25 drachmae and that he would call for me again at about 7 o'clock. I did not visit madame but went to have a look round the town going for the first time to FLOCAS the famous pastry shop known by all who have been in Salonica. I was back again in front of Madame's house at 7 when the General picked me up and he was surprised that I had not availed myself of his offer. The Staff at Divisional Hqs was very efficient. My opposite number was quite an important individual for he was Chef du II Bureau and as such had a large staff of photographers, map makers, statistic holders, battle order makers etc. etc. Maps and diagrams were everywhere yet they did not know where the front line was nor that we were miles ahead of them. I altered their maps, traced our proposed work, made a rough tracing of the road to Suho and gave them as much information as I could on the general situation. My stay there was a nice change and although I did not learn much it was interesting.

The promise of spring brought fresh plans for attack. There had been thoughts in the high commands on both sides for renewed action early in the year, but those ideas were generated in France and Germany, many miles from the front concerned and, as would be the case again, in complete and unimaginative ignorance of the physical realities. German ideas neglected the availability of only a single rail line that terminated 60 miles (100 km) away from the scene of the intended action to carry all supplies. The French did not take into account the fact that, in their retreat of the previous year, they had torn up the railway to the border. It was not until mid-March that the Allies began to move, for the roads needed a great deal of work. Collinson Owen commented:

There were three more or less main routes leading into Salonika – the Monastir, the Naresh and the Seres Roads. They were all – from the modern European requirements of heavy traffic – in a shocking condition. . . . We had to make roads before we could use our vehicles.

The road up to Monastir did not at first much concern us. It was chiefly an affair for the French, and also that region was served by the railway. There was also a railway to Doiran, in which direction ran the Naresh road. But there was no railway up to the Struma Front, and there we had an Army Corps, consisting varyingly of two or three Divisions. . . .

In the later summer of 1916 we began to take the road in hand. Previous to this there had been a colossal amount of work within the region of the 'Birdcage'. Heavens, but how our poor infantrymen had to dig in Macedonia! Their first task was to construct all the defences and trenches which ran along the edge of the steep line of hills covering the town, and the 10th (Irish) Division particularly had some very heavy strategic road-making to do on the steep slopes of Mount Hortiach (nearly 4,000 ft [1,220 m] high) which, in case of an attack to drive us into the sea, would have been the chief bastion of our defence. . . .

That completed, the poor infantry had to start on the roads to support the move forward, particularly the 45 miles (70 km) over the hills to the Struma front. This

A British supply wagon negotiating one of the roads built with such difficulty the previous winter.

A composite photograph of the Vardar River valley with Macukovo this side of the river on the left and the Crête des Mitrailleuses on the right. *(Turrall)*

work, started during the winter months, was dogged by bad weather and the mud that resulted from heavy rains. The road was washed away in a series of mud slides and ton after ton of hand-broken stone, smashed into fragments by local women, were tipped into the greedy earth. Even that was insufficient, as Collinson Owen observed: 'When the lorries came to their final morass the mule transport took on. Imagine the scene with the bottom of the road fallen out, the rain dropping in torrents, and the long trains of limbers struggling forward. Imagine the tugging and shoving, the shouts and bad language and despair, with limbers sunk over their axles and the mules in the liquid mud to their bellies.'

On 13 March the French 243rd Brigade moved up the River Vardar towards the border. They drove the Germans from the village of Macukovo and a front line was formed to the south by the French with their enemies occupying the high ground north of the village which they called the Crête des Mitrailleuses, the Machine-gun crest. It was thought to be a hammer-shaped feature with the head forming the crest along the Donsale to the west and running to the striking surface at the Grand Piton in the east, the southern part of which was called 'The Nose' by the British. The land rose from the river past Macukovo to the Double Hill, on the north–south shaft of the hammer shape and fell away once more to the east. In fact, once properly mapped, the hammer shaft was much less coherent a ridge than had been supposed and the differences between the maps of September and November 1916 are striking. The British moved to a line south of Lake Doiran, overlooked by the high ridge of the Grand Couronné beyond Jumeaux Ravine. In April the Serbian forces, rested and re-equipped, started to arrive from Corfu, coming by sea, the Greek government denying passage overland. By the end of May 112,000 men and more than 8,000 horses were encamped south-east of Salonika, leaving 25,000 unfit Serbian troops behind.

With the approach of summer two hazards grew in importance: heat and sickness. Sir Ronald Ross wrote to the British Army Medical Director General to warn him that, in two months' time, 'General Malaria comes in the field . . .' and that quinine should be given to the troops and other steps, such as swamp drainage, taken to counter the spread of the mosquitoes carrying the infection. The area most affected was the Struma valley, and it became necessary to withdraw from the lowlands in summer, each side viewing the other across its wide expanse with only a few standing patrols in between. The battle against malaria continued throughout the war and after it Collinson Owen wrote:

> The summer of 1916 . . . was particularly fierce in its heat. There is no need for the summer to be more than usually hot for the malaria mosquito to do its worst, but undoubtedly this factor contributed considerably to the wave of sickness that passed over the Army. Under the severe conditions imposed on them by month after month of blazing heat, the men were used up and of low vitality. In every battalion men went down by the hundred, and there were several cases of one or two officers and two or three score men only being left out of a whole battalion up to full strength.

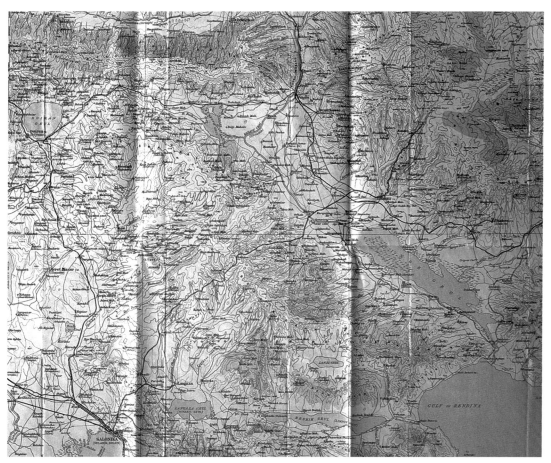

Detail from the Salonika sheet of the 1:250,000 Turkey map of 1908 which employs some placenames that differ from later usage. Contours are at 250 ft vertical intervals up to 2,000 ft and 500 ft above. Salonika is shown bottom left and Doiran top left. The Struma River flows through the Rupel Pass, top centre, and runs to the Gulf of Orfano, here named Rendina. Stavros is at the western extreme of the gulf. *(Turrall)*

In a fortnight the South Notts Hussars were reduced to 45 officers and other ranks and never went into action at all in Macedonia, though they saw plenty later in Palestine. And one infantry battalion was reduced to one officer and 19 men. The difficulties of evacuating this flood of sick men, a large proportion of whom were extremely ill and helpless as babies, were extreme. Most of them fell ill when they were far from convenient means of transport, and had to be carried two at a time in *cacolets* on the back of a mule, or had to be dragged along in a *travois*, a sort of litter made of canvas stretched between two shafts which trail on the ground behind a mule; or carried on a litter suspended between two mules. The personnel of the Field Ambulances were worked to death at this difficult and exhausting work. The sudden outbreak overwhelmed the medical services, which were not then organised up to the point of dealing with the startling problem of a fit army suddenly turning into a sick one. Again the Seres Road, which from right and left on the Struma, received the main flood of patients, was still largely in its primitive state, and the men had very exhausting journeys down to the Base.

The number of malaria cases in the summer of 1916 soon approached 30,000. The established hospitals could provide only 11,500 beds. As Collinson Owen reported, a solution was found:

As the generous establishment of hospitals was insufficient to deal with all the malarial cases under treatment, and the fresh ones which constantly came rolling in, patients were sent off to Malta by hospital ship. Some twenty thousand were dealt with in this way during 1916, and some of those who were more or less themselves again felt, as they sailed over the blue sea *away* from Salonica (but not when they were sailing back) that malaria had its compensations. But the unrestricted submarine warfare of 1917, in which the Germans showed themselves base enough to attack hospital ships, put a stop to all this. As a consequence more and more hospitals were brought to Salonica, and soon the great medical settlement of Kalamaria, where the big hospitals gathered together near the sea, formed a large-sized town, was rivalled by the new settlement which sprung up on the lower slopes leading up to Hortiach.

And 1916 was by no means the end of our troubles from malaria. It was only the insignificant beginning. The problem was tackled most energetically and the medical authorities initiated preventive measures on a very large scale in the way of oiling and draining stagnant waters, cutting down and burning great tracts of brushwood, making sluggish streams flow swiftly. The healthy men were protected in every way possible – mosquito-proof huts, gloves, head nets and nasty ointments; and the men already infected treated with all the medical skill which a close acquaintance with the disease on a large scale had given us. But the chief difficulty about dealing with malaria on such a scale is that the patient is subject to frequent relapses. Again each fresh summer gave us, in spite of all the hard work and devotion displayed, many new patients in addition to those who were constantly going sick as a result of their infection one or two summers previously . . . in spite of . . . improved methods, the total admissions for malaria rose with each summer . . . the thirty thousand of 1916 had become sixty-three thousand in 1917 and sixty-seven thousand (in a much-depleted Army) in 1918.

On 10 May Lieutenant-General George Milne replaced Mahon, also reporting to Sarrail, but still within the limitations of the defensive entrenched area. The French, however, were set on a summer campaign and sent their plan to the British four days after Milne arrived in Salonika. This was not accepted and Robertson was entirely opposed to an offensive in this theatre. Then, on 27 May, the Germans and Bulgars were yielded Fort Rupel, the gateway through the mountains north of the Struma valley, by a compliant Greek garrison. The Bulgarian Seventh Infantry Division occupied the western bank of the river at Demirhissar, rendering the destruction of the bridge irrelevant. Sarrail determined to make a counter-attack, but Milne held firm to his orders and declined to have his troops involved. That did not prevent the Frenchman from bringing his own forces up for the purpose, or from declaring Salonika as being under siege and thus subject to his military government. The French then went on to blockade all Greek ports and force a change of government to one compliant with the objectives of the Allies; an act it was difficult to square with the claim to be protecting Greece from the domination of a foreign power.

Shortly after this the 81st Brigade were moved to Stavros, the little port on the Gulf of Orfano that marked the eastern end of the Birdcage enclave. Orders then came for someone to be sent to find out what the situation was in the Greek-held town of Kavala, the port close to the Turkish border to the east. A boat was placed at Lyster's disposal and, in spite of his protests that it would be more prudent to conduct his investigations in civilian clothes, he was sent off in uniform. On his arrival he asked for the British Consul, a gentleman who was very embarrassed by his appearance, refused to help and sent him to the Khedivial Hotel for the night. He checked in and then walked to a café and ordered a beer. The other customers stared at this curiosity.

I ordered some beer and pretended not to notice the attraction I had created. I actually started reading a book, when a civilian approached me and asked whether I minded him joining me, I said I would be delighted and asked him to join me in a beer. He gradually moved his chair nearer and nearer to me and eventually whispered that I should leave the place discreetly and go to another place for my meal when a certain Greek Officer would meet me and give me some information.

This advice I took seriously and after thanking my unknown friend and after he had left, I also paid and left. I found the other restaurant and entered casually asking whether I could get some food. I was shown a table far away from the door and somewhat retired from the rest of the tables. In the ordinary way

I would have refused to be so segregated from the rest of the diners but presumed that this was done on purpose, which proved correct for soon a door behind me opened and a Greek Captain beckoned to me to enter another room. He said that [while] he was a Venezilist Officer that most [of] the Gunners were Royalists and that as a result the guns were being secretly dismantled and sent to the Bulgars – 'so that when the Bulgars attack this place we shall not be able to resist'. He added, 'Please inform your people of this and if you want proof go up tomorrow morning at such a spot and you will see with your own eyes that the gun positions are already empty there.' He suggested my being there at about 10 when there would be a friendly sentry on the spot as it was a prohibited area and I might get into trouble if caught there by any royalist sympathisers.

Warned that his hotel was run by two ladies in the pay of the Germans, Lyster passed the night lying fully dressed on his bed, the door propped shut with a chair and his revolver ready to hand. Next morning he went to the gun positions and found them empty, the sentry turning a blind eye as arranged. He was drawing and making notes when an officer approached and warned him to make haste before any Royalists turned up, so Lyster returned to town. There he was quizzed by curious crowds and replied that he was checking for suitable billets for the British who would come soon. He was picked up by his boat at 1800 hours as arranged and departed safely. His report was not believed and Kavala fell into Bulgarian hands as predicted.

The uncertainties of the times led to many Greek soldiers deserting and becoming, in effect, bandits. One such group was led by a man Lyster identifies as Pandofevgho who, with some 2,000 men, was robbing British convoys. A Yeomanry unit was sent to apprehend them and Lyster was attached as Intelligence Officer. He found the major in command a man lacking enterprise. When news was acquired of a feast the deserters were to hold, the CO sent for permission to mount an ambush instead of acting on his own initiative. Approval came too late and all they found was the evidence of cooking fires and a wonderful party. Lyster made up his mind to act on his own.

I therefore one morning left the camp unarmed and made for the hills. After about two hours' ride I was halted as I hoped I would be by two sentries and I informed them that I had come to speak to their chief. I pointed out that I was unarmed to prove that I had come on a mission of peace. I was blindfolded, placed on my horse again and led on. Arrived at a certain spot my bandages were removed and the sight I saw was really extraordinary. Well armed troops were standing about all round me and tents also were seen well camouflaged. A man I took to be Pandafevgho came forward and asked me if I spoke Greek. On answering in the affirmative I also asked if I could speak to him privately. We then went into a tent where the traditional cup of coffee was brought me. He laughed and said that they got the sugar from our convoys. Well I said I am glad you mention our convoys for it is about these I have come to speak to you. Our Hqs are getting fed up with your actions. As long as you were Greek deserters we were not interested in your movements and ideas, but now that you are attacking our troops we consider you enemies and we have decided to exterminate you. 'Now,' I added, 'this is a pity as I would like to prevent the shedding of unnecessary blood.' I had come on my own initiative to suggest to them to give themselves up and I would try and get our people to promise them a free pardon if they returned, each with his rifle, to our lines. I also asked Pandofevgho to allow me to speak to his men about this scheme and to my surprise he readily agreed more or less making it plain that he could not keep them much longer. He gave some orders and men seemed to spring from everywhere. I spoke to them for some time suggesting that it was time they realised that they could not remain in the hills all their lives and the best thing was for them to return to their units. This was not well received, but I went on that my idea was for the British to bring pressure to bear on the Greek military authorities for a general amnesty provided they returned to duty through our hands bringing with them their rifles. I made a special point that I would only accept men who brought their rifles with them. A few stated that they did not take their rifles and in that case I added they would be sent separately and if it was proved that their rifles were still in their units they would be accepted. I told them that so far this was only my idea and I would have to get permission from our GHQ to agree to this suggestion. I asked that a parliamentary be sent me in a week's time to whom I would give the answer. We agreed on the time and a place to meet. I was again blindfolded and led back to the spot where I had been 'captured', and I parted with my two guides on very friendly terms.

The major was furious, but he could not prevent Lyster reporting to GHQ and the scheme was approved. Compounds were made of barbed wire to hold the men and shipping was organized to remove them to Salonika from Stavros. The rendezvous was fixed and, with rifles at the slope, the Greek deserters began to march in. All of a sudden firing broke out and the Greeks began to fall. Lyster rushed towards the source of the gunfire and found an excited officer of Marines urging his men to greater efforts. '[He] thought it a wonderful idea and good fun.' It was some time before Lyster could prevail on him to cease fire, after which, naturally, no more Greeks were to be seen. The Royal Navy had no knowledge of Lyster's operation and were, independently, taking action to wipe out the maverick Greeks. Those that escaped sought refuge on Mount Athos where they were hunted by the French. It was a sad outcome for a peaceable initiative.

The situation of the war in the Salonika theatre was changed by military and political action elsewhere. On the Russian front the Brusilov Offensive was sapping the strength of Austria while Roumania was at last making up its mind which side to join in this war. The Austrian setback brought Roumania in on the side of the Allies, thus threatening the Bulgars on another front and encouraging an Allied offensive in Salonika. Further, a Russian contingent arrived to reinforce Sarrail's force and he reorganized his front line. Collinson Owen reported developments:

Russian troops marching to the front, August 1916. *(Imperial War Museum Q32402)*

The French occupied the centre, from the Vardar westwards, and the Serbs took up the line from the left of the French on towards Monastir. And on July 30th the first of the Russians came. That was a wonderful morning. They marched up the *Place de la Liberté* eight abreast, their bayonets on their long rifles; magnificent looking men whose firm tread, in their heavy boots, seemed to make the earth shake. Here, one felt, was the might of the Czar, with his inexhaustible legions. Here was Great Russia, with her boundless primitive strength allied to the civilisation of the West. As the men marched they occasionally broke out into wonderful and inspiring chants. The Balkan campaign promised well as they tramped past. These, no doubt, were but the forerunners of many more. Roumania was coming in from the north. The enemy would be pinched like a nut between crackers. . . .

Twelve days later the first of the Italians arrived, Alpini and Bersaglieri amongst them – fine looking troops who drove the Italian inhabitants mad with joy. And gradually, in the never-ceasing heat and dust, the line of the Allies was formed far away beyond the line of the 'Birdcage' – French, British, Serbs, Italians and Russians taking up their posts over mountain and valley in a continuous trench line across more than half of the Balkan Peninsula.

The pressure on the enemy became more aggressive with the French 17th Colonial Division's successful attack on the hill known as La Tortue, overlooking Jumeaux Ravine, south of Doiran on 16 August. To the west the British in support took Horseshoe Hill but the ruined village of Doldzeli between those two positions remained in Bulgar hands. However, far to the west, the Bulgars anticipated the Allied offensive by taking the town of Florina, south of Monastir. On 17 August two Bulgarian columns had attacked the Serbian Third Army's Danube Division and took the railway station to the east of the town. More troops followed up this success to raise the Bulgar strength to 18,000 men and the Allies had to hurry up reinforcements to prevent a breakthrough to Lake Ostrovo. Meanwhile, in the east, the Bulgar Second Army began operations on the River Struma.

General Sarrail, typically, saw attack as the best form of defence. On 20 August he held a conference of his commanders and had the Italians take over the mountain front in the north-east while the British were to mount attacks on the Struma and destroy the bridges. The French relieved from the mountain line, together with the Russians, moved west to support the Serbs.

The Bulgars rejoiced in their victory at Florina and threw themselves against Serbian positions west of Lake Ostrovo. On 22 August they made five assaults at great cost and no gain. The next day they took one position, but that was the end of their advance. By 26 August the infantry battle here had ceased, leaving fighting to the artillery.

The British activity on the Struma was witnessed by Lyster, but he fails to record the exact dates of the attacks and it is possible that he is mistaken in thinking the three assaults he describes were made on successive Sundays. His impressions are none the less valuable for that. It was the 10th Division that he saw go into action first. His Brigade HQ were ordered to observe the action and they positioned themselves on a ridge about half a mile (800 m) further to the rear to get a good view. A meal was prepared, tables and chairs set up and the officers assembled to see what happened. Lyster wrote:

> It was really ghastly to be sitting there eating and drinking whilst our own people were being killed only a few miles away. Every one of our party had to make notes on what he saw and this eventually became a lengthy report sent to Corps Headquarters. The poor Irishmen were badly cut down by the Bulgars and had to retire protected by a barrage from our divisional guns. The next Sunday the same attack took place and once more we went for our 'picnic' and once more the Irishmen had to retire after losing severe casualties. . . .

The next week it was 81st Brigade's turn to assault Karajakoi Bala and Karajakoi Zir. They had learned from the experience of their unfortunate comrades in the 10th Division, in particular that a large, deep pond protected the eastern side of Bala. Lyster's duties started on the evening before the attack. While his recollection is that it was a Saturday, the official records have it that the main attack was made on Saturday 30 September, and so the preliminary work would have been done on the Friday night. Lyster led a party of Royal Engineers to throw a bridge over the Struma. He had reconnoitred the area thoroughly and reported the location and its characteristics in detail, so the Engineers arrived with all their gear ready. The Bulgars saw and heard nothing. When the bridge was in place straw was spread to muffle the sound of the

The Struma valley and the hills behind the British line seen from Cole's Kop, a large tumulus near the village of Orlijak (Orliak, and now Strimoniko) on the British side of the river, west-south-west of Seres. *(Alan Wakefield, Simon Moody and Andrew Whitmarsh)*

infantry crossing and the rumble of gun wheels going over. The Argylls and the Camerons were to lead the attack with the Royal Scots in reserve.

At dawn the artillery opened up and Lyster was impressed with their accuracy and effectiveness; they, too, had benefited from the previous attempts. The Argylls on the right were over at once, but the Bulgar machine-guns opened up a heavy fire and the attack began to lose momentum.

By noon we still had not dislodged the enemy who was putting up a stout resistance and the Royal Scots were told to charge. The pipe-major started his pipes and walked quite calmly at the head of his unit. The poor chap had not gone very far when he was hit, he fell but went on playing his pipes as if nothing had happened. The Bulgars kept on firing at him and he received several more bullets so that when he eventually was carried away by the stretcher bearers almost by force he looked a sorry sight. I placed a cigarette in his mouth for which he thanked me and I am glad to say that he was able to recover after a long spell in hospital. The evening came none too soon. The enemy had at last retired and the R.E. were now in front putting up wire in front of our new positions. The next morning the Bulgars did try and retake the two villages but coming against the wire they were stopped and suffered very heavy casualties and would have had many more if two of our machine guns had not jammed owing to sand getting into the works.

Among the prisoners the 81st had taken was a captain who was put in a ruined church and offered food. He refused it, saying he would not be bribed with fancy fare, but would eat only what his captors ate. Lyster spoke to him: 'Asked what he meant by this he replied that he knew that we were starved, all our ships bringing in food having been sunk by German submarines. I assured him that no special food had been given him, that on Saturday and Monday morning he had actually had the men's food but that as from then he would be served from the officer's mess. This he could not believe, so I took him to our cookhouse and showed him. . . .' The man was enraged that he should have been told lies by his own people, and demanded to be set free to return and report the plenty – but permission was not given. What did happen was that Lyster began to leave loaves of bread forward of their lines with messages inviting the Bulgars to come over and eat 'this sort of bread'. The number of deserters increased somewhat as a result, yielding, as the Intelligence Officer remarked, quite useful information.

The attack of 30 September was timed to coincide with the final effort on the front to the west. The Allied counter-attack had begun on 12 September at 0600 hours when

A modern view of the Struma at the position of Jungle Island Bridge, built for the attack on Karajakoi Bala and Karajakoi Zir. *(Alan Wakefield, Simon Moody and Andrew Whitmarsh)*

A contemporary photograph of the shelling of Karajakoi Bala and Karajakoi Zir, on the right of the picture. It can be seen that trees obstruct the view of the river in front of these objectives and that the land is uncultivated. *(Imperial War Museum Q32432)*

the French and Serbian artillery opened fire near Lake Ostrovo. The Bulgars were established beside the Serbian–Greek border which ran along the peaks of the Kaymakcalan mountain complex, a position from which the Serbian First Army was determined to remove them. It was a formidable undertaking, but if it could be done the valley of the River Crna (Tcherna) beyond, leading to the River Vardar, would permit the line on the latter river, blocking the principal route northwards, to be outflanked. The French 156th Division attacked westwards, towards Florina, and the Serbs took the foothills of the mountains north of Lake

Graves of men killed in August 1916. On the left F. Bovington, 7th Ox & Bucks, who died of wounds. In the centre, Lance-Corporal D. Davis, 11th Worcesters, killed in action, and on the right Driver D. McDonald, 108th Field Company, Royal Engineers, aged twenty-two years. *(Turrall)*

Ostrovo. On 14 September the Serbs took Gornichevo, west of the northern end of the lake, but progress towards the heights of Kaymakcalan was poor. On 17 September the Russian Brigade and the French 57th Division regained Florina.

On the flanks of the mountain the fighting continued in the beech woods, a grim business of hand-to-hand, man-to-man combat. Once through the trees the bare mountainside faced the Serbs while their enemies opposed them from the natural clefts and gullies in the rocks. In the early hours of 19 September the Serbs attained the eastern summit of the ridge, a position within their homeland. On 26 September the Bulgars counter-attacked and expelled the Drina Division from Kaymakcalan. On 30 September the Serbs took it back yet again and added the second of the mountain's

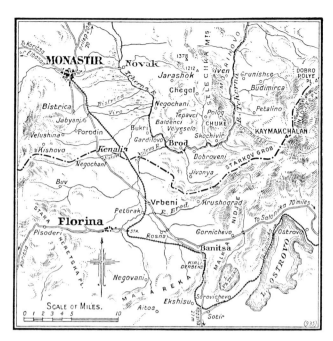

Map of the country between Lake Ostrovo and Monastir. (from The Times History of the War)

two peaks to their gains. On the lower ground progress had been more than equal to that of the Drina Division above and, outflanked, the Bulgars pulled back.

General Sarrail was, however, displeased with the progress of the French and Russian forces under General Emilien Cordonnier. It had taken too long for the town of Florina, dominating the valley route from Ostrovo to Monastir, to fall. Now progress up the valley to the north was no better. What Sarrail either did not, or did not care to, appreciate was that the Bulgars had constructed elaborate trenches at Kenali running as far east as Brod and that they also were still in possession of the monastery of St Mark, overlooking Florina. A simple, frontal assault would be as prudent as a repetition of the first day of the Battle of the Somme. The attack was postponed until 3 October in response to Cordonnier's letters of detailed explanation, but Sarrail accompanied his concession with a threat to relieve Cordonnier of his command. The two men met at Banica (Banitsa) railway station on Sunday 1 October and it was agreed that St Mark's must be taken first. The monastery fell the next day. On 5 October Cordonnier occupied the observer's seat in a French reconnaissance aircraft over the Bulgarian positions and identified opportunities to outflank the defences both east and west. He never got the chance to exploit his knowledge. Sarrail issued firm orders for an attack the next day.

The assault was no more successful than Cordonnier expected. The Serbs achieved some modest inroads near Brod, but the main Bulgar position held. Not that the

The Struma Military Cemetery near the modern village of Kalokastro in which the fallen of September to October 1916 lie alongside those who died in the constant patrol activity on this front. *(Alan Wakefield, Simon Moody and Andrew Whitmarsh)*

Bulgarian forces were much cheered by their stand, for a battalion facing the Serbs mutinied and the Germans were forced to rush three battalions from the Vardar front to shore them up. But the French and Russians had lost heavily. On both sides the pressure from headquarters to make progress intensified. The Central Powers made General Otto von Below Army Group Commander for Macedonia on 10 October and six additional battalions were allocated to him immediately. Sarrail was looking for the vital breakthrough at Monastir. On 14 October Cordonnier reluctantly laid on another frontal attack and lost some 1,500 French and 800 Russians in the process, gaining one trench line. Before he could return to his flanking scheme he was dismissed.

On 18 October the Serbs took the village of Veljeselo (Velyeselo), north of Brod but three days later the rain turned the Crna valley into a wide, shallow lake of mud. The Italian Cagliari Brigade started to struggle west from their positions east of Lake Doiran, but the conditions alone almost halted them. The weather closed down operations on the Monastir front for the time being.

The British had not been inactive while the French had been battering on at Kenali. On 23 October a substantial raid was made on the German line at the Dorsale, the western end of the Crête des Mitrailleuses, north of Macukovo and east of the River Vardar. It was undertaken by the 11th Welch Regiment, 67th Brigade, to which Lieutenant Guy Turrell, RE was attached. He was responsible for framing orders for four dug-out parties for blowing up enemy positions and leading the one working with 'C' Party. The Brigade Diary declares that '. . . our artillery cooperation was magnificent. Infantry showed great dash, endurance & steadiness under heavy shell & machine gun fire. RE did most plucky & useful work.' It also notes that 22nd Division were asked to send copies of the orders issued for the operation to Army Headquarters because the French, impressed by the raid, had requested them. It does not record that, of 300 men sent into action, 34 became casualties.

Turrall wrote about the action three times, but he also scribbled, in pencil, a letter to his parents the night before the raid.

Dear Mother & Father
Am in a show tomorrow night & hope to come off with honours if it is in my power. [Here a sentence scratched out.] My job tomorrow is a good one & we will be the last to leave the trenches. I haven't had cold feet yet & tomorrow I hope to ['bag' deleted] get a Boche. If you get this [two words crossed out] the bullet with my number on it will have been fired & you *must* take my last present of records in memory of me & enclosed copies of letters will explain all my accounts etc etc

Well au revoir & very best love
from your loving son
Guy

There are two brief notes apparently made by Turrall immediately after the raid and a longer piece produced later. The first of these read:

Before DORSALE Raid. Poor X's remark, his last cheery words to me, amid the trying shellfire, 'Come into the office, Turrall!' said with a laugh in the bare exposed hillside.

The railway up from Salonika into Serbia ran along the Vardar River through Karasuli, south of Macukovo, where a line branched north-east towards Lake Doiran. The town was an important supply depot and became the location of the Karasuli British Military Cemetery. The town is now called Polikastro. *(Alan Wakefield, Simon Moody and Andrew Whitmarsh)*

British dug-outs,
captioned 'Happy Valley'
by Guy Turrall. *(Turrall)*

A close-up of the Mess in 'Happy
Valley'; evidently the Officer's
Mess. *(Turrall)*

> After DORSALE Raid. Flatness. The events despite their rack & ruin seem not to come anywhere up to one's imagination. Alone dull day somewhere. Clouds moving low & fast overhead air damp & raining. Self shut in this arid slopes, alone amid nature & one's feelings of appreciation. How they depend tho' on one's stomach being fed.

The very incoherence of Turrall's note is moving and informative. His later writing is characteristically atmospheric and, perhaps, a little overdone. The transcription of his handwriting is not easy and uncertainties are shown with a question mark. Here he describes his experience on reaching the Dorsale:

> The smoke has lessened, disclosing, as far as night will allow, the nature of the ridge. The Dorsale is in fact a narrow promentory [*sic*], in places a mere razor edge, thrust

out from background masses, which one cannot see from here, & ending at last abruptly on three sides in yawning space. Shell blasted, shell heaped throughout its length, bare of any living thing, it resembles in its desolation some barren height of volcanic ash. A few steps to the N as one gazed into the pit of night; & here to the S, beyond this dark line of shattered parapets, night yawns again across the Ravin du Dorsale [?] dusky & vague & seeming in one's imagination to loom [?] the vague projecting mass of the Chapeau de Gendarme. Gough & I are now quite alone: our search has disclosed the emplacement or what our artillery has left of it. The retreating voices have sunk below us almost out of hearing. G urges me to come away. A cold air drifts over the crest. It is eerie here alone. We put the [Bangalore] torpedo in position & I hold it while G finds a splintered fragment for a prop. The prop fails; the torpedo with fuze & detonator falls into the trench. We pick them up & start to try again. It has begun to seem very still, unaccountably so; the demolished gaping trench straggles its emptiness away back rising unevenly in the direction that must be taking it swinging back towards the Dome. Suddenly a swift feeling comes that the enemy is sneaking back on us; further demolition of the emplacement would anyway be useless: clambering over the parapet we dip steeply down, blunder through matted wire & we are descending still amid a litter of stones & potholes & metal fragments of all descriptions. We have proceeded thus but 50 paces down the declivity when suddenly, from one of 3 figures below comes a savage 'Who goes there?' A revolver is thrust in our faces: it is Eyron [?] in the rear of the decending infantry believing himself to be the last. We recognize each other & in the same instant a ragged fire opens as from the trench above. The raid is over: the Bulgar is once more in possession. . . .

Another entry, possibly about the same raid, tells of Turrall's return to his own lines, accompanied by a comrade who did not manage to complete his mission.

Before us as we stumble away from Stoney Hill the forms of L & M sections are looming close & dark. In that very stillness seems to reign a menace & with the guilty feeling of one wrongly suspected we are as a raiding party alert for the first sign of betrayal. Along those hill sides, seen through a blue distant atmosphere of which the luminosity is momently increasing a gibbous waning moon had risen red & mournful. Hitchens labouring alongside beneath a disappointment as keen as the first high hopes alludes again bitterly to his misfortune. We begin to rise: our feet catch continually in rank unyielding grass: perspiring & breathless we become aware of a fatigue that in the heat of action was unknown. Straggled piquets of slope entanglements appear in silhouette: and now at last out of the dark rings harsh & near & threatening a challenge: out rings our reply. After a brief, expectant pause Hopkins is recognized: a solitary sentry admits us through the wire & we are home. Our way leads hence up a steep rocky shallow and unfamiliar sap that I imagine to be on or near Pitou Avancé & now, hot and breathless, we are on the bare open roof

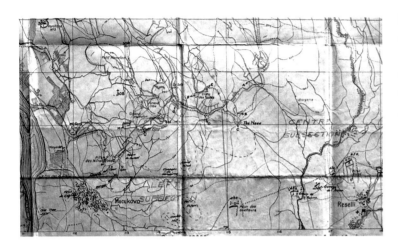

Detail from Turrall's 1:20,000 map, Sheet J, dated 10.9.16, showing the enemy front line on the Dorsale. He has marked the wire in front of the British positions with blue crosses at the foot of the map. The Chapeau de Gendarme, which he mentions in his account, is above the red crayoned word 'Left'. Cardiff and Bangor Ravines have been noted above the village of Macukovo, near the fold of the map. *(Turrall)*

of our front defences. H & I together enjoying cold air, gazing back on the dark expressionless gulf of no-man's-land & across to the dusky outlines of the enemy.

November brought a renewal of the fighting. On 10 November two Serbian divisions and some French Zouaves attacked in the bend of the Crna, capturing a thousand Germans and ten guns. Then the fog closed in and two days were lost before the assault could be pursued, but at 1500 hours on 13 November the fog lifted and another 600 Germans were captured. The Serbs were now well along the ridges east of the Crna and Monastir. The French struck at the trenches at Kenali again the next day and were again thrown back, but the Germans were coming to the conclusion that their allies, the Bulgars, were losing heart and were no longer to be relied on. The weather became colder. The Italians, to the left on the hills above Monastir, were suffering in blizzard conditions. Away to the east the British carried out yet another trench raid below the Dorsale. Lyster was incorrectly reported to have retired early and it was not until 1932 that he managed to have the record set straight. On 17 November the skies cleared and in the west the Allies moved forward through the snow. Hills fell to the east and west of Monastir. The town was untenable and the Germans and Bulgars began to pull out. On Sunday 19 November the Allies entered the town having carried out almost exactly the series of flanking attacks the unfortunate Cordonnier had suggested many days before. Raids and counter-raids continued for a while along the front but, by 11 December, winter had its hold and operations were suspended.

The fighting of 1916 had inflicted what were, compared to the slaughter on the Western Front, trivial casualties. Since August the Serbs had suffered the loss of 27,551 men killed, wounded or made prisoner. The French total came to 13,786 and the Russian to 1,701. Italian losses were 342 men. The British had battle casualties of 5,048 and hospital admissions of 29,594 malaria cases, of which 21,902 were evacuated. The Bulgar casualties came to some 52,000 men of whom 6,500 or so were captured, while the Germans had lost about 8,000 men including 1,500 made prisoner. The front had scarcely moved.

Nine

Balkan Victory

The winters of the Balkans were something of which the British had little or no idea. Collinson Owen made a journey to the Serbian headquarters, in the direction of Monastir, that winter. There were three of them in a Ford, well west of the Vardar by 1000 hours, and hoping to see the Serbs for lunch and be back in Salonika by teatime. They were told to take a particular road as it was in much the best condition. As they travelled through mud a foot deep, Collinson Owen wondered what the other road was like:

> In a very short time, in spite of fur gloves, my fingers are aching, and in spite of a rampart of sheepskin rug round the legs, my toes follow suit. The sky is a dull grey; the mists that hang over the mountains swirl aside occasionally to show their snow-covered tops. It must be dreadful manning the Serbian trenches up there.
>
> Three-quarters of an hour through the mud, which here and there is being flattened out by small gangs of native labourers shrouded in all manner of strange garments, and we come to the village of Subotsko. It is as typical a Balkan village of the larger size as could be found in the whole of the Peninsula. As we turn into the main broad street a minaret stands out, sharply silhouetted against a *massif* of the big mountain range beyond – a pleasing picture-postcard effect. A stream runs through the street, and of course there is deep mud everywhere. . . .
>
> A sharp turn out of the village and we have the wind behind us. The change is astonishing, and for a moment it is hard to believe that the blast is still blowing with the same strength and bitterness. But the grass and rushes at the roadside that flatten away before us show that there is no change except to ourselves, and even more so is this shown by the demeanour of the local Macedonians who come trotting along towards us on their donkeys to market. Some of them sit backwards on their miserable little mounts, preferring to meet the weather that way. Those of whose faces we get a peep as they sit humped and shrouded, have the appearance of men who are being frozen alive and detest the process. But in spite of their crying misery, they cannot help looking picturesque in their many-coloured garments. Doubtless they are quite unaware of it, and would be very angry if they knew of it, but to the Western eye they bring a touch of comfort into that cheerless landscape.

A little further and we come suddenly on one of those British camps of light motor transport which have done such great work on the Serbian front. There are, apparently, many hundreds of extremely small, black motor-cars all in action at the same moment, and the sudden impression, as we round the side of a hill, is of nothing so much as an ants' nest suddenly disturbed. Perhaps they are swarming or something. . . . And yet these strange little creatures, which have apparently popped out of holes in the ground, gave the Serbs the vital help that was necessary in their victory away up on Kaymakchalan, for no other transport could have done the same arduous work. . . .

The party arrived safely at the Serbian headquarters and had lunch and a long talk before it was time to turn for home.

We take the road again at last. The wind seems colder than ever. Half-an-hour or so along a good side-track and we strike the main Monastir Road – the chief artery for the French, Italians, Serbs, Greeks and Russians in this part of the world. There are about 45 miles [72 km] of it before we get to Salonica, and it is a bleak prospect even with the wind behind our backs. It is a flat and dreary countryside, largely marshland, and much of it subject to inundations. The mountains are behind us, and there is nothing worth looking at. . . .

Lieutenant Turrall was in the line east of the River Vardar, the sector in which he had been involved in the trench raids of the previous autumn. He wrote of the comforts he arranged to endure the winter.

This evening I have a hot bath inside the dugout. Outside it is cold & dark & a long unseen monotony of autumn cloud obscures the stars. Pitch dark it is but for the instant flicker of the very lights & cold & raw: But winter has its compensations. How snug & safe inside here the dugout is, if lit by an extravagance of two candles, & what a cozy glow the charcoal brazier is giving from the floor. Oh! That brazier what a precious thing it is! Just an old tin with perforated sides & wire handle – & how powerful that charcoal with its glowing sunshine gleaned on mountain glades to warm the cockles of the heart. One can almost greet the winter thus, that can give such genial compensation. I would not change this rough old dugout with the finest room I've ever seen: this is an honest fact. With its old bed in the corner (four by two [1.2 m × 0.6 m] & a wire mattress) & the old box with my dry sunwarmed clothes & souvenirs & books (Tennyson & Scott) what could one wish for more. The ceiling is of rusty corrugated iron, the floor of earth, the walls of earth and wooden uprights; yet in this subdued & rosy light they might be oak panelling, brown painted ceiling and Turkey carpets for all I know or care. Washing is strung across above to dry & see the glowing charcoal is spluttering forth a shower of sparks as if to say look this way. . . .

Outside the cold & very lights & watching trenches & the short sharp flash of bursting shell. Thud! Thud! Thud! Thud! – four dull air compressions in this warm interior – as old glen small sends four 18 pdrs over to the Dorsale or perhaps Les Muriers – even as you ponder on the contrast. Where in civil life could you find this contrast? Crash! Below there somewhere in this same ravine as an HE tears into its whining metallic fragments; but it sounds dull & powerless from here; & what care you? As if anything would hit this isolated spot. No rich man hearing the rain dashing on his study windows could experience the same security & warmth as one cannot fail to here. The very sounds of war seem as tho devised to emphasise the homeliness & warmth of your retreat. Tis a wonderful thing indeed, a DO in the line, & a careless happy life. When it is all over, if I get thro', I wonder how the old peaceful life will seem? Oh! I shall miss all <u>this</u>.

General Sarrail was obliged to consider wider issues than the comfort of a dug-out. The politicians and supreme commanders in France and Britain continued to blow hot and cold on the exploitation of the Allied bridgehead at Salonika. At a conference in

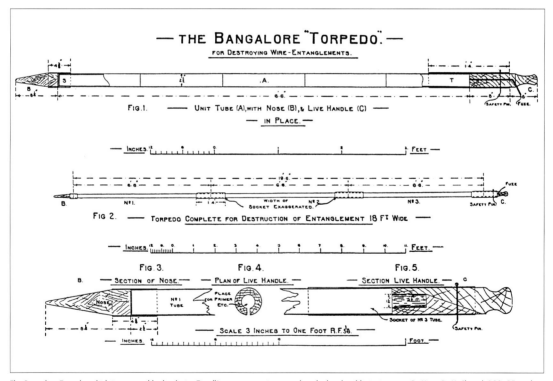

The Bangalore Torpedo, which is presumably the device Turrall's men were using, was described in detail by its inventor, Bt Major R. McClintock DSO, RE, in the *Royal Engineers Journal*, March 1913, from which this diagram comes. Sections of 6.5 ft (2 m) could be fixed together to destroy wider bands of barbed wire, as in Fig. 2. The 'Nose' fitted on one end to penetrate the entanglement and the 'Live Handle' contained the fuze to set it off. *(Stand To!, No. 66, January 2003)*

Rome on 5 January 1917 the French general managed to persuade the British Prime Minister, Lloyd George, to support the plan for an active front outside the confines of the Western Front and he returned to plan accordingly.

In the field the troops endured terrible weather. Rain reduced the eastern front on the Struma River to a wilderness of mud and water and the front itself was almost cut off from Salonika. The painfully built road over the hills was washed away in many places and what survived was not much use. The last part of the road, down from the hills, could not be used by motor transport at all and had to be serviced by mules. To the west snow compounded similar conditions. In spite of this the lethal repetition of trench raids and larger attacks went on. On 10 February the British raided the Petit Couronné near Doiran and took twenty-seven prisoners. In the southern bend of the Crna River where it turns north towards the Vardar the Germans launched an assault with flame-throwers on the Italians at Hill 1050 on 12 February. While much of the ground was recovered, the summit of the hill was not. On the night of 20/21 February the Piton des Mitrailleuses, north of Makucovo near the Vardar, was raided by the 11th Royal Welch Fusiliers together with men of Turrall's RE unit, 127th Field Company. Captain J.A. Warburton reported:

> . . . torpedoes . . . were not as effective as had been expected. The wire was all barbed very heavy, too thick for small wire cutters, with long barbs, about 2″ to 2½″ apart. When gaps were made torpedo party withdrew . . . Lt Chasserau & the 2 demolition parties then advanced with the Infantry search parties. . . . When the signal was given the sappers withdrew in good order. Lt Chasserau had been slightly wounded on entering the trenches. During the withdrawal he came across Lt Craig who had a broken leg. Lt Chasserau helped him as far as the other belt of wire, where he himself was wounded a second time. After talking the matter over Lt Chasserau crawled in alone. He got as far as the *Yellow House*, MAKACOVO but could get no further. He was picked up by a search party for the 11 RWF. . . .

The diary of the Fusiliers says that neither Lieutenant Craig nor Private Mee could be found and lists both of them as missing. The diary of the 7th South Wales Borderers reports that the Fusiliers brought back prisoners of 2nd Battalion, 59th Regiment who confirmed what they thought they knew of German dispositions. This is just another incident considered too trivial to be included in the official history books, but typical of the constant conflict that marked so-called quiet periods on the front.

Before the month was out Sarrail had formed his overall plan. The Bulgarian positions south of Monastir on the heights south-east of the valley of the Crna were to be smashed by the Serbs. Then they were to move north-east along the valley to occupy the Central Powers' supply centre at Gradsko, at the confluence of the river with the Vardar. The French and Italians were to attack to the west of the Serbs, and the British would go for the Belashitza (Belasica) Mountains north-east of Doiran and the eastern side of the Struma valley. The Western Front was, however, getting preference from the commanders back home and the Serbs were not that steady here. They were dealing with the problem of secret societies concerned with variations on the theme of 'Greater Serbia', a dominance of a broad swathe of the Balkans, which divided the loyalties of their soldiers. On 30 March the Serb Third Army was broken up and the constituent units distributed between the other two armies while suspect officers were interned or put on trial. They had also suffered from the premature uprising on 1 March of 8,000 Serb irregulars at Niš, far to the north, that would have been appropriate if undertaken at the same time as the intended attack further south. As it was more than 2,000 Serbs were executed by the 1st Bulgar Division.

British preparations went on apace, but the operations near Lake Ostrovo were jeopardized by the weather; snow fell. The attack was postponed from 15 to 26 April, with General Milne's British troops scheduled to go into action two days earlier. On the morning of the day of the attack intelligence was received that the Bulgars were bringing reinforcements into the area to be assaulted, but this was accepted as inevitable given the view the enemy enjoyed from the mountains of all British movements between Doiran and the sea. The area was, in fact, one of more than military importance to the Bulgars. Here the borders of Greece, Serbia and Bulgaria met and holding this position was politically and emotionally vital to them. In 1918, after the end of the war, Collinson Owen wrote of this location:

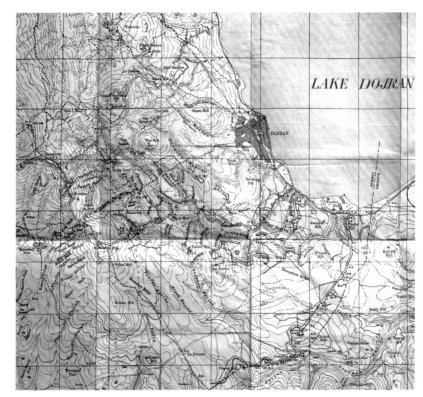

The 1:20,000 'Dojran', this version showing Bulgarian trenches in red as at 26 June 1917. The green dotted lines are Turrall's additions made about 11 September 1917 to show British wire and he used the purple lines to show British trenches. Jumeaux Ravine and the Petit Couronné are two squares south of Doiran town. Pip Ridge can be traced from P2 four squares west of Doiran on the edge of the sheet down along the dash and circle line marking the Greek–Serb boundary. *(Turrall)*

For weeks and months on end the same infantry manning our trenches up in these hills would wake to the same scene; the tumble of brown stony hills stretching for miles on either side; with the two main Bulgar bastions, Pip 2 and Grand Couronné, ever frowning down; with entrancing peeps down towards the ruined town of Doiran and the big circular lake, reflecting the most wonderful colours at early morning or at sunset; and beyond the lake the 5,000-feet [1,525-m] crests of the impressive Belashitza Range, standing up like a purple wall. On all the nearer hills, amid which the scene of the fighting was set, there was not a single tree, hardly a green blade of grass. Only in the ravines was there to be found occasional scrub clothing the steep sides. And yet with all their unvarying barrenness it was a magnificent prospect amidst which our men lived for so long; with a view that extended far beyond the shining ribbon of the Vardar on the west, away to the mountains overlooking Monastir; with the broad valley running eastwards from the lake, bounded by the Belashitza and the Krusha Balkan Hills and, behind, the flat plain as far as Janesh [aka Janes, now Metallikon], with the heights that enclose Salonica to be seen on clear days. One forgot the absence of trees after a time. The effect of light was so magical that there was beauty and to spare, of a wild untamed kind, even for English eyes.

The formidable terrain was clear for the British to see and the positions of the Bulgar defences were no secret either. The appreciation of the strength with which they were held and the artillery support available was less developed and of the thirty-three searchlights that the Bulgars had installed between the Vardar and Doiran there was no knowledge at all. On the British maps two ridges were marked, 'Pip' which

A contemporary picture of the terrain at Doiran from the eastern shore of the lake. Wooded Point juts into the water halfway to the town and Basing Hill rises just inland of the Point. Further left the dark cut of Jumeaux Ravine appears with the Petit Couronné to its right and Pip Ridge forming the skyline beyond. *(Turrall)*

comprised a series of summits labelled P1, P2 and so on, and a second ridge on which the hills were given the designations O6, O5, etc. The objectives for 24 April were, for the 22nd Division, the line from Pip Ridge to Hill 380 north of the remains of the villages of Krastali and Doldzeli, and for the 26th Division the line from Point O6, to the east of Hill 380, along the ridge to the lake, including the position the other side of Jumeaux Ravine the French had dubbed the Petit Couronné. While this was happening a diversionary attack would take place on the Crête des Mitrailleuses north of Macukovo near the Vardar River.

After the heaviest bombardment the slender artillery resources allowed, the British attack went in at 2145 hours in the hope that darkness would conceal their movements from Bulgar eyes. On the left the 7th South Wales Borderers of 22nd Division with 127th Field Company, Royal Engineers, was commanded by Lieutenant-Colonel J. Grimwood, who wrote in his report that they had moved off at 2030 hours and transferred to Dougal Ravine where, being ahead of time, they laid up for a while before entering the enemy wire at 2150 hours. About 20 minutes later they advanced towards Krastali but the Lewis gun opened up almost at once and red signal lights went up from the enemy side. Shell-fire came down at once about 150 yd (137 m) east of Rhyl Ravine and a searchlight was turned on them from the direction of Devedzili, a mile and a half (2.4 km) to the north-west. They called for artillery cover and it was given immediately. The officer commanding the raiding party, Major P. Gottwalz, wrote:

In face of heavy shell fire & in the light of the searchlight the party pushed for'd to Rhyl Ravine. By this time several men were wounded, & taking into consideration the shell fire, the searchlight, & the fact that it was impossible to

Doiran from the eastern shore today. The decline in goat-herding has allowed considerable tree growth. The old town is just below the dark rectangle of trees in the centre of the picture with the Grand Couronné, the highest peak, above to the right and the Petit Couronné, showing slightly darker than the hills beyond, above the rectangle to the left. *(Alan Wakefield, Simon Moody and Andrew Whitmarsh)*

come to close quarters with the enemy, I ordered withdrawal. Lieut MACPHERSON RFA was hit about this time, & died in a v. few minutes, 2/Lieut Whitehorn stayed with him till he died, & had the body put behind the rock in order that the Search Parties might find him easily. . . .

Grimwood noted: 'The death of Lt Macpherson RFA, the F.O.O. of the party is regretab. He was killed by a direct hit from a shell which blew off both his legs. When hit 2/Lieut Whitehorn 7SWB went up to him & he appeared in NO great pain, & merely remarked "I am killed", & died within a couple of minutes.' The commander of 67th Infantry Brigade was not as satisfied with the outcome as Grimwood, but as the object of the exercise had been to draw fire from other units, he accepted the situation without further comment.

The other units of the 67th succeeded in taking the hill called Mamelon, north of Doldzeli, and Hill 380 and held them against counter-attacks, but their tenure was made impossible by events to their right. The 7th Wiltshires and 10th Devonshires crossed the stream at the bottom of Jumeaux Ravine and clambered up the other side only to be caught in the beams of two searchlights suddenly switched on. Machine-gun and enfilading shell-fire did great damage. To their left the 7th Berkshires and the 11th Worcesters met a similar fate. Some small parties penetrated as far as the Bulgar trench lines on the Petit Couronné, but it soon became clear that they could not take the positions and the men were recalled. The British sustained 3,163 casualties and, although they comforted themselves with the fact that the 13th Manchesters and 8th King's Shropshire Light Infantry fought off the Bulgar counter-attacks with great effectiveness, no significant ground was gained. What was more, the adverse weather to the west continued and Sarrail cancelled the main attack which this sacrifice was intended to assist.

General Sarrail now decided to undertake the offensive early in May, but no longer as part of a scheme to invade Bulgaria, but merely to take Monastir. The British were again to move first, on 8 May, and the Serbs, Russians and French would begin their attack the next day. The British plan changed slightly, in that a thrust would be made along the side of the lake forward of Swindon Hill where Patty Ravine, at right angles to the line of Jumeaux, offered shelter from shelling instead of a trap. In addition a shorter, better targeted, barrage would precede the attack. At 2200 hours the infantry moved forward. Men of the 11th Scottish Rifles crossed Patty Ravine and

The bottom of Jumeaux Ravine, a picture annotated '19-5-17 Grotto'. *(Turrall)*

were swallowed up in fog. The poor visibility led their commanders to believe they had seen men up in the ridge and the 7th Oxford & Bucks Light Infantry and the Berkshires were sent forward to Jumeaux Ravine earlier than planned to exploit the apparent advantage. It was a mistake. In gaining the Petit Couronné they met not only the fire of the Bulgars but became embroiled in their own barrage. Shell-fire cut the telephone wires and fog and smoke prevented visual signalling, so what was actually happening was a mystery to commanders and front-line attackers alike. The 9th Gloucesters, unknown to anyone else, had seized a length of Bulgarian trench above Patty Ravine. The British hung on to some small gains the next day, but their positions were terribly exposed and insecure. The attack had been more successful than the previous attempt, but it was again necessary to withdraw, with about another 2,000 men added to the casualty lists.

On 9 May the Serbian Second Army attack went in on the Moglena Mountains and the French 16th Colonial Division, with the Russian Second Brigade on their right and the Italian 35th Division to their left, struck at the Crna loop. Valiant efforts brought some progress but much of what was gained was lost again by the end of the day. On

A view, possibly from Stable Hill but perhaps from the front line, of Pip Ridge and the Grand Couronné in the distance and the hump of La Tortue in the centre. *(Turrall)*

10 May the Italians and some of the French hurled themselves into action once more at 0800 hours. They found themselves alone, for half an hour earlier, with most of the French forces late in getting ready, the attack had been postponed. The Italians, isolated, withdrew with great loss and a lasting mistrust of French commanders. The Serbian attack stalled after the taking of their first objectives and the unfortunate troops huddled under a storm of German and Bulgarian counter-fire. The French artillery replied and there was British support as well, using two 4.5-in naval guns that had seen action in the Boer War. On 11 May the Sumadija Division was thrown into the battle and by 14 May had gained a hold on two spurs of the Dobropolje massif, but they could go no further.

On the Struma River, to the east, the British XVIth Corps under Lieutenant-General C.J. Briggs launched an attack on 15 May. The broad river valley contrasted markedly with the rocky mountain slopes on which the other battles of the Spring Offensive were fought. The flat, often marshy, country dotted with trees and standing crops was not entrenched like the Western Front, but scattered with dug-outs and look-outs, sparsely manned. The 10th (Irish) Division took its objectives almost without firing a shot and the 28th Division, although it ran into rather tougher resistance, also achieved what it was asked.

In all this the Serb First Army, to the left of the Second, remained still. Sarrail asked for action and got delay; until the heights had fallen to the Second Army the First was, it was said, too vulnerable. Then the Serbs asked for the whole campaign to be halted and Sarrail had no option but to agree. Some 14,000 men had become casualties for very little purpose. This failure was obscured by the massive disaster of the Chemin des Dames venture of General Robert Nivelle in France and Sarrail's position as commander-in-chief in this theatre was secure in consequence.

The front lapsed back into its usual state of boredom and occasional lethal activity. Guy Turrall spent a good deal of time fishing for carp in Dobrovica Ravine, south-east of Doiran, from which the stream runs down to the lake at Doiran Station. He even wrote an article for the *Field* magazine about the experience, though there is no record of it having been published. He was also involved with a raid on a Bulgarian dug-out north of P4½ which was reported by Major J.A. Warburton, his CO, on 22 June. Turrall used 20 lb of guncotton, 8 lb of ammonal, 11 detonators and 10 dry primers to blow up the dug-out and leave a hole like a mine crater in its place. He clearly enjoyed himself. A scribbled note says:

Get in through opening; & take good care to ensure that the sapper guard there cover every crevice before we inside flash the light on. The opening faces the enemy, & must confess it is a little unpleasant even tho there is a covering party to be thus alone & underground in No Man's Land with only a rabbit hole to get out by should anything be seen or suspected of us. . . . Shelling is going on outside all the time we are laying charges. – – –

Up in the trench, our cable laid to the detonator at my feet. Inf'y rather wondering at our strange weapon of destruction. Gough & I tense with

British tents, possibly in Dobrovica Ravine or perhaps in Vladaja Ravine. *(Turrall)*

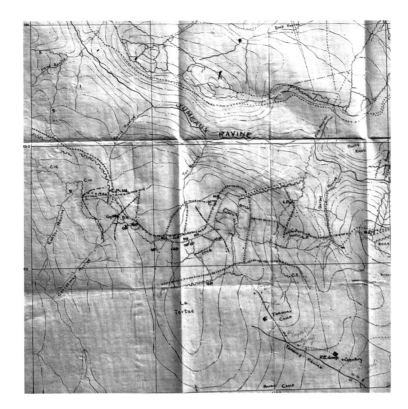

This detail of a plan, dated 8 July 1917, shows works in hand for the enhancement of British defences above Jumeaux Ravine undertaken by the Royal Engineers of 22nd Division. *(Turrall)*

expectation & trust that the current will be strong enough. All clear, all clear. With feelings much more concentrated than the next cast over a risen fish I shove the handle hard down with one great thump! – – – Hooray! She's gone. G & the boys agog with pleasure. Inf'y plainly impressed & admiring. . . . Truly we expect retaliation or worse after this bit of cheek under their very nose.

They lost no time in scampering back down the communication trench, gathering up their cable and other kit and heading back to their own trenches for a well-earned sleep.

The miseries of winter were long past, but the summer brought hazards of its own. Collinson Owen wrote of a journey he made from Salonika towards the Struma valley:

An unflecked sky of perfect, dazzling blue overhangs the world as we roll out of the little Greek village of Ano and begin the long descent down to the shore of the Gulf of Orfano. We are in a region where insect life abounds in astonishing quantities and where enormous thistles grow to eight feet high, so that the Scotsmen in the Brigade whose Headquarters we are just leaving feel strangely humble as they have never done before. It is pleasant to sit in the big open Vauxhall in which D.A.D.O.S. [Deputy Assistant Director of Ordnance Services] does his rounds for the Division. On such a hot day as this an enclosed Ford van would be like a stove. We pass odd soldiers on the road, and little strings of transport. All our men are wearing sun helmets, open shirts, and 'shorts'. They are really half naked, and their arms, knees, chests and faces are baked a dark brown. The shorts can be let down, and in the evening, when the mosquitoes begin to bite, are tucked into the puttees for protection.

It is a blazing, glaring, sizzling hot day – a Macedonian midsummer day at its very worst. Down on the sea shore we halt for a little while in a dump, where D.A.D.O.S. has something to do. The bare, ugly ground is red and baked as hard as a brick and the heat strikes off the corrugated iron sheds in waves. As one sits there in the car, inert, a wandering M.O. drops off his horse for a chat. I mention casually that both D.A.D.O.S. and myself had a bad night, in our little whitewashed rooms at the Brigade H.Q. owing to the exasperating attentions of innumerable tiny sand flies. 'Keep a watch on yourself,' says the M.O., 'there's a lot of sand-fly fever about.' As D.A.D.O.S. climbs back into the car the M.O. says he will take a photograph of us as a souvenir. 'Never know what may happen to you, you know,' he laughs. He tells us that our faces are in deep shadow. 'Take your helmets off.' We do, and the heat scorches our unprotected heads. The helmets are back again within five seconds, but it feels none too soon. . . .

It is comparatively cool among the trees of the Rendina Gorge, but soon we are out in the open at the beginning of the long valley in which lie the big lakes of Beshik and Langaza. There are large herds of goats spread across the narrow, bumpy track, which scatter with great fright and scuffling as we approach. And, before we have gone very far we become aware that, even with the wind of our passage to temper the heat, the early afternoon of mid-July is not the time to travel along the Langaza Valley. The wind that fans our faces has nothing fresh and invigorating in it, but is languid and stifling. The dust whirls up from our wheels and hangs in dense clouds behind us. With the exception of an occasional goatherd, there is not a soul to be seen. The earth is one monotonous dun khaki colour. The short, burnt grass is alive with

British lorries on the move in a cloud of dust that obscures the mountains just visible top left. (Turrall)

shrilling, leaping grasshoppers. Theirs is the predominant noise by day. The hoarse croaking of frogs fills the air at night. These are the two voices of Macedonia in summer time. . . .

A little further on we see, climbing a steep gradient, a long convoy of motor-lorries winding in and out, now in view, now disappearing. In a little while we catch it up. The gradient is very stiff, and we seem almost to creep past the rumbling monsters. The hillside is shaking as we go by. Ten – twenty of them, all nicely spaced out; shall we never get rid of them? The dust thickens the further we advance up the convoy, until we are in a dense cloud which gets in the eyes and mouth and tastes hot and nasty. We pass another ten of them, and still we are rolling up the hill alongside – a small atom engulfed in a whirl of dust and noise. Each driver as we pass turns a whitey-brown face towards us. The dust is caked thick on them all, encumbers their eyebrows, fills their ears, and gives their eyes a wild, bloodshot, strained look. Eight more lorries, their engines growling like monsters held by the throat, their vast bulks quivering and shaking as they thunder along. And then at last the officer's motor car ahead, which shows, thank Heaven, that we are at the head of the convoy at last. Thirty-eight three-ton lorries, grinding and forcing their way up a sun-baked mountain road, and stretching along nearly a mile of it! . . .

And in a little while we are on the last stretch of the hill road before it dips down into the Struma Valley. As we turn here and there we catch glimpses of a wonderful panorama, and in another moment the whole prospect is open to us; the wonderful wide sweep of the Struma Valley with the sun of early evening shining full on the great ranges of mountains held by the Bulgars; the river winding up to the gateway of the Rupel Pass, marvellously distinct in detail; Lake Tahinos to the East, and Seres shining white and clear twenty miles away. It is difficult to think that such a fair valley can have such an evil reputation, but such is the danger in the hot season of malaria that now, having learnt by experience, all our troops except a few advanced posts on the river line are withdrawn to the hills. The men left on the plain, who must have suffered there in this day of baking, steaming heat, are protected by face masks and gauntlets, so that they look like some mediaeval survival; and at night have to smear their hands and faces with thick, dark ointment. It is but a detail of our discomforts in our Watch on the Struma. Think of wearing face nets and gauntlets on such a day as this!

August was marked by an event that was not of the war, but came of an accident – fire. The northern quarter of the town, up towards the citadel and against the old city wall, was a warren of little streets and crammed-together houses with balconies which, as in medieval towns, almost touched across the street. They were baked dry in the summer heat, so when a cooking stove overturned, if that was indeed the cause, the flames took hold quickly. At first the news was limited to the few neighbours and the town's fire provision was a couple of mobile water-tanks which were brought by a

Part of a contemporary plan of the city of Salonika. The Citadel is on the east and the White Tower is on the harbourside in the south. The Rue Egnatia, emphasized by the tram line, runs from the north-west to the south-east. *(Turrall)*

gaggle of busy citizens as fast as possible, but it was a puny response to the crisis. People hurried from their houses, carrying what they could, and crammed the little streets. The military were at play, 18 August being a Saturday, but as evening came and the fire grew the two British fire engines that had arrived recently were brought into action. More soldiers joined the fire-fighting. It then became apparent that the newer part of town, south-west of the Rue Egnatia which ran from the Porte Vardar to the Arc de Triomphe, was threatened. At 2200 hours the fire crossed the road and the modern installations such as the gas pipes added to the blaze. The hotels, clubs and restaurants emptied and ships in the harbour evacuated people apparently trapped on the quayside. In the end it was Tuesday before the conflagration had been brought under control and by that time some 80,000 people were homeless though very few had been killed. With the houses had gone the places of entertainment and to all the privations of the campaign the prospect of a diet of exclusively do-it-yourself entertainment was added.

Lieutenant Lyster had been planning an outing with his brother, who was also with the army, as an interpreter:

On the 19 August 1917 my brother and I were granted two days leave to go and spend [time] with my Father in Salonica. We rode to Corps Hqs leaving our horses there to return to their respective units telling our grooms to return on the third day. We hitchhiked to Lembet and there heard for the first time that there was a fire in the town. This did not mean much to us so we waited until we could find something to take us into town. We did manage this but on arrival at the entrance we found a picket who asked for our passes. This we produced but the N.C.O.

The fire rages through the old town in Salonika on 18 August 1917. The White Tower is prominent on the quayside just left of centre. *(Turrall)*

said it was not valid. This we did not understand so asked to see an officer, this request was granted and the officer informed us that only passes dated by the C.I.C. were valid because the town was out of bounds to everyone. We explained our privileged position but to no avail. He told us to go back at once. This rather upset me so I suggested to my brother to take the bull by the horns and get into Salonica by the path over the hills. This he refused to do and we had to get back. What a journey we had. We must have changed cars a dozen times and walked miles and miles finishing up at Corps Hqs after midnight and having to wait until about 5 in the morning for our horses to turn up. The Salonica fire was a major disaster and hundreds of people were rendered homeless as a result. I also was hit by the fire. I had been collecting from Greek churches silver filigree works which had been presented to the churches as ex-votive. This apparently can be sold by the priest after a certain amount of years and the price was 1 drachmae per gram irrespective of the workmanship. Needless to say I picked on the best I could find. I had also put in the two boxes I had stored in the Ottoman Bank a beautiful wooden ikon given me by a monk from Mount Athos. This consisted of a piece of olive tree 4 by 4 inches. It had a centre picture consisting of the Mother and Child and on each side were three smaller engravings all depicting some phase of the life of Christ. In each picture one could even see the fingernails in the fingers. This complete work took the monk 6 years to do and he did the whole thing with an ordinary penknife. The two cases were sent to the Ottoman Bank and I had asked the Manager to insure them but he replied that as my Father and myself were bank's officials he would not charge me anything for warehousing but would place my two boxes amongst his private goods in his flat situated just above the

The area north of the White Tower after the fire. *(Turrall)*

Bank Offices. As a result of this kind gesture on his part I lost all my precious collection, for the goods in the vaults of the bank were not damaged whereas his flat was burnt completely.

General Sarrail's lack of aggressive zest during the summer was explained by his distraction with the situation to the south, in the Greek capital. When his Spring Offensive fizzled out he turned his attention to the unsatisfactory relationship with the Greek monarchy which appeared to be supportive of the Central Powers. It also prevented overland passage to the Allies so that men and *matériel* had to run the gauntlet of enemy submarines around the Greek peninsula in order to reach Salonika. A change of government in France gave Sarrail the authority he desired to resolve the problem. Charles Jonnart was sent as Allied High Commissioner to Athens to give King Constantine an ultimatum – he was to cease ruling as an absolute monarch. The once and future Prime Minister, Eleutherios Venizelos, wanted a reconciliation with the monarchy, but this could not be achieved with Constantine in place. The King was forced to abdicate and his second son, Alexander, came to the throne and Venizelos headed the government once more. As a result Greek troops were to join the Allies' forces.

Another distraction thrust itself to the fore over the problem of leave for the troops. It had been the case that the French had no home leave, but changes within France bestowed rights that the Army of the Orient felt they should share. Given the journey time the long sea voyage required, this was not practical for half the army would be absent from the front at all times. The French 57th Division, which had been here since October 1915, was the source of trouble. A number of regiments mutinied, demanding home leave. They were, apart from a few dozen men, persuaded to return to their duties. The fall of Constantine meant that the overland route was now available and, only a week after the mutineers had abandoned their protest, the first batch of Frenchmen arrived in Salonika by the new route.

As autumn approached there was little cause for cheerfulness among the Allies on the Salonika front. The British had lost two divisions and a number of guns to the demands of the Palestine operations and the remaining units were weakened by sickness and fatigue. Guy Turrall, who had spent three weeks in hospital in April, was invalided home on 18 November. His Company commander had reported 'much recurrent fever' among his men in the previous month, but the precise nature of Turrall's illness is not stated in the Company Diary nor does he mention it in his notes or letters. The British had 21,434 men in hospital on 16 October. The French had been forced to merge formations to compensate for the men on home leave. The Serbs and the Russians were unreliable, the former because of political problems in the army and the latter because of what was happening at home. Sarrail made some progress on the Albanian front, but the impact on Salonika was negligible, other than to stabilize the adjoining flank.

In the Struma valley the autumn was marked by the descent of the 27th Division from the hills where they had spent the summer to avoid malaria. On the night of 13/14 October they took Homondos, south-west of Seres, and two adjacent villages to establish their winter line. They killed 79 Bulgars and captured 74, as well as taking 3 machine-guns. On 25 October they took another 3 villages east of the river and took more than 100 Bulgars prisoner, but the main force escaped them.

In France the government changed again and with it Sarrail's star went into swift decline. He was recalled and General Marie Louis Adolphe Guillaumat was put in his place. The two men did not even meet and the new commander-in-chief arrived in Salonika on 22 December carrying more precise instructions from France than Sarrail had received. The Allied Armies of Greece, a new name for them, were to be a force based on Greece as a whole, not just Salonika. They were to prevent the Central Powers from occupying the country and were to hold their existing lines. Guillaumat was charged with consolidating the defensive lines immediately and, for the longer term, with planning an offensive, bringing into play the Greek forces. It was a positive approach to the coming year. The campaign in Palestine was going well as a result of which a battery of 8-in howitzers was released for Salonika and four batteries of 6-in howitzers lost to the Middle East were returned. This gave some hope of the British being able to make an impression on the Bulgar fortifications above Doiran. The Greek Army was re-formed and became a significant part of the Allied force, and the Serbs recruited Croatian and Bosnian troops captured from the Austrians by the Russians. The Serb Volunteers, who began to arrive at the end of March, numbered some 18,000 men.

SURVEY C9? R.E. B.S.F N?.364

A card made for Christmas 1917 did little to dispel the impression of leisure on the Salonika front held by people at home. *(Turrall)*

The British troops spent their time building defences, digging trenches and getting bored. Lieutenant Lyster found some entertainment in the activities of the balloonists:

That Spring an observation balloon had appeared on our front. It was actually on the 28th Divisional front but could be seen quite clearly from our Headquarters. The rumour went round and it proved correct that the Bulgars had sent a message telling us that on a certain Sunday a plane would come and destroy it. True to their word on Sunday at about 11 in the morning a Boche plane appeared suddenly and as suddenly fired on the balloon which came down in flames whilst the observer came down slower in his parachute. Later in the week another message was sent over asking us to put up the second one when it would be brought down at the same time on Sunday. To us this meant a picnic for we took some food and drinks with us and went back to a small hill behind our camp to watch proceedings. True to his word the German pilot appeared once more at 11 and brought down again the balloon. We were furious with our A.A. for they started firing only after the German plane was almost out of sight. A third message was sent over telling us this time that they knew we had a third balloon in Salonica and that the German pilot would be delighted to burn that one too on the following Sunday. This was too good to be true so once more we all went to our picnic lunch and started scanning the sky at about 10.45. It was a perfect day without a cloud anywhere. We thought that this time our A.A. would try and do better, yet hoping in a way that the German might get away with it, for his pluck and audacity. All of a sudden we all shouted 'There he is, there he is, shoot, for God's sake shoot' but not a single gun fired, the plane dived straight for the balloon and his tracer bullets could be seen piercing the sausage, when all of a sudden a terrific bang took place and one of the wings of the plane was separated from the rest of the body and the two pieces fell with a crash to the ground. We almost all said 'Dirty'. What had actually happened was that four different sighting posts had been prepared round the balloon, which this time did not carry an observer but a charge of explosive matter and when the four posts pressed a button a spark set the explosives on fire and this blew the plane almost to bits. The body of the German pilot was buried with full military honours and flowers were placed on the grave. Photos were taken of the proceedings and the grave and copies flown and dropped over the Bulgar lines. As a punishment for this sort of fraternising the Squadron of R.A.F. who did all this was sent to the Western Front.

There were other innocent amusements on offer.

Life was now getting boring and the Staff had to entertain the troops. This took the form of travelling theatrical parties and some of these were really very good. The 27th and 28th Divisional Hqs had their own shows and so had the 738 M.T.Co who had a very good show called 'Slip your Clutch'. Our Division ran races, mostly riding, whereas our Brigade organised a sports meeting when our regulars were very upset by being beaten by our Territorial Unit. We also had

On his trip back to England, Turrall saw and photographed the unique British submarine monitor, *M1*, in Valetta, Malta. *(Turrall)*

A halt on the long rail journey back to Salonika. *(Turrall)*

a polo ground. Our Brigadier Gen. Widdrington asked me why I did not take part seeing that my mare was a typical polo pony. I told him that she had a mouth like a steel trap and that no one could ride her with spurs. He laughed and asked to use her the next day. I agreed and rode over to the polo field. I handed Nan to the Brigadier who as soon as he was on Nan must have touched her with his spurs for the last we saw of them for some time was a lot of dust disappearing into the distance. The game was nearly over when they returned, the Brigadier very angry and he shouted to me, 'You better have her shot for she is a bitch.' I liked Nan and she liked me, for we understood one another.

Guy Turrall was fully recovered from his illness. Now he was under orders to embark at 1400 hours on 1 May. He wrote to his parents with details of the arrangements for the journey:

The railway route lies as follows:–
(1)   Cherbourg. Camp in tents.
(2)   St Germain (518 miles). Near Lyon. Train halts 24 hours. Camp in tents.

(3)   Faenza (961 miles). Train halts 12 hours. Camp in tents.

(4)   Taranto (1,446 miles). Camp in tents.

Officers are recommended to provide themselves with tea or lunch baskets. Rations issued on the train consist of bully beef, bread, tea, butter and cheese. Boiling water is provided at Halte Repas stations. Officers are recommended to supplement rations by purchasing stores at the Expeditionary Force canteen at Cherbourg, also to lay in a stock of mineral water. A spirit stove & small folding table are found very useful. Keep a rug & pillow for use in the train. . . . The journey to Taranto takes about 5 (FIVE) days.

After Taranto I understand that we cut across the Adriatic in about ½ day & thence up into the mountains of 'Old Greece' where we again encamp for a night, & thence again eastward. . . .

Lyster was to make this same round trip in May and June on leave.

During the spring and summer the British were involved in a number of actions of modest size. On 14 April an Anglo-Greek force crossed the Struma and held seven villages for a short time. The Bulgars counter-attacked with vigour and caught the Cheshire Regiment in the open, inflicting heavy casualties. The Rifle Brigade was similarly in the open during their withdrawal and suffered accordingly. The British casualties numbered 349 killed, wounded or missing and the Greeks lost half of their 33 dead to premature grenade explosions. On 18 April the British undertook a 4-day artillery harassment of the line at Doiran, backed by 3 trench raids, suffering 136 casualties against a Bulgar loss of about 100.

A much more substantial assault was planned to secure Skra di Legen, a remote Bulgarian border stronghold some 10 miles (16 km) west of Gjevgjeli on the River Vardar. The ridge of the mountain top runs from north to south, covering the frontier east and west with enfilading firepower, and thus it secured the Bulgarian positions on both sides. The task of taking it was given to the Greeks using their Crete and Archipelago Divisions. In spite of the difficulties caused by poor road and rail access, heavy guns were moved up to the area around the village of Ljumnica and guns on either side of the intended objective were made ready. On 28 May barrages fell on Bulgarian positions all along the front line, disguising the sector in which the attack would take place. At 0455 hours on 30 May the Greeks went into action against the Bulgar 49th Division on Skra di Legen. At the cost of 2,659 casualties they cut the defenders to ribbons. Counter-attacks failed. Guillaumat relieved the Greeks quickly and sent French troops to hold the position, but no further efforts were made by the Bulgars to regain the crucial position.

Just as success roused enthusiasm in the Greek population the Allies suffered losses from another cause. The startling advances made by the German storm-troop attacks in France triggered the recall of 20,000 British and French troops from Salonika to stiffen the Western Front. Guillaumat was also recalled and General Louis Franchet d'Esperey was sent out to replace him. D'Esperey was an aggressive fellow and had

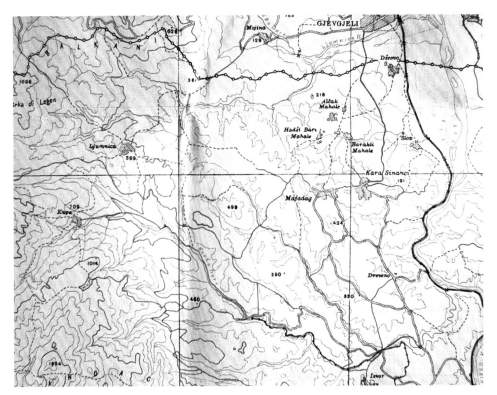

Detail from the Vardar valley 1:100,000 map of 12 September 1918, showing Skra di Legen west of Gjevgjeli. The railway from the south-east swings round Izvor and then stops. From there roads, shown by continuous lines, straggle north-west but the final access to Ljumnica is by track, indicated by dotted lines. *(Turrall)*

lost his post in France because of his unsuitability for the defensive battle that had been required in the spring of 1918. Here he inherited the foundation of an excellent plan for a major assault on the Bulgarian and German Armies, an enterprise much better suited to his temperament and abilities. He threw himself into the task, mastering every detail and also getting out into the field frequently to make swift visits to his men. In particular he forged a sound relationship with the Serbian leader, or Voïvode, Zivojin Mišić (Mishitch). On 29 June the French and Serbian generals met, together with Prince-Regent Alexander of Serbia, the future King of Yugoslavia, and rode slowly up the height of the Floka, the mountain north of the hard-won Kaymakcalan. From this height they could see the mountains along the border: Sokol, Dobropolje, Vetrenik and Kozyak. The Serbs assured the new commander that they could break through here. The plan was agreed. There would be strong assaults elsewhere to prevent reinforcements being moved to hold the Serbs, but this was to be the main thrust. The deliberations of the national leaders in France cast doubt on the future of the scheme for a while, but eventually, and in part because of American support, it was accepted.

In due course two coded signals were sent out. From the Serbian leader early in the morning of 14 September, *Mettez en route quatorze officiers et huit soldats* ('Send fourteen officers and eight soldiers'), confirming that 14 September at 0800 hours the artillery bombardment would commence. The barrage was fired by 650 guns on a line

from Monastir to the Vardar, but with the Sokol to Vetrenik sector taking the heaviest
punishment. The firing went on all morning, paused in the afternoon and then began
again. The German commanders had assumed that the main attack would come on the
River Crna with a diversionary action on the Vardar, and so far there was no evidence
that they were wrong; indeed, another battalion was moved down towards Monastir
in readiness for the expected strike. The Germans and Bulgars could do nothing but
shelter from the shell-storm and wait. A report came in of the Bulgarian
30th Regiment running into a French force on Dobropolje late that night, but when
the real assault began at 0530 on 15 September, the defenders of Sokol, Vetrenik and
Dobropolje were all surprised. The fighting was extremely tough. Although the largest
artillery concentration this front had seen had been brought to bear, the rock-fast
emplacements of the German and Bulgarian machine-guns had survived and the
mountain guns were unharmed.

The Serbian Sumadija Division struggled up the Vetrenik against such hazards, but
managed to secure the mountain by early afternoon. The French 17th Colonial
Division battled against positions on the heights between Vetrenik and Dobropolje for
much of the day and it finally fell to them when the Serbs had taken Vetrenik and
joined them. Against the emplacements on Dobropolje the French made their first use
of flame-throwers which quickly gave them the mountain. Sokol fell after dark and the
Serb Volunteers, constituted as the Yugoslav Division, were in a position to assault
Kozyak the next morning. It took them the whole day to conquer the Bulgars there,
and even then they could not take the entire position because the 13th Saxon Jäger

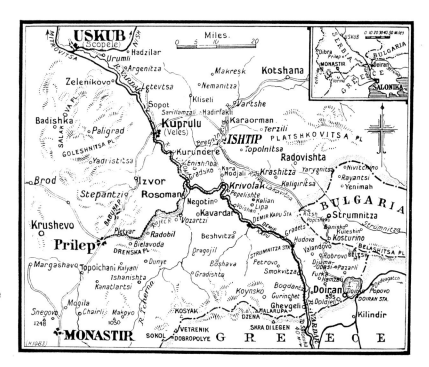

Map of the territory assaulted by the
Allies in September and October
1918. (from The Times History of
the War)

Battalion was hurried up to hold the line. The Germans were forced to recognize that the Bulgars were no longer the solid force they once had been. By 17 September, with the Allies now some 6 miles (9.6 km) inside their lines on a front of 20 miles (32 km), they were forced to fall back.

The British contribution, that of holding the crack Bulgarian 9th Division in place on the heights above Lake Doiran, commenced on 18 September. Guy Turrall, now acting Captain and commanding 99th Field Company, Royal Engineers, noted the Order of the Day from the commander of the 22nd Division, Major-General J. Duncan.

I have just come from an interview with the Commander in Chief, who has informed me that the Franco-Serbian Forces have entirely broken through the whole of the Bulgarian defences on a front of 15 miles, & are pressing towards the VARDAR, to our north west.

The Bulgars opposed to them are in full retreat, 4,000 prisoners & 50 guns have already been taken. Aeroplanes report sings of disorganization everywhere behind the Bulgar Army.

The success of the whole combined operation now depends entirely on our own attack. The eyes of the French & Serbians are on us, they are anxiously awaiting our success.

The honour of the British Army is in the hands of the 22nd Division & the gallant 77th Brigade & 3rd Greek Regiment attached to us. Everything depends on us. We must, & will succeed. Success is in the air – on every front the Allied Armies are driving back the enemy. At all costs we must do likewise. Good luck to you in your attack.

Stirring stuff, indeed, and to enthuse the men for another assault on the Grand Couronné it was needed. The axis of the attack was not the same as it had been the previous year and perhaps the change engendered optimism. On the other hand all the British divisions were seriously undermanned as the result of illness and many of those present were either not fully recovered from their ailments or were about to succumb; the spirit was willing enough, but the flesh was weak. The general direction of the assault was towards the north-west. Along the lakeside, leaving the town of Doiran on the right, the Greek Seres Division was to push forward as far as possible. On the extreme westerly flank, beyond Pip Ridge, the 26th Division would support the main attack by demonstrating against the line running towards the Vardar. On the north-eastern side of the lake the Crete Division, supported by the 28th, would attempt to outflank the Bulgarian line. The main attack, in the centre, was divided into three sectors. The Left Brigade, the 66th of the 22nd Division, was to attack Pip Ridge. The Centre was the responsibility of the Greek 2nd Regiment, heading for the Sugar Loaf, the Tongue and the Plume to gain position on the western flank of the Grand Couronné. The Right Brigade, the 67th, had to take O.6 first, and then fight their way up to the Grand Couronné itself.

Turrall thought well of the Greeks attached to his division:

A Bde of the Greek Seres Div'n has come to reinforce us & is bivouacked in the Morraine camp of the 9th Border Regt. Am detailed as liaison officer & to escort them to the various parts of the trenches. Arrive at Greek Colonel's D.O. at the same moment as a distinguished brilliant haughty Staff Officer from Corps Hq. The Greek Col X is eager to know if we have G Couronné; his persistent enquiries concerning it are met with evasive replies that at least do not reveal the truth that at this moment weighs like lead upon us all. . . . Am much impressed by the Greek who is obviously a man of character & would not brook foolery. He & his officers are all keen as blazes to be up and doing . . . the whole crowd impress me very much as <u>men</u>. Officers devouring new maps.

In fine, sunny weather the artillery pounded away at the Bulgar positions in the mountains and at 0508 on 18 September it concentrated on the enemy front line. The 67th Brigade Diary records:

. . . at 0511 the 11 Welch attacked & took the FANG, O.6 being taken by the 11 RWF [Royal Welch Fusiliers] after stiff hand to hand fighting at 0630. At 0628 hrs the 7 SWB [South Wales Borderers] attacked the ROCKIES having come along the FEATHER up to time & with few casualties. At the ROCKIES however they came under a terrific cross fire from machine Guns from both flanks which caused them very heavy casualties. The survivors had to withdraw leaving many wounded, including Lt.Col. BURGESS.

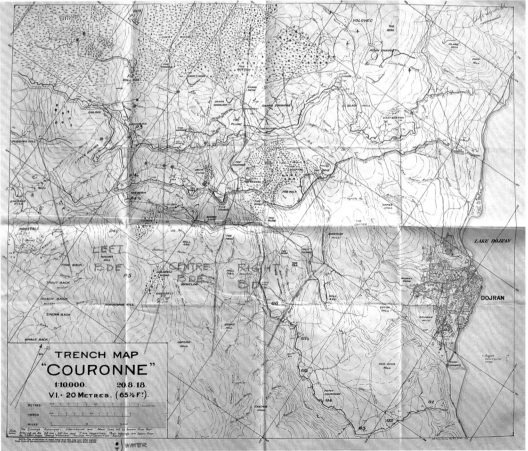

The specially prepared Couronné trench map of 20 August 1918, marked up to show the sectors to be attacked by the Left, Centre and Right Brigades. *(Turrall)*

The Bulgarian view of the Doiran front. From the height of the Grand Couronné, from which this picture was taken after their retreat, the defenders could see for many miles. The scale of the challenge to the attackers is clear. The town of Doiran is on the left and Pip Ridge on the right. *(Turrall)*

A modern view of Lake Doiran from P4 on Pip Ridge, showing Jumeaux Ravine between the Petit Couronné on the left and La Tortue on the right, all to the right of the paler green bushes in the centre. *(Alan Wakefield, Simon Moody and Andrew Whitmarsh)*

Part of the problem was the fire coming from Pip Ridge. The 12th Cheshires had assaulted P4½ from Jackson Ravine with reasonable success when suddenly a huge explosion caused many casualties. They regrouped and pressed on against growing machine-gun fire and mortar fire from P4, which was crossed by the Bulgarian trench line. Eventually they got though the line and B and C Companies advanced towards P3. They were now enfiladed by machine-gun fire from the spur of Little Dolina as well as fired upon by the Bulgarian front-line trench behind them. The 9th South Lancashires came on behind them no less courageously and were also cut down. The 8th King's Shropshire Light Infantry took up the strain, but now heavy Bulgar counter-attacks rolled them back and off Pip Ridge. The Brigade had lost 37 officers and 800 men in this fight, about two-thirds of its strength. The initial success of the 3rd Greeks on their right in taking the Sugar Loaf on the front line and the Plume and the Warren on the second line was undermined by the failure on Pip Ridge. Supported by fire from there the Bulgars managed to oust the Greeks and force them back to their starting place.

On the right the Seres Division, together with the 2nd King's Own Regiment, outflanked the Petit Couronné left and right and poured forward to seize Hill 340, Teton Hill and Doiran Hill. Soon after 0900 hours they moved on to take the main line positions of the Orb and the Hilt, but the East Bastion, to their right, could still bring fire to bear on the Welsh battalions of the 67th Brigade. The Greeks could not hold on and at 1050 hours Divisional HQ received a message that they were retiring to Hill 340.

The Crete Division on the other side of the lake advanced with enthusiasm. Lieutenant Lyster, back from leave in England, later wrote:

At last we had made all preparation for the BIG ADVANCE. My assignment was to be the liaison officer with the Greek corps on our left. To this effect I went over to Greek Hqs and was agreeably surprised to find as G.O.C. my old friend General Yoannou, who was also pleased to see me as I could speak Greek whereas no one else he had seen so far could do so. We worked out details and all seemed to be ready for a perfect collaboration. Things did not work out as smoothly as all that however. After the preliminary bombardment which was the heaviest I had ever heard the order to attack arrived and off I went on my mare to take up my position on our extreme left. I easily got contact with the Greeks and reported this back to Corps through Division. The Bulgars seem to have given up pretty soon for I suddenly found that instead of being in touch with the Front line Greeks I was with their reserves. I reported this at once and was told to keep in touch specially with the front units. In trying to do this I almost lost touch with my British units and soon I found a huge gap between the two forces. The Greeks were pushing on whereas we were advancing cautiously. The gap having increased I again wired corps about this afraid that Johny Bulgar might make a sudden attack between both forces. I got a reply ordering me to tell Yoannou to hold back and not advance any more until we caught him up. I never contacted him personally but got a message through to him and he replied that if we could not march HIS troops could and he would not stop until he reached Sofia for which he was making. Then I had a shock, I was ordered to return at once as I was urgently wanted at G.H.Q. Now that was a blow. But an order is an order and I had to comply. I rode back to Division where I was again told that I had to report to G.H.Q.

What Lyster was wanted for he never found out, for on the way back he lost consciousness and woke two days later to find himself in hospital. The attack itself succeeded in overcoming the village of Akindzali but came under heavy artillery fire and the dry fields caught alight; the troops were withdrawn.

The gains for the day had been small and the losses high; an outcome that surprised nobody. All had shared Turrall's fears, and all had fought magnificently none the less. The Bulgarian 9th Division was still in place, giving no thought to supporting their comrades who were folding under Serbian and French pressure beyond the Vardar, so perhaps the price was worth paying. The Diary of the 11th Battalion the Welch Regiment for 18 September reads, in its entirety: 'On the 18th the Bn went into action 15 officers & 409 ORs [Other Ranks] strong. Objectives were reached but by the evening of the 19th only 1 officer (the C.O.) & 40 ORs remained of those who went into action.' The 11th Royal Welch Fusiliers sent 20 officers, 1 Medical Officer and 480 other ranks into action on 18 September and ended the day with 3 officers and 100 men unwounded.

The next day the attacks were resumed with no greater success. New troops were thrown into the fight but the 12th Argyll & Sutherland Highlanders, 8th Royal Scots Fusiliers and 11th Scottish Rifles achieved no more than their comrades had the day before and, what was worse, some fell victim to their own artillery fire. The Zouaves were ordered to take Pip Ridge from the east and made the attempt in spite of the incredible optimism of the plan. They had no chance of success and this explains the Bulgar flanking fire on the Scots as they gained positions in the front-line fortifications through the Tongue and the Hilt. The 9th East Lancs were sent to the aid of the Zouaves with a similar outcome. The 9th King's Own (Royal Lancasters) never got the message cancelling their assault on Pip Ridge and they got as far as P4 where they ran into solid and effective resistance. By the end of the day the British casualties had risen to 3,871 killed, wounded and missing; not many by the standards of the insatiable Western Front, but when set alongside their 23,762 battle casualties for the whole Macedonian campaign from 1915 to 1918 the impact is clear.

The morning of 20 September was quiet. Two aircraft of 47 Squadron, RAF reported in the late morning. The roads to the rear of the Bulgarian line through Rabrovo (Robrovo) and Kosturino to Strumica (Strumnitza) were thronged with troops marching north. The French and Serbs to the west had broken the enemy line and reached as far as their supply centre at Gradsko; the whole position of the Central Powers was unstable and they were forced to withdraw. The RAF harried the Bulgars mercilessly. On 21 September 45 aircraft attacked the Bulgarian columns as they squeezed through the Kosturino defile, bombing and machine-gunning,

The view from Hill 340, an objective of the Seres Division, towards the Grand Couronné, right, and Pip Ridge, left. *(Alan Wakefield, Simon Moody and Andrew Whitmarsh)*

The remains of Bulgarian second-line trenches on Hill 340. The Grand Couronné is beyond. *(Alan Wakefield, Simon Moody and Andrew Whitmarsh)*

The remains of a Bulgarian machine-gun bunker on Hill 340. *(Alan Wakefield, Simon Moody and Andrew Whitmarsh)*

killing more than 700 and destroying over 300 wagons. To the west Franchet d'Espery gave the cavalry their head at last: the 1st and 4th Chasseurs d'Afrique went into action with a section of armoured cars and six squadrons of Moroccan Spahis. They were at Prilep, north of Monastir, by 1300 hours on 23 September and moved on the Babuna Pass the next day. Here the Serbs had made a stand when they were retreating three years earlier and resistance was expected. In the early hours of 25 September the Spahis made their cautious climb but met no enemy until the very summit. They let the Serbian infantry take up the fight along with the armoured cars and took to the hills, the Spahis acting as rearguards. On 28 September, with the Spahis now rejoined, the Chasseurs descended towards the valley of the Vardar and arrived at the river just 7 miles (11 km) south of Uskub (Skopje). At 0900 on 29 September they entered the town, the remaining German troops making their escape on their armoured train.

To the east the British and Greek troops were advancing also. On 25 September the Derbyshire Yeomanry entered Bulgaria near Kusturino with the 79th Infantry Brigade close behind. The next day the Yeomanry encountered a huge German staff car flying a white flag; the Bulgars were seeking an armistice. Hostilities ceased at noon on 30 September.

That was not the end of the campaign as far as the British were concerned. To the east was another enemy, Turkey. On 4 November Captain Turrall wrote to his mother:

Sarigol British Military Cemetery, to the rear of the Doiran front at a place now called Kristoni. *(Alan Wakefield, Simon Moody and Andrew Whitmarsh)*

. . . Firstly no cake etc. thank you as I may be ANYWHERE by XMAS! Desperate fighting on both sides marked the final days of action on the P Ridge & if the tale is ever told the 22nd Division will be a respected name. Since those days much has happened. . . .

My Company & another were the only two of the English forces to march <u>on foot</u> from SERBIA thro MACEDONIA & BULGARIA to the TURKISH frontier at DEDE AGHATCH, & I think you will agree it wasn't a bad effort. From here we can see SAMOTHRACE – the island which we used to see from GALLIPOLI. . . .

The Central Powers seem to be rapidly disintegrating now, thank goodness! The date of my own exit from the army is what I must wish to know; may it be very soon. . . .

Hoskins [Turrall's driver] is in hospital with malaria & dysentry: his brother died out here the other day which is very sad as he had never had leave & was a robust specimen of humanity until he got a sudden & fatal dose of Spanish 'Flu.

Hoskins, it is good to know, survived his illness, for among Turrall's papers is a copy of a letter he wrote some four years later to his former driver to congratulate him on his wedding. It was not necessary for Turrall or any of his comrades to fight on the Turkish front for the armistice had been signed on 30 October. On 8 December an Allied Military Administration was set up in Constantinople (Istanbul) and there Lyster was to serve for some time to come, for his mastery of languages included Turkish.

BIBLIOGRAPHY

UNPUBLISHED

The Memoirs of Henry N. Lyster MBE, MC
The papers, notes and letters of R. Guy Turrall DSO, MC

PUBLISHED

Anon. *American Armies and Battlefields in Europe*, Washington, DC, US Government Printing Office, 1938

Anon. *The Story of the 91st Division*, San Mateo, Calif., privately published, 1919

Anon. *The War in Italy, Vols I–III*, Milan, Fratelli Treves, 1916

Anon. *The Yser and the Belgian Coast*, Clemont-Ferrand, Michelin, 1920

Ashurst, George. *My Bit: A Lancashire Fusilier at War 1914–1918*, Richard Holmes (ed.), Marlborough, Crowood Press, 1987

Banks, Arthur. *A Military Atlas of the First World War*, London, Heinemann Educational Books, 1975 and Leo Cooper, 1989

Bennett, Geoffrey. *Naval Battles of the First World War*, London, Batsford, 1968 and Penguin, 2001

Butcher, Bob. 'The Battle of the Silver Helmets', *Stand To!*, 63, January 2002

Carpenter, Alfred F.B. *The Blocking of Zeebrugge*, London, Herbert Jenkins, 1921

Coombs, Rose E.B. *Before Endeavours Fade*, London, After the Battle, 1994

Durlewanger, Armand. *Sites Militaires en Alsace*, Strasbourg, La Nuée Bleu/DNA, 1991

——. *The Linge 1915*, M.A. Cooper (trans.), Ingersheim-Colmar, Editions SAEP, 1993

Edmonds, Sir James E. *Military Operations, France and Belgium, 1914*, London, Macmillan, 1929

Gray, Randal with Argyle, Christopher. *Chronicle of the First World War, Vol. I: 1914–1916*, New York, Oxford and Sydney, Facts on File, 1990; *Vol. II: 1917–1921*, New York, Oxford and Sydney, Facts on File, 1991

Hammerton, Sir J.A. (ed.). *A Popular History of the Great War, Vol. I, The First Phase: 1914*, London, Fleetway House, 1933; *Vol. V, The Year of Victory: 1918*, London, Fleetway House, 1933

Holt, Tonie and Valmai. *Battlefields of the First World War*, London, Pavilion, 1993

Innes, T.A. and Castle, Ivor (eds). *Covenants with Death*, London, Daily Express Publications, 1934

Keegan, John. *The First World War*, London, Hutchinson, 1998

Le Goffic, Charles. *Dixmude: The Epic of the French Marines*, Florence Simmonds (trans.), London, William Heinemann, 1916

Livesey, Anthony. *The Viking Atlas of World War I*, London, Viking, 1994

Malins, Geoffrey. *How I Filmed the War*, London, Herbert Jenkins, 1920

Marix Evans, Martin (ed.). *Retreat Hell! We Just Got Here! – The AEF in France 1917–1918*, Oxford, Osprey, 1998

——. *American Voices of World War I*, London and Chicago, Fitzroy Dearborn, 2001

Monelli, Paolo. *Toes Up*, Orlo Williams (trans.), London, Duckworth, 1930

Moore, John. *Jane's Fighting Ships of World War I*, London, Jane's Publishing, 1919 and Studio Editions, 1990

Owen, H. Collinson. *Salonika & After*, London, Hodder & Stoughton, 1919

Palmer, Alan. *The Gardeners of Salonika: The Macedonian Campaign 1915–1918*, London, André Deutsch, 1965

——. *Victory 1918*, London, Weidenfeld & Nicolson, 1998

Pope, Stephen and Wheal, Elizabeth-Anne. *The Macmillan Dictionary of the First World War*, London, 1995

Powell, E. Alexander. *Fighting in Flanders*, New York, Scribners and London, William Heinemann, 1914

Price, G. Ward. *Extra-special Correspondent*, London, George G. Harrap, 1957

Price, Julius M. *Six Months on the Italian Front*, London, Chapman & Hall, 1917

Roze, Anne. *Les Champs de la Mémoire, Paris*, Les Éditions du Chêne-Hachette Livre, 1998 and in translation as *Fields of Memory*, London, Cassell, 1999

Saint Julien, Christian de. *The Vosges Offensive, History of the First World War, Vol. 2, No. 8*, London, Macdonald, repr. in the *Bulletin of the Western Front Association*, 1992

Samson, Charles Rumney. *Fights and Flights*, London, 1930 and Nashville, Battery Press, 1990

Seth, Ronald. *Caporetto: The Scapegoat Battle*, London, Macdonald, 1965

Stallings, Laurence. *The First World War: A Photographic History*, London, Daily Express Publications, 1933

Strachan, Hew. *The First World War, Vol. I: To Arms*, Oxford, Oxford University Press, 2001

Swinton, E.D. and Percy, the Earl. *A Year Ago*, London, Edward Arnold, 1916

The Times History of the War, Vol. II, London, *The Times*, 1915; *Vol. III*, London, 1915; *Vol. VI*, London, 1916; *Vol. VII*, London, 1916; *Vol. XII*, London, 1917; *Vol. XIII*, London, 1917; *Vol. XV*, London, 1918; *Vol. XIX*, London, 1919; *Vol. XX*, London, 1919

Tuchman, Barbara W. *August 1914*, London, Constable, 1962

Wakefield, Alan, Moody, Simon and Whitmarsh, Andrew. 'Salonika: First World War Battlefields of Greece', *Battlefields Review No. 11*, Barnsley, 2001

Wilks, John and Eileen. *The British Army in Italy 1917–1918*, Barnsley, Leo Cooper/Pen & Sword, 1998

——. *Rommel and Caporetto*, Barnsley, Leo Cooper/Pen & Sword, 2001

INDEX

Italic references are to illustrations or maps

Aachen Battery, *60*
Adamello, *131*, 132, 174
Adige valley, 123, 132
Aerschot, *17*, 18
Albert, King of the Belgians, 3
Alexander, King of Greece, 234
Alexander of Serbia, Prince-
  Regent, 240
Allenby, Lt Gen Edmund, 12
Altkirch, 102
American Expeditionary Force,
  53, 59, 95
  1st Division, 95–102
  32nd Division, 102–7
  37th Division, *55*
  42nd (Rainbow) Division,
    102–7
  77th Division, 107–8
  91st Division, 53–6
  332nd Infantry, 178, 179
Antwerp, 3, 11
  fortifications, *21*, 22
  siege of, 22–8
  sortie from, 16–17, 19–21
Aosta, Duke of, 139, 166
armoured cars, 14, *31*
armoured train, *18*, 19, 26
Arsiero, 134, 135
Arthur, Baron Arz von
    Straussenberg, Gen,
    150, 158
Ashurst, Sgt George, 49–51
Asiago, 112, 134, 135, *136*,
    139, 153, 171, 174–8
Audenarde, 53–6
Austro-Hungarian Army, 114
  First Isonzo Army, 161
  Second Isonzo Army, 161,
    167

Third Army, 130
Fifth Army, 139, 158
Sixth Army, 182
Eleventh Army, 130
VIIIth Corps, 132
XXth Corps, 134
12th Division, *158*
22nd Division, 163
1st Mountain Brigade, 171
10th Mountain Brigade, 132
Austro-Hungarian cemeteries
  Caporetto, *168*
  Slagenhoft, *181*

Babington, Maj Gen Sir J.M., 179
Badoglio, Lt Gen, 151
Badonviller, *104*
Bainsizza plateau, 151, *156*,
    157, 162
balloon, observation, 236–7
Bangalore Torpedo, 215, *219*
Barrenkopf, 90–5
Bathelémont, 99, *106*
Belashitza mountains, *186*, 187,
    220, 222
Belgian Army
  Cavalry Division, 6–8, 16, 34
  1st Division, 6, 8, 16, 35, 37,
    42
  2nd Division, 16, 19, 26, 34,
    35, 38, 44
  3rd Division, 16, 19, 26, 44
  4th Division, 24, 34
  5th Division, 16, 34, 35
  6th Division, 16, 19, 26, 34
  Guides, 15
Belgium, defence of, 3
Belgium, innundation of, 42–4
Belgrade, 187, 190

Below, Gen Otto von, 160, 162,
    167, 171, 212
Berendt, Lt Gen Richard, 162
Bernadin, Sgt J.A., 94
Berrer, Gen A. von, 160, 162,
    167
Beseler, Hans von, 22
Beshik Lake, 229
Billyard-Leake, Lt Edward, 71–3
Birdcage, the, *192*, 193, 196, 199
Blazer, Gen, 85, 86
Boissondy, Jaj Gen de, 53
Bonham-Carter, Lt Stuart, 71
Boroevich von Bojna, Gen
    Svetosar, 114, 139, 158
Boselli, Paolo, 149
Briand, Aristide, 149
Briggs, Lt Gen C.J., 226
British Expeditionary Force, 10,
    12–14, 30
  Intelligence Branch, General
    Staff, 194
  IInd Corps, 30
  IIIrd Corps, 30
  IVth Corps, 30
  XIVth Corps, 135, 174, 179
  XVIth Corps, 226
  3rd Cavalry Division, 30
  1st Division, 49
  7th Division, 26, 30, 179
  10th (Irish) Division, 189,
    199, 207, 226
  22nd Division, 190, 223,
    242, 250
  23rd Division, 160, 170,
    175, 179
  26th Division, 223, 242
  27th Division, 235
  28th Division, 226, 243

32nd Division, 49
41st Division, 169, 170
48th Division, 175
Royal Engineers, 207
    99th Field Company, 242
    101st Field Company, 180
    108th Field Company,
        210
    127th Field Comapny,
        191, 220, 223
Royal Marine Brigade, 23,
    24, 26
31st Brigade, 196
67th Brigade, 212, 224
81st Brigade, 197, 203, 207
Derbyshire Yeomanry, 249
4th Irish Dragoon Guards, 12
Argyll & Sutherland
    Highlanders, 208, 247
7th Berkshire, 224, 225
9th Border, 243
Cameron Highlanders, 208
10th Devonshire, 224
12th Durham Light Infantry,
    176–8, 181
13th Durham Light Infantry,
    176–8
9th East Lancashire, 247
9th Gloucestershire, 225
1st Honourable Artillery
    Company, 180
King's Own (Royal
    Lancaster), 176–8, 246,
    247
King's Royal Rifles, 50
8th King's Shropshire Light
    Infantry, 225, 246
16th Lancashire Fusiliers, 49
13th Manchester, 225
4th Middlesex, 12
1st Northamptonshire, 50, 51
10th Northumberland
    Fusiliers, 176–8
11th Northumberland
    Fusiliers, 176–8, 181
4th Ox & Bucks Light
    Infantry, 176–8
7th Ox & Bucks Light
    Infantry, 210, 225

1st Queen's Own Royal West
    Kent, 13
Rifle Brigade, 239
4th Royal Fusiliers, 12
4th/3rd (City of London)
    Royal Fusiliers, 191,
    194
2nd Royal Irish, 13
Royal Scots Fusiliers, 208, 247
Royal Sussex, 52
1st Royal Welch Fusiliers,
    180
11th Royal Welch Fusiliers,
    212, 220, 243, 247
1st/7th Royal Worcestershire,
    177
11th Royal Worcestershire,
    210, 224
11th Scottish Rifles, 225, 247
11th Sherwood Foresters,
    176–8
9th South Lancashire, 246
7th South Wales Borderers,
    220, 223, 243
11th Welch, 247
7th Wiltshire, 224
Brod, 211
Bruges, 58, 61
Bulgaria, 185
Bulgarian Army, 185
    Second Army, 190, 207
    1st Division, 221
    7th Division, 203
    9th Division, 242, 247
    49th Division, 239
Bülow, Gen Karl von, 4

Cadore, the, 111, 115, 123, 146
Cadorna, Gen Luigi, 113, 115,
    126, 129, 132, 144,
    149, 156, 163, 166, 170
Camp Retranché de Salonique
    (Birdcage), 193
Campbell, Lt H.G., 68
Capello, Gen Luigi, 139, 150,
    156, 162
Caporetto, 113, 115, 161, 162,
    170
Carpenter, Cdr Alfred, 65–74

Carso, the, 113, 126, 139, 142,
    148, 150, 151
Castelgomberto, 134, 173
Castlenau, Gen Noël de, 78
Cauriòl, the, 146
Cavan, Lt Gen the Earl of, 169,
    170, 179, 182
cemeteries, Commonwealth War
    Graves Commission
    Barenthal, 177
    Karasuli, 213
    Ramscapelle Road, 52
    St Symphorien, Mons, 13
    Sarigol, 249
    Struma, 212
    Zeebrugge, 72
Cesuna, 176
Churchill, First Sea Lord
    Winston, 23, 26
Cima Dodici, 128, 132, 133, 154
Col de la Schucht, 82 94
Col de Wettstein, 82, 88, 91
Col di Lana, 123, 127, 132
Col du Bonhomme, 82, 83
Collet, Lt, 22, 58
Collinson Owen, H., 187, 193,
    199, 202, 205, 217,
    221, 228–30
Colmar, 78, 82, 83
Colovrat mountains, 161, 162
Conrad von Hötzendorf, Field
    Marshal Franz, Count,
    114, 130, 150
Constantine, King of Greece,
    185, 234
Cope, Sgt Benjamin, 51
Cordonnier, Gen Emilien, 211,
    212
Corfu, 191, 200
Cortina d'Ampezzo, 123, 124
Couture, Charles Thomas, 42–3
Crête des Mitrailleuses, 200,
    212, 223
Cristallo Ridge, 145
Crna River, 185, 210, 212, 220,
    225, 241

Dankl, Gen, 130
D'Annunzio, Gabriele, 151

Davies, Lt R.B., 58
Demirhissar, 203
Devedzili, 223
Diaz, Gen Armando, 170, 179, 182
Dixmude, 34, *48*
Dixmude, Battle of, 34–7, 39–40, 42–5, 46–7
Doberdo, 142
Dobropolje, 240, 241
Dobrovica Ravine, 227
dog batteries, 7, *20*
Doiran Lake, 187, 200, 206, 220, 222–3, 227, 242, *244–5*
Doldzeli, 206, 224
Dorsale, the, 200, 212–15, 219
Dubail, Gen Auguste, 78, 82, 94
Duncan, Maj Gen J. 242
Dunkirk, 58–9

Emmich, Gen Otto von, 5
Eugen, Archduke, 114, 132

Falkenhayn, Gen Erich von, 21, 33, 130
Fanshawe, Maj Gen Sir Robert, 178
Fecht valley, 82, 86, *88*, 91–2
flame-throwers, 95, 241
Floca's, *197*, 198
Florina, 207, 210, *211*
Foch, Gen Ferdinand, 29, 42, 78, 169
Forcola, 122
Fort de Loncin, 6, 8, 9, *8–9*
Fort Kessel, *21*
Franchet d'Esperey, Gen Louis, 239–40, 249
francs-tireurs, 11, 39, *41*
French Army
 First Army, 78
 Second Army, 78
 Third Army, 78
 Fourth Army, 78
 Fifth Army, 10
 Army of Alsace, 78

Army of Belgium, 53
Army of the Vosges (former Seventh Army), 82, 84, 87, 92
 VIIth Corps, 78
 XIIth Corps, 175
 XXth Corps, 78–9
 Colonial Corps, 79
 41st Division, 53, 85
 42nd Division, 40, 42, 44
 47th Division (Alpine) Division, 84, 86, 87, 89, 90–5
 57th Division, 82, 85, 190, 235
 64th Division, 169
 65th Division, 169
 66th Division, 82, 86, 89
 129th Division, 90, 92–3
 156th Division, 190, 210
 16th Colonial Division, 225
 17th Colonial Division, 206, 241
 1st Chasseur Brigade, 87
 3rd Brigade, 91
 5th Brigade, 92
 81st Brigade, 82
 Marine Brigade (Fusiliers Marins), 30–2, 34–7, 39–40, 44–5, 46–7
 Schlucht Brigade, 82
 Chasseurs Alpins, 82, 83, 84, 87, 91, 94, 95, *96*, 171
 Chasseurs d'Afrique, 249
 Goumiers, 45–6
 Spahis, 249
 152nd Regiment, 95
French, FM Sir John, 30
Fulleren, 105

Gallipoli, 185
Garda, Lake, 112, 115, 121, 132, 169
Garibaldi, Peppino, 115, 126
gas, 95
Gaulle, Charles de, 10
Gaythorne-Hardy, Brig Gen the Hon. J.F., 169

German Army
 First Army, 4, 12, 21
 Second Army, 4, 78
 Third Army, 78
 Fourth Army, 33, 78
 Fifth Army, 78
 Sixth Army, 22, 34, 78
 Seventh Army, 78
 Fourteenth Army, 160, 167
 IIIrd Reserve Corps, 19, 22, 33, 35, 40
 IXth Reserve Corps, 16, 19
 XXIInd Reserve Corps, 35, 40
 XXIIIrd Reserve Corps, 40
 cavalry, 6–8, 12, 17
 8th Bavarian Ersatz Division, 92
 6th Bavarian Landwehr Division, 89
 12th Bavarian Landwehr Division, 89
 4th Ersatz Division, 40
 1st Marine Division, 51
 Münster Bavarian Division, 87
 19th Reserve Division, 89
 37th Landwehr Brigade, 24, 26
 1st Reserve Ersatz Brigade, 24
 3rd Bavarian Life Guards, 165
 12th Brandenburg Grenadiers, 12
 84th Infantry, 12
 123rd Landwehr, 82
 Mecklenburger Regiment, 92
 202nd Regiment, 39
 13th Saxon Jäger, 241
 Württemberg Mountain Battalion, 163–6
German military cemeteries
 Vladslo, *56*
 Zeebrugge, 72
Ghelpac River, 175
Ghent, 30–2
Gibbs, Cdr Valentine, 68
Gondrecourt-le-Château, 95
Gorizia, 116, *120*, 126, 139, 140–2, 148, 159
Gradsko, 220, 247

Grand Couronné, *188*, 200, 222, 243
Grand Couronné, Battle of, 79
Greek Army, 235
    Archipelagos Divison, 196, 239
    Crete Division, 239, 243, 246
    Seres Division, 243, 246
    2nd Regiment, 243
    3rd Regiment, 242, 246
    Greek deserters, 204–5
Grimwood, Lt Col J., 223
Grosetti, Gen, 40
Guillaumat, Gen Marie Louis Adolphe, 235, 239

Haelen, Battle of, 6–8
Haig, Lt Gen Sir Douglas, 12
Happy Valley, *214*
Hartmannswillerkopf, *80*, 82, 85–7, 95
Hausen, Gen Max von, 78
Heeringen, Gen August von, 78
Helloco, Abbé le, 35, 42
Hemingway, Ernest, 178
Hill 340, 246, *248–9*
Hofacker, Gen E. von, 167
Hood, Adm Horace, 35
Horseshoe Hill, 206
Hudson, Lt Col C.E., 176

Isonzo, Battle of
    First, 119
    Second, 119
    Third, 126
    Fourth, 127
    Fifth, 130
    Sixth, 139
    Seventh, 144
    Eighth, 146
    Ninth, 148
    Tenth, 151
    Eleventh, 156
Isonzo River, 113, 139–41, 161, *164*
Italian Army, 114
    First Army, 114
    Second Army, 114, 116, 148, 150, 156–7, 166

Third Army, 114, 116, 139, 144, 148, 150, 151, 156, 166
Fourth Army, 114
Fifth Army, 139
Eighth Army, 179, 181
Tenth Army, 179, 181
Twelfth Army, 179
Gorizia Defence Command, 150, 156
IInd Corps, 151, 158
IVth Corps, 162
VIth Corps, 139, 151
VIIIth Corps, 156
IXth Corps, 171
Xth Corps, 174
XIth Corps, 139, 170, 179
XIIIth Corps, 175
XVIIIth Corps, 170, 182
XXth Corps, 175
XXIIIrd Corps, 158
XXIVth Corps, 167
XXVIIIth Corps, 170
4th Division, 151
5th Division, 132
35th Division, 225
45th Division, 139
Alessandra Brigade, 162
Alpini, 114, *115*, 116–18, 122–3, 127, 130, *131*, 146, 154–5, 173, 206
arditi, 156
Bersaglieri, 121, 157, 165, 206
Cagliari Brigade, 212
Casale Brigade, 140
Catanzero Brigade, 156
Cuneo Brigade, 139, 140
Florence Brigade, 158
Napoli Brigade, 162
Pallenza Brigade, 158
Pavia Brigade, 140
Ravenna Brigade, 116
Roma Brigade, 132
Salerno Brigade, 166
Sassari Brigade, 127

Joffre, Gen Joseph, 10, 29, 77, 78, 86, 92, 94

Jumeaux Ravine, 200, 206, 223, 224–5
Karajakoi Bala, 207, *209*, *210*
Karajakoi Zir, 207, *209*, *210*
Karl I, Emperor, 150, 158
Kavala, 203
Kenali, 211, 216
Kent, Samuel M., 102–7
Keyes, Vice Adm Roger, 63, 65, 66–7
Kluck, Gen Alexander von, 4
Knox, Lt Col, *177*
Kogge, Charles Louis, 42
Kosovo, 190
Kostanjevica, 151, 158
Kosturino, 247
Kövess, Gen, 130
Kozyak, 240, 241
Krafft, Lt Gen Konrad, von Dellmensingen, 162
Krauss, Maj Gen Alfred von, 132, 160, 162
Kyler, Pte Donald Drake, 95–102

Langle de Cary, Gen Ferdinand de, 78
Lanrezac, Gen Charles, 10
Latisana, 166, 167
La Tortue, 206, *226*
Leavell, Capt John H., 55
Le Linge, 82, 86, 87, 89–95
Leman, Lt Gen Gérard, 3, 6
Liège, fortifications, 6, 8–10
Ligne, Prince Henri de, 14
Littlejohn, Lt Cdr, 19
Lloyd George, David, 149, 220
Lombartzyde, 36, 49
Louvain, 17–19
Ludendorff, Maj Gen Erich von, 5, 6
Lunéville sector, 102
Lys, River, 30
Lyster, Lt Henry N., 191, 193–6, 203, 207, 232–4, 236–8, 250

Macukovo, 200, 220, 223
Mahon, Lt Gen Sir Bryan, 189, 193, 203

malaria, 201–3, 235
Malins, Geoffrey, 38–9, 45–6,
    47–9, 83–4
maps
    Belgium
        Antwerp/Brussels, *20*
        Antwerp, forts, *22*
        Audenarde, *54*
        Dixmude/Nieuport, *32*
        Flanders, *29*
        Liège area, *4*
        Liège, forts, *4*
        Zeebrugge, port, *62*
    Italy
        Asiago, *176*
        Carso, *152*
        Isonzo front, *138*
        Isonzo front, centre, *156*
        Isonzo front, south, *120*
        Ortigara, *152*
        Piave front, *174*
        Setti Communi, Trentino,
            172
        Trentino and Cadore, *111*
        Val Sugana, *128*
    Salonika
        Birdcage, the, *192*, *193*
        Couronné, August 1918,
            244
        Doiran, June 1917, *221*
        Dorsale/Mackovo, *216*
        Jumeaux Ravine, *228*
        Monastir/Doiran, *241*
        Ostrovo/Monastir, *211*
        Salonika city, *231*
        Salonika/Doiran/Struma,
            201
        Salonika front, *186*
        Vardar/Skra di Legen, *240*
    Vosges
        American sectors, *97*
        Badonviller, *104*
        Fecht and Soultzeren, *88*
        Verdun/Toul, *77*
        Vosges front, *79*
Marix, Lt Reggie, 26
Maud'huy, Gen Louis Comte
    de, 87, 90, 92, 94
Melle, action at, 31–2

Metzeral, 89
Milne, Gen Sir George, 149,
    203, 221
Mišić, Voïvode Zivojin, 240
Moglena mountains, 185, 225
Moltke, Gen Helmuth von, 21, 78
Monastir, 185, 206, 216, 218,
    220, 225, 241
Monelli, Paolo, 127–8, 129–30,
    133, 137, 146, 147–8,
    150, 153–5, 169,
    170–1, 173
Monfalcone, 119, 132, 142,
    144, 151, *152*
monitors, 35, 36, 50, 63, 65, 151
    submarine, *237*
Mons, Battle of, 12–14
Monte Grappa, 170, 171, *173*,
    178, 182
Monte Kuk, 151
Montello, 170, 171, 178
Monte Maggiore, 163
Monte Matajur, 161, 162, 166
Montenegro, 190
Monte Nero, 113, 116–18, 161
Monte Piana, *148*
Monte San Gabriele, 158
Monte San Michele, 119, 126,
    130, 139
Monte Santo, 151, 158
Monte Tomba, 171
Monte Tondarecar, 171, 173
Montuori, Gen L., 163
Mount Kaymakchalan, 185,
    210, *211*, 218
Mrzli vrh, 161, 165–6
Mudros, 187, *189*, 193
Münster, 82, 86, 89
Mulhouse, 78, 82
Mussolini, Cpl Benito, 150

Na Gradu, 161, 163–5
Namur, fall of, 10–11
National Redoubt, Belgium, 11,
    22
Nieuport, 34, *49*
Nieuport, Battle of, 49–53
Nieuport–Dixmude railway, *33*,
    42

Nish, 190, 221
Nivelle, Gen Robert, 149, 150,
    227
Nollet, Gen, 90, 92, 94
Nova Vas, 144–5

O'Connor, Lt Col Richard, 179
Oppacchiasella, 142, 151, *152*
Orbey, 82
Ortigara, *152*, 153, 154
Ostend, 30, *57*, *58*, *59*
    raid, 74
Ostertag, Sgt Paul R., 107–8
Ostrovo Lake, 207, 210, 221
Oudenaarde, 53–6

Pal Grande, 125
Panarotta, *127*, 128, 133
Papadopoli Island, 170,
    179–81, *182*
Paris, Maj Gen Archibald, 23, 28
Patty ravine, 225
Pau, Gen Paul Marie, 78
Pecori-Giraldi, Gen Count, 132
Percy, Capt the Earl, 45
Petit Couronné, 220, 223, 225,
    246
Piacentino, Gen, 150
Piave, Battle of
    First, 170
    Second, 174
Piave River, 167, 170, 174, 181
Pinzano, 167
Pip Ridge, 222, 226, *245*,
    246–7
Plan XVII, 77–9
Plumer, Gen Sir Herbert, 170
Podgora, 139, 140
Pouydraguin, Gen d'Arman de,
    87, 90
Powell, E. Alexander, 10,
    11–12, 14–28
Pozzuolo, 167
Price, G. Ward, 166, 167, 170
Price, Julius, 114, 119, 132,
    135, 139–46
Pristina, 187, 191
Putnik, FM Radomir, 191
Putz, Gen, 82, 86

Ramscapelle, 39, *40*, 44
Raversijde Museum, *60*
Rawlinson, Lt Gen Sir Henry,
       26, 30
Robertson, Gen Sir William,
       149, 169, 203
Rommel, Lt Erwin, 163–6
Ronarc'h, Rear Adm Pierre, 30,
       34, 35, 43, 47
Ross, Sir Ronald, 200
Route des Crêtes, *80*, 82
Royal Air Force, 178, 237
    47 Squadron, 247
Royal Navy
    HMS *Attentive*, 35
    HMS *Daffodil*, 64, 68–9, 73–4
    HMS *Erebus*, 65
    HMS *Foresight*, 35
    HMS *Humber*, 35
    HMS *Intrepid*, 63, 67, 71–3
    HMS *Iphigenia*, 63, 71–3
    HMS *Iris*, 64, 68, 71
    HMS *Mersea*, 35
    HMS *Severn*, 35
    HMS *Sirius*, 63
    HMS *Terror*, 65
    HMS *Thetis*, 63, 71–3
    HMS *Vindictive*, 64, *65*, 66,
       68–74
    HMS *Warwick*, 65, 66, 73
    HM Submarines,
       C1, 65
       C3, *65*, 69–70
       M1, *237*
    Royal Naval Air Service, 22,
       26
    Royal Naval Division, 24, 28
       1st Naval Brigade, 24, 28
       2nd Naval Brigade, 24
Ruffey, Gen Pierre, 78
Rupel Pass, 187, 203
Rupprech of Bavaria, Crown
       Prince, 78
Russian Army, 206, 235
    Second Brigade, 225

Salonika, 149, 185, 191
    fire of, 230–4
    journey to, 238–9

Sambre, River, 10
Samson, Cdr Charles, 22, 24,
       58–9
Sandford, Lt Cdr F.H., 70
Sandford, Lt Richard, 69–70
San Martino del Carso, 143
Sarrail, Gen Maurice, 149, 185,
       190, 193, 196, 203,
       207, 211, 219, 220,
       225, 234–5
Scheldt, River, 11, *22*, 26, 30, 53
Schlieffen Plan, 4
Schratzmännele, 90–5
Scotti, Gen K. von, 160, 162, 167
Selva di Ternova, 157
Serbia, 185
    uprising, 221
Serbian Army, 200, 206, 235
    First Army, 226
    Second Army, 225
    Third Army, 207, 221
    Danube Division, 207
    Sumadija Division, 226, 241
    Yugoslav Division (Serb
       Volunteers), 235, 241
Skra di Legen, 239
Smith-Dorrien, Gen Horace, 12
Sneyd, Cdr Ralph, 71–3
Sokol, 240, 241
Sommerviller sector, 96
Spencer-Grey, Lt, 26
Stavros, 203
Stein, Gen H. von, 160, 162
Stelvio Pass, 112, 120–1
Struma River, 187, 199, 207,
       209, 220, 226, 239
Struma valley, *208*, 230
'Sulzern Line', the, *88*, 90
Swinton, Lt Col E.D., 45

Tagliamento River, 163, 166, 170
Tête des Faux, la, 83, *84*
Thompson, Donald, 10, 18, 19
Tolmino, *112*, 126, 161
Tomkinson, Lt Col F.M., 178
Torre River, 167
Treaty of London, 112
Trentino, 113, 132–4, 139, 148,
       153, 170

Treviso, 179
Trieste, 151
Turrall, Lt R. Guy, *190*, 191,
       212–16, 218, 220,
       227–8, 235, 238, 243,
       249–50

U-boats, *57*–8
Udine, 115, 167
Uskub (Skopje), 187, 190, 249

Val d'Astico, *133*, 134, 135,
       137, 174
Val Sugana, 112, 128, *132*, 133,
       153, 171
Vardar River, 185, 193, 200,
       210, 241
Veliki Hrib, 158–9
Venice, 114, 170
Venizelos, Eleutherios, 185, 234
Vetoenik, 240, 241
Vieil-Armand, 82
Vittorio Veneto, Battle of,
       179–82
Vosges mountains, 77

Wales, HRH the Prince of, 169
Walker, Lt Isaac G., 102
Warburton, Jamor J.A., 227
Wemyss, Adm Sir Rosslyn, 63
Wilhelm of Prussia, Crown
       Prince, 78
Wilson, Gen Sir Henry, 170
Witte, Gen de, 7
Wolfsohn, Robert, *85*, *86*
Württemberg, Albrecht Grand
       Duke of, 78

Yoannon, Col, 195, 246
Youll, 2nd Lt J.S., 178
Ypres, 34, 36, 40, 45
Yser, Battle of, 34–47
Yser, River, *32*, 34, 47

Zeebrugge, 30, 58
    port, 59–62
    raid, 59–74
Zeppelin, attack, 6, 14
    sheds, 22, 26